DRAWN TO THE GODS

Drawn to the Gods

RELIGION AND HUMOR IN *THE SIMPSONS*,
SOUTH PARK, AND *FAMILY GUY*

David Feltmate

NEW YORK UNIVERSITY PRESS

New York

NEW YORK UNIVERSITY PRESS
New York
www.nyupress.org

© 2017 by New York University

References to Internet websites (URLs) were accurate at the time of writing. Neither the author nor New York University Press is responsible for URLs that may have expired or changed since the manuscript was prepared.

ISBN: 978-1-4798-2218-8 (hardback)
ISBN: 978-1-4798-9036-1 (paperback)

For Library of Congress Cataloging-in-Publication data, please contact the Library of Congress.

New York University Press books are printed on acid-free paper, and their binding materials are chosen for strength and durability. We strive to use environmentally responsible suppliers and materials to the greatest extent possible in publishing our books.

Manufactured in the United States of America

10 9 8 7 6 5 4 3 2 1

Also available as an ebook

For Dominic and Ashlynne

CONTENTS

ACKNOWLEDGMENTS

A lot of work goes into a scholarly book, especially a first book. My mentor, Douglas E. Cowan, deserves the biggest debt of gratitude as he was able to see the value of my work before this project really took shape. He nurtured my intellectual development during my time at the University of Waterloo. Doug set a high bar for me, both with his expectations and his personal example, and I am forever grateful that he saw studying the animated TV series *The Simpsons* as a valid dissertation topic. Thank you Doug, your guidance is something I cherish and draw upon daily.

Other scholars were also invaluable in the development of this book. At the University of Waterloo, Lorne Dawson and Scott Kline gave me valuable feedback on this project in its earlier incarnations. S. Brent Rodriguez-Plate has been an invaluable influence on my thinking about blasphemy and its importance for understanding religion. Philip Tite has moved from being an early editor of an article to the best kind of critic of my research agenda. His criticisms and continuous engagement with my work within the broader field of the study of religion are always welcome and my work is sharper for thinking through his reflections on the relationship between religion and humor. Behind the scenes, Gary Laderman's, Eric Mazur's, Sarah McFarland Taylor's, and Elijah Siegler's support has prompted me to push through with some of the more difficult writing phases involved in finishing this book. There are also academic friends who did not directly comment on my research, but whose support and encouragement have helped me through the process. Although they are many, Rebekka King and Joel Thiessen deserve special mention for their friendship. My conversations with Rebekka at the American Academy of Religion and the Canadian Society for the Study of Religion have become a regular part of my thinking about the place of this work in the broader study of religion. Without her as a sounding board, my thinking about the field would be impoverished. Joel has been my best friend in academia since we first met in 2006 in a class at the

University of Waterloo. Our friendship has matured over the last decade and I am eternally grateful for his presence in my life as a professional and personal sounding board. I hope to someday give as much support to Joel as he has given me. Words cannot express how thankful I am for Jennifer Hammer, my editor at New York University Press. Her tireless patience has pushed me through the multiple revisions this manuscript has undertaken. I am a better writer for her steady assistance. Lastly, I would like to once again thank all of the anonymous reviewers and journal editors who have given their time to previous publications that have been reworked into different parts of this book. Their comments and criticisms have shaped my thinking over time and their hard work is much appreciated. The anonymous reviewers of this manuscript deserve additional thanks as their comments and criticisms helped to make this a better book. To anybody not directly mentioned by name, I can only beg forgiveness for my mental lapse. Your support and friendship are much appreciated. Any mistakes and errors in this manuscript are mine, but they are far fewer thanks to the help I have received along the way.

At Auburn University at Montgomery I need to thank Michael Burger, my former dean in the School of Liberal Arts, for his financial support in the form of Dean's Grants that enabled me to acquire research materials, to travel, and to present my research. Without his help I could not have received the feedback and intellectual engagement that makes the long road to writing a book possible. My current dean in the College of Public Policy & Justice, Kievan Dervai, also deserves a debt of gratitude for his unwavering support and promotion of my research. I would also like to thank my previous department chair, Terry Winemiller, for his help funding my travels and research. Finally, my deepest thanks go to Kimberly P. Brackett, who has helped me in her roles as department chair, associate dean, sometime collaborator, and friend. Words fail to describe the impact and importance of her friendship and collegiality on the process of bringing this book into the world. Thank you, Kim.

I would like to thank the library staff at the University of Waterloo's Dana Porter Library and Auburn University at Montgomery. Their help locating the materials I needed to complete my research was timely and invaluable. I could not have written this book without their tireless work. Financially, this work was supported by a Social Sciences and Humanities Research Council of Canada Doctoral Fellowship held at the

University of Waterloo in 2009–2010. Their funding was much appreciated and has helped bring this project to completion.

My family deserves a great deal of thanks for their support of all kinds during the long road from this book's conception to its completion. Bill and Gwen supported me from a distance in what can sometimes look like a fool's errand. My mother and father have been unshakable in their faith and belief in me. Their love and support have sustained me through the highs and lows of the writing and research process. I am truly blessed to have such wonderful people in my life to reach out to in the storms that came with the long process of writing this book. My children, Dominic and Ashlynne, have grown up with this book in the background. Their lives and laughter gave me hope and drive when writing. They continue to inspire me to greater heights just by being alive. Thank you both for your love and for motivating me just by being yourselves. Finally, Krista deserves a deep debt of gratitude. She was a dissertation and book widow while I brought this work to completion and I am grateful for the sacrifices she made to help me make this book a reality.

I would like to thank the following presses for their permission to use parts of the following in the writing of this book:

Some material presented in chapter 3 reflects updated and revised ideas that first appeared in David Feltmate, 2013. "'It's Funny Because it's True?' *The Simpsons*, Satire, and the Significance of Religious Humor in Popular Culture." *Journal of the American Academy of Religion* 81 (1): 222–248. doi: 10.1093/jaarel/lfs100. © 2013 Oxford University Press.

Some material presented in chapter 4 reflects updated and revised ideas that first appeared in David Feltmate, 2013. "Cowards, Critics, and Catholics: The Catholic League for Religious and Civil Rights, *South Park* and the Politics of Religious Humor in the United States." *Bulletin for the Study of Religion* 42 (3): 2–11. doi: 10.1558/bsor.v42i3.2. © 2013 Equinox Publishing Ltd.

Some material presented in chapter 5 reflects updated and revised ideas that first appeared in David Feltmate, 2011. "New Religious Movements in Adult Animated Sitcoms—A Spectrum of Portrayals." *Religion Compass* 5 (7): 343–354. doi: 10.1111/j.1749-8171.2011.00287.x. © 2011 Blackwell Publishing Ltd.

Some material presented in chapter 5 reflects updated and revised ideas that first appeared in David Feltmate, 2012. "The Humorous Reproduction of Religious Prejudice: 'Cults' and Religious Humour in *The Simpsons, South Park*, and *King of the Hill.*" *Journal of Religion and Popular Culture* 24 (2): 201–216. doi: 10.1353/rpc.2012.0017. © 2012 University of Toronto Press. Reprinted with permission from University of Toronto Press (www.utpjournals.com).

Introduction

If you have ever watched *The Simpsons*, *South Park*, or *Family Guy* and laughed uproariously before asking "Why did I find that funny?" then this book is for you. Within its pages you will find a theory of satire that will help you to understand why you laughed and what you learned. If you have never watched these programs and are horrified that somebody would find depictions of God aiming a sniper's rifle at your head, Jesus miraculously increasing his friend's wife's breasts, or the Virgin Mary "shitting blood on the Pope"[1] humorous, this book will help you to understand why these jokes tell you significant things about yourself and American society. It will guide you through the process of analyzing how humor teaches people about different religions' beliefs and ideas while defining what constitutes good religious practice in twenty-first-century America.[2] Analyzing humor matters because popular culture is an important vehicle for teaching people of all ages about religion and its place in our society.[3] The ideas presented here will help you to understand jokes that are broadcast through television programs around the globe, how they reflect social divisions in the United States, and how their humor reflects social, political, and religious biases.

This book focuses on *The Simpsons* (FOX 1989–present), *South Park* (Comedy Central 1997–present), and *Family Guy* (FOX 1999–2002, 2004–present) because they are wildly popular, have had a significant impact on cultural consciousness, and are brimming with religious references. Each has produced more than two hundred episodes, is beloved by countless fans, moves billions of dollars in merchandise annually, is syndicated globally, and is recognized for its wit, intelligence, and social commentary. More than 95% of *Simpsons* episodes, roughly 84% of *Family Guy* episodes, and about 78% of *South Park* episodes contain explicit references to religion. Without these programs the current television landscape would look very different. Inspired by these shows, syndicated animated sitcoms for adults have proliferated and have helped to teach audiences how to think about religious diversity.

These programs are also contentious. Moral watchdogs have targeted each series for its portrayal of the family, religion, sex, and drugs, and *South Park* has been singled out for its use of profanity. These controversies help to shape the programs' humor, giving them material for further jokes and helping them to establish their place in America's culture wars.[4] The humor in these three programs is not inherently funny. Indeed, nothing is "funny because it is funny." Our mental maps of the world shape our sense of humor. This cultural foundation makes humor interesting and significant because jokes tell us about their tellers' assumptions.

This book explores three questions: (1) *What do you have to believe about different groups classified as "religions" and the role of "religion" in society to find jokes in the three sitcoms humorous?* (2) *What do the patterns in these programs tell us about the popular construction of "religion's" significance in America?* and (3) *What can a critical assessment of religion in the public sphere through popular culture tell us about American civil life?* These questions are related to the overarching argument of this book, which is that jokes about religion are tools for teaching audiences how to interpret and judge religious people and institutions. If we want to understand how popular perceptions of religion are taught to large segments of society through popular media, we need to take humor seriously. This book analyzes how jokes about religion communicate a worldview concerning religion's proper place in American society. Each of the three programs discussed portrays, in a different way, what it means to be a good religious American through its humor. This volume examines the ways in which each program presents core morals and values, arguing for humor's importance in transmitting these ideas about religion's place in American life. Drawing on this analysis, the book offers a new theoretical model of religious satire that is based on the sociologies of knowledge, religion, and humor and that helps us to understand how these three programs and other humorous popular media contribute to larger discussions about religion in American public life. This book also explains how creators of satirical media craft and manipulate public knowledge about different religious groups.

Why focus on television comedy to make the case for how satirical media presents interpretations of different religious groups and communicates what good religious practice is in America? Television entertainment is useful because of its ubiquity. The Nielsen Company, which remains the gold standard for measuring television consumption, reported that 116.3 million American homes had a television in 2014, reaching an estimated 296 million people over the age of two.[5] Even with new viewing options on smartphones, tablets, and Internet streaming, the average American adult (18+) spent four hours and thirty-two minutes daily watching television in the third quarter of 2014.[6] Television remains a socializing force in American life, reaching massive audiences with its content delivered through entertainment genres such as dramas, game shows, and sitcoms; these compete for viewers' attention with more informational formats such as news and documentaries, which are becoming more entertaining in order to compete with entertainment programming.[7] As successful television programs adjust to new content arenas, they are still streamed online, highlights are watched on YouTube, and episodes are downloaded. Television's content remains relevant, though it is now being consumed across multiple platforms.[8] When we also take into account that American broadcast media is syndicated globally, a successful program's ability to spread its message to millions—if not billions—of people is reason enough to continue paying attention to the medium.[9]

Why focus on these three programs? There are other relevant animated sitcoms, such as *King of the Hill*, *Futurama* (a product of *Simpsons* creator Matt Groening and *Simpsons* writer David X. Cohen), and *American Dad* (by *Family Guy's* creator Seth MacFarlane) that could have been included, among others. This book also could have focused on other sitcoms that are not animated, but two factors make focusing on *The Simpsons*, *South Park*, and *Family Guy* particularly instructive. First, animation allows for a much broader and more vivid world than live action. Rather than being limited by casting costs, the creation of sets, or the necessity of relocating a cast and crew for a "special" episode, animation is limited only by the artists', writers', and voice actors' imaginations and abilities. Thus, each of these programs is able to expand well beyond a few fixed locations, allowing them to showcase a variety of religious situations, characters, and settings. *The Simpsons*, *South*

Park, and *Family Guy* are frequently compared in popular discourse, are among the longest running animated sitcoms, and combined they total in excess of 1,000 episodes. This is a rich source of data and allows for a thorough comparison.

In teaching religion, I have found that when I start quoting examples from *The Simpsons, South Park*, and *Family Guy*, students respond. They know Apu Nahasapeemapetilon, the Indian immigrant who runs the local Kwik-E-Mart in the Simpson's hometown of Springfield and has a Shrine to Ganesha in his store. They can make sense of "spirituality" in Homer Simpson's spiritual quest in the episode "Homer the Heretic." They understand cult jokes in *South Park* and quote *Family Guy* to me. It is significant that these young adults do not know the basics of most world religions but they have learned something about how to interpret different religious traditions from these television shows. Boston University religious studies professor Stephen Prothero contends that Americans are remarkably ignorant about religion—both their own (if they have one) and others'. The Pew Forum on Religion and Public Life confirmed Prothero's hypothesis with a poll about general religious knowledge, on which the average score was 16/32. Atheists and agnostics scored highest with an average score of 20.9/32, while Hispanic Catholics scored the lowest with an average of 11.6/32.[10] Arguing that this is a civic problem, Prothero suggests teaching biblical literacy and world religions in secondary schools and making world religions part of postsecondary studies' core curriculum.[11] Yet, my students apparently learned *something* from shows like *The Simpsons* and *South Park*. But what do these programs teach? How do they teach it? And what are the assumptions about religion undergirding the programs' depictions? This book answers these questions.

The programs' power lies in their popularity, pervasiveness, and recountability. They present references that contain information people from different walks of life can understand and draw upon to make sense of the world. This book uses the concept of *ignorant familiarity* to refer to widespread superficial—and often erroneous—knowledge about groups of people that other groups use to facilitate social interaction. Ignorant familiarity exists when people think they know enough about others to make decisions about how to treat them, but that familiarity is based in ignorance.[12] Among the different types of incomplete knowledge humans often employ to understand others and their religions are stereotypes (e.g., Native Americans are closer to nature and "more spiritual" than whites), theological ignorance (e.g., that Catholics worship the saints), and racial-religious prejudices (e.g., that Jews secretly run the world). Ignorant familiarity is useful for explaining why the different programs' creators use the religious humor they do, how it builds upon commonly held misconceptions, and how different religious groups in the United States have been unfairly advantaged or disadvantaged through their depictions in popular media.

The Three Programs

We can credit *The Simpsons* for launching contemporary adult-oriented television cartoon sitcoms. Before the program debuted on the fledgling FOX television network in December 1989, America had been exposed to the Simpson family through a series of shorts on *The Tracey Ullman Show* (FOX 1987–1990). Underground cartoonist Matt Groening created *The Simpsons*, which was brought to the small screen by iconic television producer James L. Brooks, who had previously worked on such hits as *The Mary Tyler Moore Show* (CBS 1970–1977) and *Taxi* (ABC 1978–1982, NBC 1982–1983). Brooks was a fan of Groening's comic strip *Life in Hell* and asked the cartoonist to turn it into bumper cartoons for *The Tracey Ullman Show*. Instead of relinquishing *Life in Hell* to FOX, Groening created the Simpson family—overweight and dim-witted father Homer, mother Marge with her blue hair and devotion to family, the bratty troublemaker and eldest child Bart, Lisa the brilliant and talented middle child, and the non-verbal baby Maggie. A new sensation was born.

The early Ullman shorts were crudely drawn and lacked the dynamic characters that *The Simpsons* would later develop, but the sketches captured people's imaginations and attracted enough attention for FOX to turn them into an independent program. After the third co-creator, Sam Simon, helped assemble the writing staff, the program was launched. In its first year *The Simpsons* made $1.4 billion for FOX and was a massive popular culture sensation. Since then the show has generated more than 550 episodes, thirty-two Primetime Emmy Awards, a Peabody Award, and *The Simpsons Movie* in 2007, which grossed more than $527 million worldwide.[13] Set in the American everytown of Springfield, the program became known for topical satire, writing that was hilarious and heartfelt, and dozens of well-developed characters. While the show's popularity has declined, it was still drawing roughly three million viewers for each new episode's initial broadcast twenty-five years after its first episode. It will go down in history as one of television's greatest commercial and artistic successes, as the writing and voice acting have been consistently recognized for their excellence.[14]

The Simpsons has been treated as groundbreaking television, pushing postmodern thought into popular entertainment through its self-referential style and stretching the boundaries of what cartoons can do while also depicting the world beyond animation in a realistic way.[15] The program is seen as a site of oppositional culture.[16] President George H. W. Bush even targeted it for its depictions of family values.[17] The show has also been praised in different venues for presenting religion as family-friendly,[18] a revelation of American culture's need for reformation,[19] and a critical assessment that balances the positives and negatives of religion in American culture.[20] The two major analyses of religion in *The Simpsons* are offered by *Orlando Sentinel* journalist Mark Pinsky and theologian Jamie Heit. Pinsky contends that *The Simpsons* is "not at all dangerous or threatening to the status quo, it is a sweet funny show about a family as 'real' as the faith lives of many Americans."[21] Heit, on the other hand, argues that *The Simpsons* implores contemporary American Christians to reform their ways. He writes, "Its [*The Simpsons'*] goal is, in part, to elicit a response from its viewers to address Christianity's problems before they lose the chance to do so."[22] These two analyses are incomplete. Pinsky's analysis does not explain the implications of *The Simpsons'* critical depictions of certain traditions. Meanwhile, Heit's argument suffers from his faulty thesis that *The Simpsons* is calling on Christianity to reform. He reads his theological concerns into the program, though the program itself offers a broader look at American culture. *The Simpsons* does not set out to provide theological solutions to contemporary Christianity's situation, nor is it calling for Heit's specific solutions of moving away from the neoconservative political and economic forces that characterize conservative American Protestantism.[23] Pinsky and Heit's analysis set the stage for this book because they both show that *The Simpsons* offers insight into American religion, but needs to be analyzed critically in light of American religious diversity.

While *The Simpsons* was rising to its critical heights in the 1990s, *South Park* was born in 1997 after struggling filmmakers Trey Parker and Matt Stone—who bonded at the University of Colorado at Boulder over a shared love of *Monty Python's Flying Circus* (BBC 1969–1974)—made a short cartoon for a studio executive who had asked them to make a video Christmas card to send to his friends. They created the infamous *The Spirit of Christmas* short in which Jesus and Santa Claus fight each other over the meaning of Christmas. In this film we learn that Christmas is really about presents and we are given valuable moral advice including, "don't say pig fucker in front of Jesus."[24] After the video went viral, Comedy Central signed Parker and Stone, and upon its 1997 debut, *South Park* became the fledgling network's biggest hit.

From its inception, *South Park* has featured the antics of four fourth-grade boys (for the first three seasons and for some of the fourth they were in third grade): Stan Marsh is an average middle-class child who is usually perceptive and critical of social hypocrisy. Stan's best friend, Kyle Broflovski, is the son of a Jewish lawyer and a stereotypical Jewish mother. Kyle shares Stan's perceptiveness and without Kyle's Jewishness it would be hard to tell the two characters apart. On the other hand, Eric Cartman is an extremely bigoted, greedy, and manipulative child with self-esteem issues whose perceptiveness varies in relation to how an event affects him. Cartman always seems two steps ahead of his competition when he can manipulate a situation for his selfish interests. If he does not care, then the issue does not register in his egocentric world. Finally, Kenny McCormick is a poor boy who is dressed in a parka, who mumbles incomprehensibly, and whose weekly demise was a running gag for the first few seasons.[25]

South Park focuses on the boys' ability to see through the silliness of the adult world around them, and the show purposefully exaggerates situations so that they can be humorously explored and criticized through satire. Religion is a popular target, as the tiny Colorado town of South Park experiences everything from a Catholic sex abuse scandal, to a cult scare, to even a boxing match between Jesus and Satan.[26] While the program is easily the most scatological and vulgar of the three programs discussed in this book, it is also a critical darling. Like *The Simpsons*, *South Park* has won five Emmys and a Peabody Award for its biting satire. It ranks consistently among Comedy Central's most popular pro-

grams and it sparks political discussions, in part, due to its short production schedule—episodes are made in one week, while *The Simpsons*
and *Family Guy* episodes take roughly ten months to construct. This
schedule allows *South Park* to tackle sensitive issues which the audience
may forget if Parker and Stone had to wait ten months to bring them to
air. Their treatments of the Catholic sex abuse scandals, the 2005 controversy over caricatures of Muhammad,[27] and Richard Dawkins' rise
in popularity after *The God Delusion*[28] was published exemplify *South
Park*'s ability to critically engage topical subjects on short notice, which
is a key factor in their ability to construct religious satires.

A body of scholarly criticism has developed around *South Park*'s
depictions of religion.[29] Yet, excepting sociologist Douglas Cowan's
article on *South Park*'s "All About Mormons?" and cultural studies
scholar Ted Gournelos' critical evaluation of *South Park* as oppositional culture, scholars tend to continue to repeat the idea that *South
Park* is an equal opportunity offender when it comes to religion.[30] In
one sense this is true—many religions are satirized in *South Park*—but
just as in *The Simpsons*, some religions are fairer game than others.
Australian cultural studies scholar Toni Johnson-Woods puts it best
when she writes:

> The problem is not divine leadership—God, Jesus, Moses, and other reli-
> gious deities fare pretty well—but earthly hypocrisy. *South Park*'s secular
> humanism offers every religion equal opportunity. Belief in a higher de-
> ity or deities is fine, even encouraged, but be wary of politicized religion,
> warns the show. Religion is just another powerful institution that needs to
> have its cages rattled. The show's irreverence promotes a healthy skepti-
> cism about religious dogma. The morality of a culture is reflected in the
> ability of its adherents to learn simple moral lessons and to lead "good"
> lives.[31]

As we will see, Woods' synopsis needs more nuance. *South Park* teaches
viewers to be "good" people through a comparison of religious hypocrites and those who live according to certain moral principles. Yet, what
is "good" is contentious and needs to be unpacked through an analysis
of numerous episodes, moving us beyond a more shallow argument that
all religions are treated equally.

Family Guy is the youngest of the three programs discussed in this book. The brainchild of Seth MacFarlane, a New England cartoonist who had moved to Los Angeles to work at the legendary Hanna-Barbara animation studios after graduating from the Rhode Island School of Design, *Family Guy*'s genesis lies in two short films: MacFarlane's thesis project, *The Life of Larry*, and *Larry & Steve*.[32] While the character designs are different, we can hear early versions of *Family Guy*'s family guy—Peter Griffin—and his anthropomorphic dog, Brian, in Larry and Steve. Indeed, the bumbling New England idiot that is Peter is already apparent in Larry and the brilliant but sarcastic Brian is impossible to miss in Steve. After *Larry & Steve* aired on Cartoon Network's *What a Cartoon* series, FOX asked MacFarlane to produce a pilot, which eventually became *Family Guy*.

The program originally aired after Superbowl XXXIII on January 31, 1999, and went on to suffer one of the worst fates any new program can endure. After a successful first season, FOX constantly changed *Family Guy*'s time slot, putting it up against heavyweight programs such as *Frasier* (NBC 1993–2004) and *Friends* (NBC 1994–2004). *Family Guy*'s audience could not find the program, the ratings suffered, and in 2002 the program was cancelled. But that did not spell the end. Cartoon Network acquired the syndication rights and made *Family Guy* part of their Adult Swim lineup. With a secure time slot, the program became a hit and when DVDs began flying off the shelves, FOX resurrected the program in 2004. It has been running ever since.

Family Guy is a parody of New England and American family life. Often unfavorably compared to *The Simpsons*, the program features an edgier perspective on American life. Set in the fictional town of Quahog, Rhode Island, Peter and Brian are joined by Peter's devoted if somewhat devious wife, Lois, and their three children: Meg, the social outcast; Chris, an overweight simpleton; and their genius baby Stewie. The program has evolved over time, moving away from its infamous cutaway scenes to more plot-driven escapades. It has always been rife with cultural references ranging from the topical to the obscure and pulls as few punches as it can while being aired on a major television network. This is especially true of its depictions of religion, which have become more vicious and critical over time. Indeed, while *South Park* and *The Simpsons* present different religions as having some viability,

Family Guy has become increasingly hostile toward religious organizations and people.[33]

Toward a Theory of Religious Satire

To analyze satirical portrayals of religion we need to integrate three theoretical streams: a working definition of religion, a theory of culture, and a theory of how religion and culture are sources for making satire. We need a definition of religion so that we know what we are talking about when we discuss "religion jokes." We need a theory of culture so that we can explain how different groups of people come to create jokes by combining their ideas about religion with their sense of humor. Finally, we need a theory of satire to explain how those jokes are composed from different stocks of knowledge for competitive social purposes.

A Working Conception of Religion

Religion is hard to define. It is not that most people do not have some notion of what constitutes a "religion," but rather that those conceptions are blurry.[34] Scholars of religion are no better, having turned disagreement about the definition of "religion" into intellectual blood sport. For the purposes of this book, however, we need a working definition of religion. Recognizing that there are numerous definitions that could be employed, this book builds upon William James' definition from the third lecture in *The Varieties of Religious Experience*, "the belief that there is an unseen order, and that our supreme good lies in harmoniously adjusting ourselves thereto."[35] For James, religion starts with a conviction that there is something more to this life than what our senses tell us is present. This belief in the world's inherent order allows humans to adhere to a religion despite what would be taken as disconfirming evidence in other situations.[36] James' definition is valuable because it encompasses a wide range of activities without being unnecessarily restrictive. The unseen order is psychologically powerful without relying upon the existence of gods, spirits, or the supernatural. It is also a fully human conception in that we believe in the unseen order's existence and change our behavior according to the order's standards.[37] That said, James' definition suffers from being too individualistic. Someone who hears a voice they think is God providing ethical instructions has a belief in an unseen order, and if they change their behavior to reflect these convictions they are harmoniously adjusting themselves to it. The community that supports and cultivates religious action is absent in this example, but communities are essential for our understanding of religion. They support, shape, and project the unseen order—making it seen in this world to the best of human ability.[38] If this caveat is taken into account, then our new definition is: *A religion consists of the social structures and institutions that facilitate, support, and protect the belief that there is an unseen order and that our ultimate good relies on harmoniously adjusting to it.*

This definition is broad enough to encompass the traditions that are commonly considered religions. It can also include phenomena that are not widely treated as religions (e.g., sports fans).[39] This ambiguity is useful and throughout this book the term religion will flow between traditions such as Christianity, Hinduism, and Islam and "religious" behaviors that guide us to adhere to an unseen order. We still need to narrow what we are discussing to something manageable and comparative with everyday life in the United States. This book examines groups that are popularly considered religions or "religious" in mass media, religious studies textbooks, and, most importantly, in the programs themselves. This choice enables us to include phenomena such as "spiritual" and "New Age" beliefs and practices and some "cults" in our data set, even if some people might not consider them "religions."

Our definition of religion allows us to emphasize two issues that can be mined for humor. First, religions have to convince people that there is an unseen order, and this attempt can invite skeptical questions from non-adherents. As sociologist Peter Berger argued in *The Sacred Canopy,* "All socially constructed worlds are inherently precarious. Supported by human activity, they are constantly threatened by the human facts of self-interest and stupidity."[40] Building on his earlier work with Thomas Luckmann in *The Social Construction of Reality,*[41] Berger argues that people create religious worlds through everyday interactions in which they externalize ideas, objectivate them (treat them as objective reality instead of subjective externalizations), and reintegrate these objectivated ideas into their lives as guiding principles (internalization).[42] Religions are "plausibility structures" (the sum total of our knowledge of the real world and the explanations for why things are the way they are)[43] which draw upon our "social stock of knowledge" ("knowledge of [our] situation and its limits"),[44] a common pool of knowledge that is shared within a group and sometimes widely (although not always completely) within a society. Plausibility structures need to remain believable when questioned, so we develop legitimations—answers to questions about the "why" of institutional arrangements—as a way of intellectually protecting our religious worlds. Berger identifies four levels of legitimations: a pre-theoretical level that contains simple traditional statements (e.g., "we have always done it this way"); an incipiently theoretical level, which contains proverbs, moral maxims, and traditional wisdom; explicitly theoretical statements, which can become long and convoluted in their logic; and when the meaningful order of the world achieves a level of self-consciousness.[45] For our purposes the most significant levels are the second and third levels of legitimation because they are the explanations that comedians draw upon most often when they challenge, mock, subvert, and satirize religious groups. As legitimations are repeated they become sedimented ("they congeal in recollection as recognizable and memorable entities").[46] Eventually, these sedimentations become institutions, which are patterns of behavior and rules that exist as social standards apart from the individuals who habitually perform them.[47] These terms—externalization, objectivation, internalization, plausibility structure, social stock of knowledge, legitimation, sedimentation, and institutionalization—permeate this book because, as will be discussed shortly, humor arises when what is expected differs from what happens. When we start seeing the unseen order as something that human beings work hard to maintain, the human efforts themselves belie the idea that the unseen order is "just the way things are." This contradiction between human effort and presumed naturalness of the given order of things is rife for attack.

Religions are often presented as having a special connection to "the sacred." The term sacralization is used throughout this book to explain the ways in which humans make things sacred. This conceptualization builds upon French sociologist Emile Durkheim's work.[48] Durkheim argued that religion results first from people separating the sacred and profane, and second, from their orienting their lives around the sacred. Nothing is inherently sacred or profane. Instead, these qualities are ascribed to different objects, actions, and ideas. Things that are considered sacred are "set apart and forbidden,"[49] marking them as special. "Sacred" is a category around which groups construct their collective identities. Since sacredness is ascribed and not inherent in an object, a thing has to be sacralized in order to direct group members' responses, a goal that is achieved through rituals that enable people to attach positive feelings to the object in question.[50] Sacredness is, however, "highly contagious,"[51] which Durkheim suggests helps religions to become cognitive organizers, bringing everything together into a meaningful whole. Practically, this means that once something is identified as sacred, then this significance extends to everything else that comes in contact with the object or idea.

Sociologist Robert Bellah adds an important twist to this discussion of what can be considered sacred. In "Civil Religion in America" Bellah presents American *culture* as being infused with sacredness.[52] Political speeches are his main focus; he notes that there is a widely held belief in America that the United States is divinely sanctioned as Earth's model nation. While Bellah would later abandon the term "civil religion,"[53] others continue to find American culture deeply infused with a sense of sacredness about the nation, its purpose, and its future, a sacredness that seeps into politics and popular culture alike.[54] The belief that America and its founding ideas and documents are sacred elevates the First Amendment to the Constitution of the United States of America with its protections for religion and freedom of speech to sacred status. For religious groups, this means that they have a sacred right to pursue their religious interests. For comedians criticizing those religious groups, what they have to say is also protected—even if it is perceived as slanderous.

Civil religion and civil rights are significant forces shaping the humor in *The Simpsons*, *South Park*, and *Family Guy*, especially emerging from the tradition among comedians of interpreting the First Amendment as a license to offend dominant sensibilities. Drawing from George Carlin's fights with the U.S. Supreme Court over his infamous "Seven Dirty Words" bit and Lenny Bruce's frequent run-ins with authorities over obscenity, for many contemporary comedians the First Amendment protects and enables the comedian's power to speak freely about what he or she sees as profound social problems. Indeed, without the freedom to speak there could be no questioning of government, no deconstructions of social norms with rapier wit, and no attacking of the beliefs or actions of religious leaders without risking the wrath of public officials. Historian Stephen Kercher demonstrates that post-War comedy draws this security from the precedents set by a group of liberal comedians who dared to challenge social conventions and introduced American culture to satire that challenged McCarthyism and other forms of totalitarianism that arose when the nation's moral ideals failed.[55] Contemporary American comedy loses its ability to speak truth to power without the sacredness of the First Amendment and the belief in equality arising from the Declaration of Independence, the Constitution, and the Bill of Rights. This belief in the sacredness of freedom of speech is a powerful idea that the different programs use to organize and rank the religious groups they satirize.

The second issue arising from our definition that can be mined for humorous purposes is that religions in the United States have to deal with religious diversity. When religions encounter each other, the taken-for-granted assumptions behind their unseen orders are implicitly challenged. Sociologist of religion Robert Wuthnow argues that there are four reasons why religious diversity is socially significant: "First, there are some who believe that greater diversity poses a threat to democracy itself . . . Second, there is concern that greater religious diversity raises difficult practical questions about fairness and decency. Third, there are those who fear that increasing diversity is undermining long-held American values. And fourth, there is a set of arguments suggesting that the *religious* dimension of religious diversity is itself an important cultural challenge that needs to be taken seriously."[56] Religious diversity exposes deep anxieties about how to live as a community of people with different unseen orders, and it requires religious groups to explain others' presence.[57]

We need to keep these issues of religious pluralism, instability, and competition in mind because strange behaviors and, by extension, "normal" ones, become significant factors in determining which religions are acceptable or not in each program's satirical worldview. These distinctions are the framework upon which satirical worldviews are founded and all three programs are active participants in what has been called the culture wars.[58] America's negotiations of religious diversity are built by comparing different groups and then attacking differences rather than emphasizing similarities. The tensions and ethical contradictions that arise from these similarities and distinctions make them useful fodder for humor.

Culture and Knowledge

Our definition of religion, especially when we take Berger's and Durkheim's insights seriously, invites us to look at religion as something that touches all arenas of human life. If an unseen order has something to say about how we should organize families, regulate sexual relationships, or govern our nation-states, then making the unseen order visible extends to all social arenas. Even if the United States has a formal separation of church and state, the two are intertwined in practice and in people's lives. This book draws insights from the sociology of culture dealing with how symbols and their interpretations are used to establish moral boundaries within and between communities. Sociologist Michèle Lamont argues that moral boundaries "are drawn on the basis of moral character."[59] Moral boundaries are important because they are part of a stock of knowledge for evaluating different religious groups based on the qualities of their members. As Americans continue to equate morality with religion, each religious group's plausibility structure is infused with arguments about the correctness of their moral positions. They are, as anthropologist Mary Douglas would argue, ways of maintaining purity against defilement.[60] As we will see in our discussion of humor, hypocrisy or a moral legitimation's general inefficacy is generally sufficient to justify assaulting another group to reinforce one's own moral boundaries.[61]

Moral boundaries are contested in the mass media through the use of symbols. The cartoons in question are especially powerful in contributing to long-standing sedimented legitimations because they are constantly repeated. Successful television shows live in perpetuity through reruns on basic cable and streaming over the Internet. Their legitimations are available long after their initial cultural moment has passed. Effective use of cultural symbols facilitates the transmission of ideas to audiences decades after an initial broadcast because of how they use the tools in their "cultural tool-kits." Sociologist Ann Swidler coined the term "cultural tool-kit" to explain how people draw from their cultural stocks of knowledge to engage situations as they arise.[62] We should, however, keep in mind sociologist Michael Schudson's criticism that media tends to trade in "cultural objects" that have a host of sedimented ideas already associated with them (e.g., the different values people place on publicly displayed crosses) rather than create new cultural objects from their "tool-kits" when telling stories.[63] In other words, when writing a sitcom, the creators will draw cultural objects from their cultural tool-kits and use them in a way that they think will communicate positively with a wide audience. This approach ties back into the sociology of knowledge, as our social stock of knowledge is legitimated within our moral boundaries. We communicate which things, ideas, and traditions are sacred through the use of cultural objects.[64] Once things are sacralized, they can be arranged into what Gordon Lynch calls "hierarchies of sacred forms," which exist when sacred forms are culturally arranged in such a way that one dominates the others. When this happens subjugated sacred forms still circulate in society, but the dominant form sets the agenda for their interpretation.[65] Evaluating how cultural objects teach us about moral boundaries helps us to see which sacred forms have been institutionalized. For example, in *Family Guy*'s episode "April in Quahog," Stewie is playing with *Thundercats* and *He-Man* action figures when he turns, faces the screen, and addresses the audience, "Yeah, that's right, you buy your kids ridiculously homoerotic dolls and then ask what happened? Yep, your gay son is on you buddy. Explain that to your god." This joke explicitly attacks American masculinity and its association with heterosexuality in conservative Christian culture. *Family Guy* is generally pro-homosexuality and this joke supports its politics by turning the tables on Christians who claim that homosexuality is unnatural and caused by immorality. Taking the cultural objects of "action figures," God, and conservative Christian rhetoric about homosexuality being an abomination before God, *Family Guy* inverts the Christian moral boundaries and puts the supposed moral failure of homosexuality back onto the conservative Christians, inverting the conservative Christian hierarchy of sacred forms in the process.

The Simpsons, *South Park*, and *Family Guy* have each developed a tool-kit for representing what the series thinks of different religions by selectively appropriating cultural objects available in the wider culture. These patterns have been institutionalized over time and demonstrate moral boundaries for evaluating different religious groups. This book uses the concept of institutional resonance ("meanings that are sanctioned by, and enacted within powerful institutional frameworks"[66]), and the evaluative categories of institutional consonance and institutional dissonance to explain how different religious traditions either meet or fail the moral standards at each program's core. All institutions require ongoing legitimation, and institutional adherence is the degree to which people's behavior follows institutionalized standards. Institutional consonance occurs when new ideas that are considered legitimate and build upon already held beliefs and ideas are integrated into pre-existing plausibility structures. Institutional dissonance occurs when new ideas are considered illegitimate according to preexisting plausibility structures. Each program has institutionalized an unseen order and evaluates different religions and their moral claims from this central position. When claims meet a program's standards they are consonant, and when they do not, they are dissonant. Discerning how the unseen orders of America's religious groups resonate with the underlying unseen orders of each program is essential to understanding religious satire in these programs.

Religious Satire

This book introduces a new theory of religious satire. This theory relies on Berger and Luckmann's concepts of legitimations, sedimentation, social stock of knowledge, plausibility structure, and institutionalization; the Durkheimian theory of sacralization; the sociology of culture's insights into moral boundaries and cultural objects; and cultural studies scholar Stuart Hall's methodological insight that the style of presentation is a key to a cultural product's epistemological origins.[67] Humor and religion build upon these concepts because they are both eminently human phenomena. This theory of satire stresses incongruity, conflict, protecting one's plausibility structures, and attacking that of an opponent.

A satirist attacks an opponent's plausibility structure by humorously showing its ideological inconsistencies and demonstrating how the opponent's assumed norms are incongruous (logically inconsistent) with reality. Traditional humor theory posits three different explanations for why we laugh: superiority (we laugh at an opponent's inferiority), relief (we laugh to relieve psychological pressure), and incongruity (we laugh at the pleasant resolution of confusion).[68] Sociologist Murray Davis puts the three theories into a useful interrelationship, writing "an individual (1) who perceives through humor an 'incongruity' in the outer world, (2) expresses through laughter the 'release' or 'relief' of being subjectively unaffected by this objective contradiction, and (3) consequently feels his laughingly sustained subjective integration manifests his 'superiority' to the humorously disintegrated object."[69] Most contemporary theories emphasize incongruity. The idea is simple—humor arises from the pleasant resolution of something that we encounter as incongruous that, as folklorist Elliott Oring notes, arises in a context that is considered appropriate for humor.[70] Otherwise we are just confused or puzzled. But in order to find something incongruous we first need a sense of congruity—an ordered understanding of the world. In other words, we need a plausibility structure. The rules, powers, and basic assumptions about how the social world operates are in place from previous generations of humans interacting with each other by the time we are born. Anything that deviates from this social order is problematic. The world we are socialized into provides our sense of congruity. Yet, how we think the world works, how others think it operates, and how it actually functions can be completely different. When faced with these incongruities, we need some way of reconciling them.

Sociologist Anton Zijderveld offers us a useful set of tools for creating humor from incongruity. Building on Berger and Luckmann's sociology of knowledge and sociologist Max Weber's concept of "ideal types," Zijderveld contends that scholars and societies construct ideal types that rarely, if ever, match the reality they purport to explain. Ideal types are useful heuristic tools that are not the thing itself. Jokes build upon the discrepancies between ideal types and reality. To illustrate this incongruity between reality and ideal type, consider an example from *The Simpsons* that satirizes the well-known Christian claim that Christianity teaches people to love others as they love themselves. When the Protestant minister Timothy Lovejoy tells Ned that "there's more to being a minister than not caring about people,"[71] the joke explicitly plays upon the incongruity between a man who, ideally, tries to love others and the fact that he openly acknowledges that he does not care about them. The juxtaposition between the ideal type of a minister who embodies Christian teaching and the character of Reverend Lovejoy demonstrates how our rationalizations lead us to expect him to care about others as much as himself, but this ideal type is a rationalized behavior, not a description of Lovejoy's actual indifference toward others. That this depiction is familiar—in the sense that viewers may know a minister who has stopped caring about his flock—facilitates the way the incongruity between the ideal type of a Christian who lives by the golden rule and the lived reality of self-centered and cruel Christians is transmitted to the audience.

Zijderveld argues that humor exists when we play with institutionalized meanings in a situation defined by laughter.[72] Juxtaposing ideal types with familiar social examples that do not meet expectations allows us to see our taken-for-granted existence as something relative and constructed, rather than permanent and given.[73] Understanding humor, however, requires deep cultural knowledge. People have to share values and plausibility structures—the same social stock of knowledge—in order to play with jokes' meanings.[74]

Once a basic understanding of our world is established, we can see that joking serves a variety of social functions. It can reaffirm reality, assuring us that our assumptions about life are stable. Reinforcing reality forges group solidarity and allows humor to be used to exclude others.[75] In other words, humor reinforces and makes explicit moral boundaries. We can now incorporate superiority theory's assumptions that we laugh at an inferior's weaknesses. Humor's role in conflict situations, with the need to reinforce an in-group's reality against an out-group's, is at work in all three programs.[76] While Zijderveld did not emphasize conflict, it is an implicit component of Berger's theories about religious pluralism and the existential threats different religions pose for each other.[77] Legitimations exist for offensive and defensive purposes. They are intellectual tools meant to protect plausibility structures against opponents.[78] Jokes are, therefore, legitimations. They employ meanings, playing with them within a plausibility structure's logical confines. Even if jokes relativize reality, making us aware of our world's precariousness, in a pluralistic situation they can become effective tools for determining who is within our social group and who is not.[79]

The sociology of humor offers us a variety of useful tools for connecting humor to the "seen order" and its social differences. Sociologist

Giselinde Kuipers argues that humor conveys standards and works as a form of symbolic capital, always marking social and moral boundaries between groups.[80] Sociologist Christie Davies' theory that there are two general types of ethnic jokes in the world, stupid and canny, is also useful for explaining how social and moral boundaries become equated with inherent characteristics in excluded groups.[81] For Davies, stupidity is "a general and universal quality and has come to include and to refer particularly to an inability to understand and cope with those technical aspects of the modern world that are common to most countries rather than simply to a lack of understanding of local customs, practices, or forms of speech."[82] Ethnic groups that are marginal in society, but also closely related to the dominant group, are often considered stupid, as Pollack jokes in the United States or "Newfie" jokes in Canada demonstrate. Jokes about canniness, on the other hand, imply "cleverness and rationality, but it is a shrewd cleverness, and a calculating rationality applied in the pursuit of personal advantage. Indeed, jokes about 'canny' groups often depend . . . on their alleged disposition to use these qualities in ways and in contexts that others find ludicrously inappropriate and excessive."[83] Scots and Jews have historically been these jokes' main targets.

Davies contends that jokes about stupidity and canniness help the dominant ethnic groups who tell them deal with the tensions of modernity by deflecting their anxieties onto peripheral groups. Jokes are minor social controls because they implicitly praise majorities while explicitly ridiculing minorities.[84] However, Davies has argued that jokes do not start wars and are not usually reasons to fight.[85] He argues that jokes are "not social thermostats regulating and shaping human behavior, but they are social thermometers that measure, record, and indicate what is going on."[86] This analogy is useful because jokes and popular comedies such as *The Simpsons*, *South Park*, and *Family Guy* can give us a sense of the cultural climate. They can tell us who is considered dominant, stupid, and canny in society. For example, in *The Simpsons*, Ned Flanders, the Simpsons' evangelical neighbor who follows the Bible to the point that he keeps kosher "just to be on the safe side,"[87] is portrayed as stupid because of his inability to think apart from biblical-literalist Christian dogma. Meanwhile, the Hindu Apu is canny because he represents the model minority stereotype applied to high achieving Indian Americans and the stereotype of a greedy convenience store clerk who applies an exorbitant markup to his goods. *The Simpsons, South Park*, and *Family Guy* are thermometers that measure certain sets of values. To understand each program's jokes, viewers need to understand the way each program manipulates everyday knowledge to craft its humorous arguments, even if viewers do not agree with these presentations.

Davies, however, ignores a volatile and important element in his sociology of ethnic jokes. Omitted from his survey are jokes about hated groups. Oring's study of cartoons in the White Aryan Nation's periodical *WAR* exemplifies the extremes to which humorists will go.[88] Arguing against Freud's contention that humor is a sign of repressed attitudes and that if the attitudes were aired humor would disappear,[89] Oring demonstrates that the racist group uses humor to further its agenda. He presents a variety of cartoons from the magazine, including one depiction of a smiling African American with a stocking cap, large mouth with thick lips and a missing tooth, wide nose, and a sign that says "Will Make Excuses for Food."[90] This caricature combines some of the most gratuitous stereotypes of African Americans, including the ideas that they are lazy and make excuses while expecting handouts. The joke itself works on the association between the man's sign and some homeless people's signs, which read "Will Work for Food."[91] These jokes reflect a particular worldview, and Oring contends that *WAR*'s founder Tom Metzger would include such depictions "to imagine—rightly or wrongly—other laughers like oneself."[92] In short, *WAR*'s cartoons are another example of using humor to build community through exclusion. Throughout this book Davies' and Oring's insights are combined to show that jokes that are told about marginal groups provide us with insight into how those groups are found wanting according to the joke-teller's standards. Religious groups that are seen as central are valued, while all other groups are judged and found lacking. Stupidity, canniness, and dangerous qualities that justify hatred are all criteria that can be used to marginalize religious groups through satire.

Satirists work with a social stock of knowledge and frame it in a way that exposes juxtapositions between the joker's plausibility structure, which is treated as congruous with how the world should be, and an opponent's plausibility structure, which is viewed as incongruous. Satire is rooted in social conflict between competing plausibility structures, but the ability to disseminate an ideological position through a humorous program—say, a mass-mediated, syndicated, animated sitcom—gives certain satirists disproportionate power compared to others.[93] All knowledge workers (not just satirists) pursue and use knowledge for the benefit of those with similar perspectives, but in a pluralistic society knowledge is inherently contentious. Knowledge is not just a way of coming to know "the truth," but it is also a weapon with which to discredit opponents.[94] For example, each program discussed in this book attacks Christianity because Christians often seem to fall short of their tradition's presumed moral standards. Homer Simpson once summarized Christianity as "the one [religion] with all the well-meaning rules that never work out in real life."[95] This joke demonstrates how *The Simpsons* incorporates opposing viewpoints into its humor as a means of criticizing them. While Christians may advance ethical principles based on doctrine and tradition, this joke emphasizes the disjunction between ideal type and lived reality. It relies on a cultural familiarity with the basics of Christian belief and exposes the basics' faults for comedic advantage.

Jokes are satirical when their humor is used to attack opposing perspectives.[96] Satirical jokes bring different unseen orders and their moral boundaries into conflict and use humor to expose the inconsistencies in an opponent's viewpoint. When a joke undermines an opponent's plausibility structure, it reinforces the joke-teller's unseen order. Satirical jokes take knowledge about a religious tradition and frame it according to a symbolic system that shapes an interpretation of the religion. This satirical framing draws upon deeply held cultural differences and expresses them in a narrative format that helps us understand the situation being represented and the appropriate social response. Satire enables this transmission to take place by strategically employing ignorant familiarity and inverting social norms so that we not only learn why a satirist's opponent is inferior, but also what should be done about them.

Consider the following example of how sacredness is conducted through religion and across other institutions while satirizing Christianity in *Family Guy*'s episode "And I'm Joyce Kinney." In this episode the Griffins are identified as regular churchgoers. Indeed, Lois is the church organist and a favorite parishioner of the priest. As the episode progresses, however, we learn that in her youth Lois made the pornographic film *Quest for Fur*. Scandal ensues after her past is announced on the local news and the priest throws her out of the church. Later, she returns and tells the judgmental congregation:

> You know, I've been coming to this church for years. I've heard all the stories. Who did Jesus hang around with? Mary Magdalene. And who was she? A prostitute. Which means if they had cameras back then, I bet she would have done a porno. [*People whisper in astonishment as Peter rolls in a projector and Meg flicks a switch, lowering a projection screen that covers the cross.*] And if she did, I know that Jesus would have forgiven her. Am I any worse than Mary Magdalene? And more importantly, are you all better than Jesus?

She then plays the porno and the priest exclaims, "I know I'm a man of God, but that [*beep*] is hot!" The congregants stand and cheer as the episode concludes.

While this narrative certainly contains the standard situation comedy formula of introducing a problem, having a series of madcap adventures, and resolving the problem satisfactorily before returning things to normal for next week, it also speaks to the way in which sacredness is administered for satirical purposes. Christianity has had a troublesome history with sexuality and pornography is taboo in most congregations. Lois' story shows how the unseen order is maintained by attaching positive sacredness to the church and negative sacredness to pornography.[97] It was insufficient to claim that Lois was no longer sacred. Instead she had to be removed from the group because she was considered a threat. Her experience in pornography cannot be associated with good—it is evil. Yet, her restoration depends upon a rebuttal based on a narrative that is also considered sacred—the life of Jesus as told in the four gospels of the Christian scriptures. It is only by saying that Jesus would not have shunned her that she can make her case before the people capitulate to their base sexual instincts, reintegrating Lois into the congregation. The legitimations justifying her exclusion and inclusion were built on theoretical logic that only makes sense within the context of Christian theology and history. After all, if you are not a Christian and have no qualms with pornography, why would Lois need to be shunned from your company? How Christianity shapes other institutions such as family, sexuality, and mass media all play a role in shaping the stereotyped Christian response in this example. Presenting their behavior as ultimately hypocritical undermines the moral boundaries that many Christians draw between good Christian morality and consuming pornography. In this case, score one for the people who like their pornography and do not worry about what Christians have to say. Different unseen orders have been brought together, one plausibility structure has been attacked, and moral boundaries and *Family Guy*'s unseen order have been reinforced. This is satire's religious work.

Finally, our theoretical framework of humor rejects Berger's moralistic interpretation of humor in *Redeeming Laughter*, which echoes classic and contemporary works in religion and humor studies that see humor as a way into a "comic world" of happiness.[98] In this tradition, satirical humor mobilizes knowledge to attack moral failings and to show us the way to the divine. Earlier, in *A Rumor of Angels*, Berger argued that laughter is one of the "signals of transcendence" that affirms the existence of something greater than our socially constructed worlds.[99] The theory of satire presented in this book rejects this notion because while humor—especially satire—inverts social norms and reveals different ways of living, that interpretation's moral direction needs contextual evaluation, which Berger's analysis lacks. Any understanding of society gained in a "finite province of meaning"—experiences such as dreams, religious visions, or paranormal encounters that are by definition extraordinary—*always* has to be reinterpreted into the cognitive and institutional frameworks that shape everyday life if it is to be available as a legitimation.[100] Although Berger is aware of humor's critical capabilities, in emphasizing a finite province of meaning's universality he departs from an empirically testable theory of humor. Throughout his oeuvre, Berger theorizes humor as something that is universal not only in the sense that every society experiences humor, but that those experiences have similar content.[101] By framing his analysis in theological terms he takes us away from looking at what actual humorous instances signify. As Douglas writes, "all jokes are expressive of the social situations in which they occur."[102] Therefore, in a study of religious humor in animated sitcoms, we have to identify the social situations that a program represents, the institutionalized bodies of knowledge it draws upon, and the critical position it takes on different social issues. Whether or not they direct us toward a universal truth is knowledge unavailable to the sociologist.

Satire is the art of using one plausibility structure to attack another through humor. Satirists take appropriate incongruities that arise from a conflict between the moral boundaries established by the different legitimations that support institutionalized religious plausibility structures and reinforce their own plausibility structures by denigrating their opponents. Humor is a tool for quickly drawing upon cultural knowledge to protect one unseen order from the threat of another. Religious satire is, therefore, religious in a twofold sense. It is religious in part because its content deals with "religion" and it is religious because the desecration of an opponent is the sacralization of one's own plausibility structure. While some may see this as a moral "correction" of somebody else's error, sociologically it is evidence of an ongoing competition between unseen orders for the privilege of enforcing one definition of reality over another upon society at large. Satire is fought in an arena defined by humor, but that does not make the battle any less vicious. We can understand how satire is used in the religious arena if we pay close attention to the ways in which satirists draw our attention to institutional consonance and dissonance. To hear these institutional resonances we need an appropriate method.

Watching Cartoons as Work

Methodologically, two routes were taken to identify the patterns of how religion is humorously portrayed in spoken words, visual depictions, and plotlines in *The Simpsons*, *South Park*, and *Family Guy*. First, I undertook what Stuart Hall calls "a long preliminary soak."[103] I have watched these programs for decades and am familiar with their perspectives on religion from repeated viewings. Then, to test for religion's presence, I watched every episode of the three programs, pausing to write down references to religion in each episode that was not a "religion episode" (an episode in which religion drives the plot), and taking notes on the religion episodes. There is a tremendous amount of material that can be classified as "religious" in the three programs. Indeed, through the 2014–2015 seasons, 529 of *The Simpsons*' 552 episodes, 209 of *Family Guy*'s 249 episodes, and 200 of *South Park*'s 257 episodes contained a clear religion reference. Furthermore, I categorized thirty *Simpsons* episodes, eighteen

Family Guy episodes, and forty-one *South Park* episodes as "religion episodes." I did not transcribe the religion episodes. Instead, I made notes about their content in order to keep the narrative structure and direct quotes available the same way I would if I were using a book that was open on my desk beside me.

Among the non-religion episodes, some references are insignificant when it comes to analyzing a program's view on religion's role in public life. For example, in one *Simpsons* episode Homer Simpson's father, Abraham, accuses his son of being "no angel behind the wheel."[104] While this is, technically, a reference to religion (you have to know what an angel is to understand the expression), it is not a commentary on religious life in the United States. By contrast, there are numerous times when Cartman's anti-Semitic jokes in *South Park* or *Family Guy*'s anti-Semitic content feels less like a religious jab than an ethnic one, but because those lines are blurred in Jewish life and culture I have included them and they are discussed in this book.

That said, there is a substantial amount of material in each of these programs that comments—either with a snappy one-liner or an extended morality play—on religion's significance in modern life. Each program's perspectives on major social issues regarding religion are elaborated in two ways. The first is to pay close attention to the "religion episodes" since those are the longest, best-developed statements on religion that the programs offer. We can study their narrative structure, as which characters are presented as honest believers and which as hypocrites are telling signs that allow us to evaluate religion through fictional characters' actions. To borrow from sociologist Erving Goffman, each cartoon sets its own dramaturgical stage upon which its characters perform.[105] As a theoretical lens, dramaturgy invites us to see all of social life as a structured play. While we each improvise within our roles, to break out of them would disrupt social life. The dramaturgical stages of our lives are largely set before us and we are socialized into them (e.g., educational settings, religious performances, medical practice). The ability to modify the rules of the performance to suit one's interests is the artist's creative license. Each program's creative team crafts their dramaturgy from common elements in American culture so that viewers are familiar with the rules of social interaction that structure the programs. They are not creating social behavior from nothing. Instead, they are taking what is familiar and using familiar settings and behavior to stage their critiques. This material is also tied into controversies and cultural struggles, suggesting that the shows' creators find it useful to draw upon a body of religious knowledge for humorous purposes, even if they cannot be sure their audience will understand these references. Out of these examples, a pattern emerges for interpreting religion in each program.

Second, I took short scenes, one-line jokes, and quick visual references to religion in other episodes as corroborating evidence. If the "religion episodes" are the major performance pieces in each program, the other information is what helps to project the depth and details that allow ignorant familiarity to develop and satirize contemporary religious people. Ned Flanders, the Simpsons' evangelical neighbor, is an excellent example. Ned is a complex stereotype of evangelicals. He makes numerous references to scripture, religious politics, and Christian ethics in episodes in which he has a minor role. Those examples are significant because they continue to develop the character and reinforce the interpretations established in the religion episodes.

To arrive at the patterns for identifying the criteria for including and excluding different religious groups I used qualitative methods of content analysis common to cultural studies of mass media and religion. Following Hall, this is not a work of content analysis that finds the substantive interpretation of religion each program offers in the quantity of the references. If this was a work of purely numerical quantity, it would focus almost exclusively on God, Jesus, Christianity, and Judaism. Instead, I follow the path that Hall characterizes as the way of the literary/linguistic and stylistic analysis:

> The analyst learns to "hear" the same underlying appeals, the same "notes," being sounded again and again in different passages and contexts. These recurring patterns are taken as pointers to latent meanings from which inferences as to the source can be drawn. But the literary/linguistic analyst has another string to his bow: namely, strategies for noting and taking account of emphasis. Position, placing, treatment, tone, stylistic intensification, striking imagery, etc., are all ways of registering emphasis. The really significant item may not be the one which continually recurs, but the one which stands out as an exception from the general pattern— but which is *also* given, in its exceptional context, the greatest weight.[106]

Our interest is in how these programs deal with contemporary religious diversity in the United States through humor. That means, for example, that while they may not write many episodes exclusively about Muslims (*The Simpsons* and *Family Guy* each have one episode, *South Park* has five), Islam's importance in the contemporary United States merits an extended discussion of a comparatively small sample because how these programs understand Islam helps to explain how they understand the roles of stigmatized minority religious groups in America. Qualitative understandings of the patterned depictions of different religious groups help us to understand the different religious stratifications across the three programs with much greater clarity than sheer numbers can provide.

This type of content analysis is fruitfully used by various scholars in religious studies and the sociology of religion such as Douglas Cowan, Heather Hendershot, Kathryn Lofton, Melani McAlister, and Gordon Lynch.[107] These scholars all study the content of specific media—which ranges from religious documents, magazines, and films to news media and television entertainment—with the goal of identifying relevant cultural scripts within them that comment on the broader society while simultaneously contributing to it. This ideological criticism focuses on how cultural producers create products from a broad range of beliefs, ideas, and symbols circulating in society, an approach that differs from other methodologies for studying mass media and religion, including audience reception studies,[108] studies of fan cultures,[109] or examinations of media's use in everyday life in which the audience is the arbitrator of a cultural production's meaning.[110] These other studies use interviews and observations to determine cultural objects' meanings by examining a group's claims about an object's significance rather than investigating the object itself for the claims that people make through it.

While other methods have yielded valuable insights into the relationship between religion, mass media, and the broader culture in which we live, qualitative content analysis is employed in this book because it is best suited to answering the question of how a shared stock of knowledge is used to compose jokes about religion in the United States. This book is grounded in an approach that treats cultural products as the creations of group activities that contain their creators' ideologies. In this book these expressions are transmitted through the genre conventions of the animated sitcom and contemporary standards of humor.[111] Studying the jokes through the sociologies of knowledge and religion enables us to understand why the assumptions behind the jokes were considered humorous in the first place and they tell us a great deal about the worldviews of three different groups behind the programs. These programs are truly collaborative efforts, as writers, producers, animators, voice actors, and network executives, among others, all contribute to the final product. For this reason, this book refers to each program's "creators" because each episode is the end result of numerous interpersonal dynamics behind the scenes between people who share the goal of creating the best product they can for audience consumption. From writers' rooms to animators' decisions about how to portray a religious character or scene; from the voice actors' expressions to the producer's final editorial decisions, the "creative teams" are discussed throughout this book because unless a specific writer, actor, editor, or artist who created a particular example can be identified, each example is treated as a collaborative product that reflects a shared "sense of humor." In this, each of the three programs' humor is sociologically relevant. Their humor is a product of shared group sensibilities and reflects sociological patterns that structure that humor instead of being the product of an individual genius.

Where to Now?

The following five chapters discuss how each program presents and interprets different religions, demonstrating not only how each program uses humor to create a religious hierarchy, but also how they evaluate religion's place in the larger social fabric of contemporary America. Chapter 1 asks the simple question: *Which religious traditions are considered good and why?* Tackling constructions of "spirituality" and atheism across the three programs, this chapter demonstrates that certain features make a religion good in the worldviews of each of these three programs: It is individualistic, it is not tied to a geographic region or ethnic (read: "non-white") identity, it is not consumerist, and it is based on human reason. There are problems with this conceptualization of spirituality—namely the way disadvantaged people's religious traditions and ethnic identities are displaced from their historical and social roots so that they can be turned into consumable goods for middle-class American consumers. The purpose of chapter 1 is to establish a foundation for the framework used in these shows to judge other religions as lacking. As we will see, each series has a somewhat different worldview and promotes different values. *The Simpsons* privileges individual spiritual seeking which scientific rationality holds in check, *South Park* favors individual creativity as a spiritual pursuit, and *Family Guy* embraces atheism and scientific rationality, while also allowing for individual spiritual exploration.

Chapter 2 examines how and why other groups are excluded, starting with the problem of "ethnic" religions for the three programs. Native American religions, Hinduism, and Judaism—traditions that are intimately tied to specific ethnic groups—offer the opportunity to ask the question of whether or not non-white people can fully integrate into American society as religious participants. The answer for these programs in each case is an uneasy "no." Ethnicity is seen as exclusive and "ethnic" characters are relegated to the margins, "set apart and equal" if you will. This chapter also considers the problem of anti-Semitism and how it reproduces an ignorant familiarity that Jews are different and that there are limits to trusting them.

Chapter 3 asks when Christians can be good citizens. Using the programs' debates around the Bible, God, and Jesus and a detailed examination of Ned Flanders from *The Simpsons*, it narrates Christianity's potential in the three programs while also highlighting what they each see as Christians' failures. This chapter reveals tensions running through the three programs between moral behavior and holding beliefs that each program finds incongruous for different reasons. Chapter 3 foreshadows chapter 4, in which Christian bigotry, greed, and malevolence—in the form of Christian proselytization, sexual ethics and sexual violence, and censorship—are used as examples of dangerous behaviors that keep Christians from ever fully participating in the good civil sphere as defined by these programs.

Chapter 5 concludes our tour of the way different religious groups are represented with a consideration of those groups that are hated. We first examine cults and new religious movements and how the programs replicate the fears of "dangerous" and "evil" religions, excluding those who find meaning in these religions. Then we turn to Islam—which has made some inroads in the programs in recent years—to consider not only how the programs changed their perspective on the world's second largest religion in recent years, but also how they are constrained by post–9/11 politics that continue to stigmatize Muslims, especially in American popular culture.

Finally, the volume concludes with a discussion of why the humorous depictions of religion in these programs matter for the public presentation of religions, how their relative merits are discussed and evaluated, and what tools viewers should bring to their viewing experiences. It will help us to understand why humorists are drawn to religious life and why humor is a strategic cloak for what can sometimes be the dirty, vicious, and slanderous enterprise of publicly criticizing religion.

1

Sacred Centers

HOMER
So I figure I should just try to live right and worship you in my own way.

GOD
Homer, it's a deal.
—Homer Simpson talks to God in *The Simpsons'* "Homer
the Heretic"

In *The Simpsons* episode "Homer the Heretic" Homer skips church on a cold, snowy morning while his family attends church and freezes miserably because the heater is broken. Homer dances around the house in his underwear (parodying Tom Cruise in *Risky Business*), watches football, and eats a waffle wrapped around a stick of butter and served on a toothpick. He attributes his great morning to missing church and vows never to go again. Marge is upset, but Homer is adamant. Later, when God visits Homer in a dream and accuses him of forsaking his church, Homer defends himself, saying, "I'm not a bad guy. I work hard and I love my kids. So why should I spend half my Sunday hearing about how I'm going to hell?" God agrees that Homer has a point. He allows Homer to worship him in his own way before disappearing to appear in a tortilla in Mexico.

This encounter convinces Homer of his decision. He walks around his backyard dressed like St. Francis of Assisi, creates fake holidays to get out of work, refuses to give money to local entertainer Krusty the Clown for the Brotherhood of Jewish Clowns, insults Apu by offering his *murti* of Ganesha a peanut, and is chased by the Flanders clan who try to bring him back to the church by singing the Sunday school song "The Lord Said to Noah." Falling asleep the next Sunday morning, Homer accidentally sets his house on fire, only to have Ned Flanders and the Springfield Volunteer Fire Department—including Krusty and Apu—rescue him. Homer's explanation for the fire is simple: "The Lord is vengeful." Reverend Lovejoy disagrees, asserting that God "was working in the hearts of your friends and neighbors when they went to your aid, be they Christian, Jew, or miscellaneous [Hindu]." Reverend Lovejoy convinces Homer to return to the church and Homer is there the next week, front row center—asleep and snoring loudly. The episode ends with Homer dreaming that he is in heaven, walking with God, who consoles Homer, saying, "Don't feel bad, Homer. Nine out of ten religions fail in their first year." Homer's personal walk with God matters, not his relationship with the church.

We cannot understand satire without understanding the satirist's moral core, and we cannot get to those cores without studying episodes that present some religious behaviors positively. Evaluations of religion are based on the values each program holds sacred. These values are often teased out through comparisons between good religious practice and bad religions, with Christianity treated especially negatively. "Homer the Heretic" is the best place to start our investigation of the three programs' sacred centers.

Spiritual Seeking in *The Simpsons* and *Family Guy*

There is no shortage of interpretations of "Homer the Heretic" and each discussion highlights different religious tensions and anxieties from the broader culture that are reflected in Homer's choice. Journalist Mark Pinsky argues that "Homer the Heretic" is built around the question of how God wants to be worshipped and the intrafamily struggles about how to raise children when parents are unequally committed.[1] The small group study guide he co-authored with Pastor Samuel F. Parvin uses this episode to argue for the importance of having a relationship with God and belonging to a faith community.[2] Journalist Steven Keslowitz suggests the episode demonstrates that morality can be achieved apart from religion, but that religion is useful for forging communal bonds.[3] Religion scholar Gordon Lynch treats it as a discourse on American interfaith dialogue, arguing that it promotes different religions working together for the common good.[4] William Romanowski, a scholar of religion and mass media, uses Homer's decision to stay home to capture American religious individualism, while theologian Jamie Heit

Homer walks with God in heaven at the end of "Homer the Heretic"

employs this episode to illustrate how Americans are leaving Christianity for individualized spirituality, a position he deems perilous.[5] Journalist Chris Turner, on the other hand, thinks "Homer the Heretic" is an attempt to strike a balance between fundamentalist and faithless extremes, contending that, in contrast to the Flanders, in the Simpson household "faith is flexible, responsive, debatable, *alive*."[6] Cultural studies scholar Matthew Henry writes that the episode is an extended critique of fundamentalist, institutionalized religion.[7] For religious studies scholar Lisle Dalton and his associates it coalesces the program's many religious themes: "Against the backdrop of declining religious authority, increasing personal choice, and 'flattening' of doctrines into more palatable themes, television presents revamped morality plays such as this in which personal piety, religious pluralism, and sincere goodness rate higher than denominational adherence and church attendance."[8] Dalton and his associates hit upon this episode's significance for understanding the larger world of *The Simpsons*. To find the religion jokes in "Homer the Heretic" funny you have to at least entertain the belief that all religions are comparable and that devotion to a set of institutional guidelines is foolish. You also have to believe that a relationship with God to further your spiritual development is personally beneficial.

"Homer the Heretic" presents the common American distinction between "religion" and "spirituality." Individuals often maintain that they can be spiritual without being religious. Central to this notion is the idea that spirituality is something people craft for themselves by drawing from the world's religious traditions. Sociologist of religion Wade Clark Roof calls spiritual seekers *bricoleurs* because they "cobble together a religious world from available images, symbols, moral codes, and doctrines, thereby exercising considerable agency in defining and shaping what is considered to be religiously meaningful."[9] Personal spirituality draws upon numerous sources. For example, in *Habits of the Heart*, sociologist Robert Bellah and his associates provide the classic example of Sheilaism, named after interviewee Sheila Larson's private faith, which was crafted from various external sources and her personal experiences and constituted belief in God without attending church.[10] Yet, most conceptions of spirituality share three common characteristics. First, spirituality tends to be immanentist—its meaning and authority are found within the individual and not in institutional doctrines and dogmas. Second, spirituality often features a metaphysical connection between a supernatural force or power and the individual, with the force imparting special teaching and insight. Third, spirituality is often seen to apply to the concerns of everyday life.[11] In *The Simpsons* these characteristics are mobilized through ignorant familiarity to generate institutional consonance—as noted earlier, institutional consonance occurs when new ideas are considered legitimate and build upon already held beliefs, and ideas are integrated into preexisting plausibility structures. The trend toward a focus on spirituality versus organized religion resonates with the value Americans place on individualism and reinforces a moral boundary against traditions that require participants to stifle their individualism for dogma.

The significance of "Homer the Heretic" lies in the fact that Homer finds spiritual awareness within himself and legitimates his spirituality through his desires. When God approves of Homer worshipping in his own way, Homer has all the justification he needs to avoid things he deems undesirable—like going to church. Jokes in this episode promote relativism, thereby facilitating spiritual seeking. For example, after Homer makes his decision he asks Marge, "What if we picked the wrong religion? Each week we're just making God madder and madder." Bart, who also wants to stop going to church, claps his hands and exclaims, "Testify!," parodying evangelical revivals. On the DVD commentary, producer Al Jean suggests that Homer's question is relevant, but its importance lies in relativism's corrosive effects on religious certainty. Maintaining certainty in the face of great and legitimate religious diversity is difficult. The First Amendment's right to religious freedom ensures that there will always be challenges to religious plausibility. *The Simpsons* suggests through its jokes that we should embrace relativism and find our own ways. Through seeking, searching, and the ability and willingness to change traditions, spirituality is legitimated in this episode's jokes because it appears more authentic than the church's rote repetition. This religious flexibility is characteristic of baby boomer religion, which is hardly surprising when we consider that *The Simpsons'* writers and producers are boomers or boomers' children.[12] *The Simpsons* draws upon ideas that undermine religious exclusivity and adopts a perspective that all religions are equally valid—even ones concocted by lazy egoists who want to stay at home, drink beer, and watch television. To be spiritual Homer had to leave and find a religion that enabled him to be himself.

Family Guy's episode "The Father, the Son, and the Holy Fonz" echoes "Homer the Heretic," but *Family Guy* has Peter form his own church dedicated to the worship of Arthur Fonzarelli of *Happy Days* (ABC 1974–1984) fame.[13] Disillusioned with his devout father Francis Griffin's Catholicism and straying from the generic Christianity the Griffins normally practice (sometimes it is Catholic, other times Protestant), he decides to find his own religion. After Peter tries the Latter Day Saints (LDS), Jehovah's Witnesses, and Hinduism, the belligerent and intolerant Irish Catholic Francis challenges his despondent son saying, "You want to find religion? All you got to do is look in your heart. Who's always been there for ya, offering wisdom and truth? You've known him all along son, now worship him!" Peter has a sudden revelation and prays to Fonzie for a sign. A naked Lindsay Lohan then rings the doorbell and crabwalks into the house. Peter's new religion is confirmed as he exalts, "Fonzie be praised!"

Peter preaches in front of the Fonz suspended as if he were crucified

Like Homer, Peter starts his own religion. Peter's is different because he establishes a church and has people visit a renovated barn that has stained glass windows featuring the characters from *Happy Days* and a statue of the Fonz hanging on the back wall, smiling, with his arms stretched to the side with two thumbs pointed straight up.

The visual reference to a crucifix is intentional, as MacFarlane notes on the DVD commentary that Fonzie was originally hanging from a cross, but censors made them remove it. Peter wears a priest's robes, speaks in King James English, and tells his congregation to "all rise" before telling them to "now sit on it" like the Fonz. People are attracted to this religion. Francis, however, thinks it is an abomination and tries to drive Peter away from his newly established church—a move Brian supports. Eventually, the two convince characters from television's past to form their own religions and Peter's flock leaves him. Although Peter is depressed at the episode's conclusion, Lois cheers him up since he was "preaching honesty, friendship, courage, and if you managed to inspire even one person to embrace those values, then you were a success." Although Peter is skeptical, we learn that he inspired Francis to do just that as he prays in front of Fonzie's picture at the episode's conclusion.

As *The Simpsons*' creative team did in "Homer the Heretic," *Family Guy*'s team has Peter leave Christianity in search of a more personal faith. There are some substantial differences—Peter's founding of a church as opposed to Homer's individualism—but the basic premise of free-form spiritual experimentation remains. Homer and Peter each look inside themselves and find that popular culture and their basest desires meet their needs. Homer wants to eat, watch television, and sleep in on Sundays. Peter wants to relive *Happy Days* without the emotional baggage accompanying his father's Catholicism. These practices are not condemned in the programs, even as the religions fade away after the week's hijinks. God consoles Homer and Peter has made a substantial change in his father's life. Later, when we consider how *Family Guy* has approached religion in more recent seasons, we will see that this portrayal is practically benevolent compared with later treatments. Christianity is treated roughly in "The Father, the Son, and the Holy Fonz" as Francis is verbally abusive (he calls Lois a "Protestant whore"), but Peter's teachings are about honesty, friendship, and courage and even though everybody in the pews is ostensibly a misguided idiot, they are at least being misguided into doing something positive. Spirituality, and especially spiritual seeking, thus finds its way into the core of *The Simpsons*' and *Family Guy*'s acceptable centers. There is an institutional resonance with the general principles of American individualism in that Homer and Peter both follow their basic instincts, find a sense of personal fulfillment, and did not let anyone detract them from that pursuit. In these two programs spirituality without religion is, as Boston University sociologist Nancy Ammerman argues about spirituality in general, a moral and political position.[14]

Seekers Consume and Convert

Despite these positive portrayals of religious innovation, there is a tension around religion and spirituality's commodification in the three programs. Religion, spirituality, and consumerism are intimately linked in America's history. Historian R. Laurence Moore shows this connection's history by examining the history of American religion and consumerism from the eighteenth-century market for evangelical novels to the contemporary religious marketplace in which Christian bookstores sell CDs, books, and "Jesus junk"; televangelists populate the airwaves; and New Age stores sell an assortment of "spiritual" goods and guides to those who can afford them. Turning religion into consumable products is not *just* to make a dollar. Religious people enter the market to promote their values and shape others' perspectives. Mass-produced goods are mediated religious ideals, not things that inherently destroy the sacred elements in people's lives. This competitive drive is constantly being revised, and the market is seen as a legitimate place to argue for one's religious position, although Moore concedes that its underlying logic could keep religion from becoming a serious and elevating part of people's lives.[15] Media scholar Mara Einstein voices a similar concern that "religion isn't supposed to be comfortable, and it is through discomfort that we find new parts of ourselves."[16] Einstein's latent assumption is that religion, consumption, and financial profit cannot coexist—an assumption other scholars have criticized. Moore writes, "The mystery of agency haunts us because we want to judge the quality of the product the past has served up and to wonder whether anything we might do from this point will matter. Many who do not like the business and commercial side of religion nourish the thought that it is never too late to do something."[17]

Spirituality's commodification gets a rougher treatment from religion scholars Jeremy Carrette and Richard King, who attack the consumption of "spiritual" products. They assert that spirituality is neoliberal ideology's tool and that selling "spiritual" things numbs consumers to modern life's pains rather than challenging them to change their circumstances.[18] Drawing upon religious traditions for its material, contemporary spirituality dehistoricizes religions, using their cultural capital to sell products that run counter to what Carrette and King see as the world's religions' vital, prophetic role. For them, "the most troubling aspect of many modern spiritualities is precisely that they are not troubling enough. They promote accommodation to the social, economic and political mores of the day and provide little in terms of a challenge to the status quo or to a lifestyle of self-interest and ubiquitous consumption."[19] In other words, the search for a self-fulfilling spirituality divorces us from community, tradition, and history, and we are easily divided so that corporate capitalist enterprises continue to exploit us as individuals who cannot thus overthrow the system.

Conversely, scholar of New Age movements Paul Heelas contends that although the diffuse spiritualities lumped under the term "New Age" are commodified, this does not exhaust their meaning. He writes, "my answer to the question 'When is an act of consumption?' is that acts . . . are *never* simply a matter of consumption."[20] Heelas argues that the activities we have discussed as falling under "spirituality" are also life-affirming and important to people. He criticizes scholars such as Carrette and King for reducing all consumption to something negative, rather than seeing it as complex human activity that is part of making sense of life.[21]

Across *The Simpsons, South Park*, and *Family Guy* there are three reactions to consumerism and spirituality: Conversion to another religion, assaulting consumerism, and embracing consumer spirituality. In the *Simpsons* episode "She of Little Faith" we observe Lisa's spiritual life as she converts to Buddhism. Lisa's spirituality is a significant aspect of her character, driving her personal development and influencing her involvement in many social causes as she is a vegetarian, environmentalist, and feminist. She belongs to the high IQ society MENSA and is the family's voice of reason. *Simpsons* writer David Cohen muses on DVD commentary for "Lisa the Skeptic," "When you have an episode which has a real moral or philosophical point, I think Lisa is your go-to character. And I think you really buy her as caring about it."[22] Lisa becomes a Buddhist after the First Church of Springfield (FCOS) burns down and plutocrat C. Montgomery Burns, with his business consultant Lindsey Neagle, turns it into "a faith-based emporium teeming with impulse buy items." In the episode's second act, Mr. Burns takes the fire-gutted building and expands it to include an ornate lobby and a large neon Jesus holding a lasso outside the church. The once-floundering religious institution is now a profitable business. People appear happy in the new accommodations.

Local businessman Comic Book Guy loves the giant seats, and Marge's sister Patty is pleased that Burns put ice in the urinals. In the words of Krusty's assistant Sideshow Mel, "He [Mr. Burns] restored it [FCOS] from nave to narthex!" Lisa is unconvinced, and the corporate advertising in the lobby, the church's new Jumbotron, a rotating billboard on the pulpit, and a man yelling "Money changed! Get your money changed! Right here in the temple!" exasperate her. She finally snaps when the Noid—a 1980s Domino's Pizza spokescharacter—delivers a sermon on "the sanctity of deliciousness." She screams that FOCS's directors have dressed the church like the Whore of Babylon and then leaves, refusing to have her hand stamped so she can get back in. This scene references both amusement parks where one has to pay for admission and the Mark of the Beast that Revelation 13:16–17 claims will be "marked on the right hand or forehead, so that no one can buy or sell unless he [sic] has the mark, that is, the name of the beast or the number of its name" (NRSV). The entire act narrates a strong Christian tradition of not serving both God and mammon (Matt 6:24) through biblical and popular culture references. Lisa thinks that this change has cost the church its soul and searches for a "church that is free from corruption." In the third act she finds the Springfield Buddhist Temple, where she meets Richard Gere and decides to become a Buddhist. Turner characterizes this shift as moving from one commodified religion to another because Gere is a celebrity, but this interpretation misses the fact that in *The Simpsons*, individual spiritual pursuits through personal seeking are what make a religion good.[23] *The Simpsons* presents Buddhism as a religious tradition that enables individual seeking without encouraging people to force their worldview on others or falling under capitalism's corrupting convenience.

When Lisa enters the Springfield Buddhist Temple she finds Homer's coworkers Lenny and Carl meditating. Interrupting them, she says, "I'm looking for a new faith. One that isn't so materialistic." At this point Gere's voice is heard from off camera, "Well, you've come to the right place. Buddhism teaches that suffering is caused by desire." When Lisa, Lenny, and Carl see Gere (a Tibetan Buddhist who is tending a Zen garden), Lenny and Carl have the following exchange:

LENNY
Ooh! The world's most famous Buddhist.

GERE
Well, what about the Dalai Lama?

LENNY
Who?

CARL
You know, the fourteenth incarnation of the Buddha Avalokiteshvara.

LENNY
Who's Buddha?

GERE
It's a good thing Buddhism teaches freedom from desire because I've got the desire to kick your ass.

Lenny is clearly taken in by Gere's celebrity, and his knowledge of Buddhist celebrities is limited to Hollywood's practitioners, regardless of the Dalai Lama's fame.[24] However, Lenny's ignorance is the butt of the joke, not Gere's celebrity promotion of Buddhism.

Ignorant familiarity is at work and playing with positive themes. This episode associates humility, peacefulness, and freedom from desire with Gere and Buddhism. It is assumed that viewers know of the Dalai Lama and Gere and positively connect them with the promotion of peace and enlightenment. American Buddhism is generally seen as grappling with material desires, or at the very least their manifestations in global injustice.[25] Indeed, Buddhism's appeal to spiritual seekers lies in what theologian Harvey Cox termed the turn eastward, in which people look for the solutions to Western problems in Eastern traditions.[26] Lisa's conversion draws upon this pattern in American religious history. While she was previously characterized as a liberal Christian voice of reason in the family,[27] her conversion story echoes a history of Westerners turning eastward for spiritual purity in the face of Western materialism. Lisa's decision is portrayed as consistent with other North American Buddhist converts. She is seeking, and finding, what she wants in another religious tradition without the "cultural baggage" accompanying its lived forms. This is an ignorant familiarity that reduces Buddhism to a story of post-1960s

Western converts. It does not require extensive knowledge of Buddhism's historical, geographical, and cultural diversity. It is also institutionally consonant with *The Simpsons'* larger political and religious perspective that stresses left-wing politics and individual spiritual fulfilment.[28]

In this episode Buddhism is characterized as the ideal political-left religion. Buddhists appear to be more active and socially engaged in their practice than other religious people—especially Christians. Celebrity Buddhists with political goals and public presence in the United States, such as the Dalai Lama and Richard Gere, are Buddhism's public face in *The Simpsons* rather than Buddhists who spend their time reading popular Zen books and meditating together.[29] Religious individuals engaged in positive social causes, but not proselytizing, are the ideal that "She of Little Faith's" Buddhists embody. The contrast between the good Buddhists in the Springfield Temple (which does include a celebrity) and the collective consumerism and laziness of the Christians at FCOS is why this episode should be seen as a critique of Christian consumerism rather than an attack on materialism and religion in general. We can see this in how "She of Little Faith" uses humor to satirize the irony of Christian materialism in the form of the megachurch while not extending the same treatment to Buddhism and Gere.

The critique of Christianity and its consumerist elements and the endorsement of Buddhism suggest that *The Simpsons'* creators embrace the notion that money has corrupted Christianity but not Buddhism. We should be wary of any presentation of an Eastern religion—especially one that is represented by a white convert—as spiritually pure when compared to a Western religion. Religious studies scholar Jane Iwamura argues that imputing spiritual purity into Buddhism as a way of saving the West from itself ties into Buddhism's consumption. Her concept of the "oriental monk" describes characters who "represent future salvation of the dominant culture—they embody a new hope of saving the West from capitalist greed, brute force, totalitarian rule, and spiritless technology."[30] However, once Westerners learn from the East, they are empowered to save impotent Asian cultures. This reinforces the inequality between East and West and leaves Westerners feeling superior now that Eastern wisdom has sanctified their way of life.[31] The East provides the philosophical and spiritual insight to conquer the West's failures, and Lisa's Buddhism follows this path.

What are we to make of Buddhism in "She of Little Faith"? The episode reflects a broader cultural pattern of seeing Buddhism as socially engaged and spiritually enlightened. Buddhism is also positively juxtaposed with Christianity. Yet, Gere's celebrity status remains unsettling. Gere is well known as a Buddhist and has consistently used his star status as a way to promote Tibetan independence and Buddhist causes.[32] He founded the non-profit Tibet House, and famously spoke out against China at the 1993 Academy Awards. It seems clear that he has not adopted his religion for trendy purposes. To suggest that because he is a celebrity his Buddhism is somehow demeaned is an inaccurate assessment. For Turner, Buddhism must be demeaned because Gere is a celebrity and celebrities are consumer objects. However, if we look at this episode in light of Moore's argument, we see an active Buddhist voice using the marketplace to further his religious agenda. Religious competition in the mediated marketplace of goods allows Gere a chance to share what is meaningful to him with millions of other people, and *The Simpsons* expands his platform. Money does not corrupt Buddhism in *The Simpsons* because the religion's values and political actions are supported in Lisa's behavior.

While "She of Little Faith" shows us how spirituality can exist in the marketplace without being corrupted by crass consumerism, in other contexts selling spirituality can be treated as a cardinal sin. In *Family Guy*'s episode "Brian Writes a Bestseller" Brian is furious when his book, *Faster than the Speed of Love*, bombs. After seeing that the *New York Times Book Review*'s bestseller is *Dream Your Way to Spiritual Joy* by stoner comedian Paulie Shore, Brian launches into a criticism of the spiritual book trade. "This is why nobody bought my damn book! This is what they want! *The Secret, Chicken Soup for the Soul, The Purpose Driven Life*. I tell ya, I could crap one of those things out in a night." Stewie challenges Brian to do just that and the end result is *Wish It, Want It, Do It* (written in three hours and twenty-seven minutes). The book starts with "Wish It" and reads as follows: "What are all the things you want most in the world? Use the following blank pages to write down all of your dreams and desires." The book becomes a mega-seller and fans swarm Brian, telling him how the book changed their lives. Unfortunately for Brian, this would normally be the point where he steps in as the voice of reason and exposes other people's stupidity, as *Wish It,*

Want It, Do It is treated throughout the episode as a joke at the expense of people who think they can change the world with the power of positive thought (*The Simpsons* make a similar criticism in "Bart Gets a 'Z'"). Instead, fame corrupts Brian and his reason gives way to his hubris. Thinking that he is brilliant and important, Brian goes on HBO's *Real Time with Bill Maher* with fellow guests Arianna Huffington (founder of *The Huffington Post* blog) and comedian Dana Gould to debate the question, "Does God have a role in politics?"

As the debate unfolds, Brian positions himself for failure, saying, "separation of church and state is something I'm gonna cover in my next book, *God. Period. Dammit.*" Maher rolls his eyes and pushes Brian to explain himself. Soon, Huffington makes the first serious criticism of Brian's book when she says, "I think what's actually alarming is the fact that all this kind of pseudo spirituality is being peddled to the American people in books that have, really, less substance than an issue of *TV Guide.*" The following dialogue ensues:

BRIAN
That's a good argument. It's a very good argument. I agree. I agree.

MAHER
Really? Because I read *Wish It, Want It, Do It.*

BRIAN
Oh my God! I'm so embarrassed. Uh, gosh, next thing you know both of you guys are gonna tell me that it changed your lives.

[*The others start teaming up on Brian, before they lay down their most serious criticisms of the genre.*]

GOULD
Actually, it, it, I mean, it seems that these sort of books tend to pander to the laziest kind of self-help within the narrowest socioeconomic range. I mean, yeah, you can wish it, and you can do it, but only if you have the educational advantages, the societal advantages that, like, what, five percent of the country has?

Brian on *Real Time with Bill Maher*

BRIAN
Well, yeah, you forgot "want it," which is such a big part of the book. I mean, but, but you know, then again, you just said you haven't read it so . . .

GOULD
Actually, since I said that I did read it.

MAHER
And that's another thing I have to say, aren't "wish it" and "want it" really the same thing? I mean, your book basically makes three points and two of them are the same point.

BRIAN
Well, you know, I mean, it does seem to be helping a lot of people, Bill . . .

MAHER
Well, "help" is a strong word. How does this help people, like, with cancer or in Darfur?

BRIAN
Well, I mean, it's not really for them. It's for, like, if you want a car.

MAHER
How does this help you get a car?

BRIAN
Well, it doesn't with that attitude. I mean, you have [*Brian is cut off by laughter from Huffington and the audience*]. You have to do some of the work yourself, that's why there are fifty blank pages.

MAHER
That's why I keep it by the phone.

HUFFINGTON
I think that what this is is simple exploitation of the American people who could be using the money to buy this book to actually buy something useful like legitimate healthcare that they actually need. [*Brian and Arianna trade insults again.*]

GOULD
Look, what it comes down to is, of, like, a quick fix to any and every problem you would ever have, what books like these suggest is actually damaging to a large, gullible segment of the population.

Brian eventually reaches his limit and admits that he wrote the book in an afternoon before groveling for Maher's approval, which Maher withholds. He accuses Brian of not only being a horrible person for writing the book, but of being a fraud who just wanted to write something that would sell. Brian, destroyed, loses his cool and starts peeing all over his chair, at which point Maher chases him out of the studio with a roll of paper yelling "Outside!" while Brian barks as he flees.

Family Guy's point is that there is big money in spiritual books and goods and that they may still be insipid. For example, *The Secret* book/DVD by Australian Rhonda Byrne was released on November 7, 2006 and by 2010 had sold over 2.2 million DVD copies and made over $65 million.[33] There are also over 5.3 million copies of the book in print.[34] Pastor Rick Warren's *The Purpose Driven Life* and its spinoffs had reportedly sold 30 million copies by 2007 and were consumed outside of Warren's evangelical theological tradition.[35] These are just two examples of products that are marketed to help consumers to achieve whatever results they want in the world. *Family Guy*'s criticism is based on the assumption that this material is devoid of value, as seen in Brian's ability to write the book in an afternoon and his willingness to admit he just wrote it to make money. The panel makes his actions' dangers explicit, sharing the idea that spiritual goods can actually be dangerous to one's health. It is one thing to seek, but another thing entirely to exploit others on their journeys. *Family Guy's* moral boundary resists exploiting the individual's quest—whether that exploitation comes from an organized religion or the "spirituality" market. Unlike when Peter formed the Church of the Holy Fonz, honesty, friendship, and courage are not cultivated through *Wish It, Want It, Do It.* To find this joke funny, *Family Guy* assumes that its audience finds similar books to be vapid and stupid. Self-help literature would be funny were it not for the fact that people put a lot of personal stock in it and "spiritual" best-sellers' damage comes from readers putting their time, minds, and money into a bad product. Cheap consumer objects are, in this example, an example of religious behavior to avoid.

In a rare move, *South Park* agrees with *Family Guy* in the episode "Cherokee Hair Tampons," in which Kyle contracts a serious kidney illness that requires an operation. His mother, Sheila, is apprehensive about the procedure so Stan's mother, Sharon, suggests that Sheila try naturalistic medicines that she read about in *People* magazine—a less than reputable source for medical information. They go to the local New Age store, run by a woman named Miss Information who wears a multicolored cloak, and jewelry with strange symbols, and who has "New Age" music play in the background whenever she talks. She tells them that "the reason our bodies fail is because of toxins" and American diets are causing this scourge, but all Kyle needs to recover is a mixture of lemon juice and cayenne pepper. Stan—who, according to the DVD commentary, speaks for Parker and Stone—asks Miss Information if she has ever seen a toxin, but she ignores him and sells Sheila herbs focusing on the kidneys that she acquired from Native Americans. Sharon is excited by the idea since "they [Native Americans] know how to heal the body spiritually."

Kyle, however, does not appear to recover. The next day Miss Information and some of her admirers come to see him. She pronounces that he is making progress after waving her arms over him and saying that his chi is flowing better and his aura is lighter. Kyle then throws up, but Miss Information declares the vomit is the toxins flushing out of his system. The adults are sold (although Stan remains unconvinced) and a New Age healing boom erupts in South Park. The malicious intentions behind this boom are revealed when the two Native Americans (voiced by stoner comedy duo Cheech Marin and Tommy Chong) come to Miss Information's store and sell products such as "all natural Aspirin" and "Cherokee hair tampons." It is clear that the Native Americans are running a scam, but their goods sell. Stan then enters to say that the local doctor told him Kyle needs surgery. Miss Information interjects, saying, "Well of course the doctor told you that because he wants to make money. Holistic medicine is about nature. $233 please." She takes Sheila's money and Kyle is scheduled to come in the next day for holistic healing from the Native Americans.

Upon seeing Kyle, the Native Americans recommend that he be taken to a doctor and then reveal a fact that sends the customers in the store into a frenzy of shock, fear, and revulsion: They are actually Mexicans. Indeed, they had never claimed to be Native Americans, but Miss Information said they were because "nobody would buy anything from Mexicans." The townspeople then turn on Miss Information, mob her, and kill her. Kyle is saved by Western medicine and the social order is restored for another week.

Literature scholar Jolene Armstrong argues that the episode parodies consumer excess,[36] but if we shift focus and emphasize the episode's religious satire we can see *South Park*'s critical engagement with consumer spirituality. Armstrong writes that it is "Parker's and Stone's own refusal to respect any party lines that makes their series as successful postmodern parody. They do not offer solutions to the problems; they do not take sides; they do not even pretend to be able to step outside of the system they are critiquing, for their own critique is entrenched in the very culture they seek to dismantle. Nothing is above ridicule or parodic examination."[37] While the episode seems to be critiquing holistic medicine, she notes that what it is really doing is attacking hyper-consumerism.[38] Yet, her criticism misses how holistic medicine is satirized as consisting of worthless commercial products that have no intrinsic value and that harm people. Just as *Family Guy* strikes at the self-help, New Age book market, *South Park* assaults holistic medicine and argues from a rationalized position: If you cannot empirically prove your claims, you should not be in the healing business. The doctor's medical approach works, Miss Information's does not. In *South Park* spirituality does not override stupidity. It is critical of hyper-consumerism, but it also makes a moral point about holistic medicine and its associations with spirituality. Armstrong's characterization of this as parody and not *satirical parody* misses the way that *South Park* makes its stronger arguments about spiritual practice in the United States.

South Park's satire of the New Age store can be helpfully compared to an example from *The Simpsons* in the episode "Make Room for Lisa." After Lisa develops stress-related stomachaches, she and Homer visit the parodic New Age store "Karma-ceuticals." The windows feature various symbols that have been appropriated by New Age seekers, including the medieval-style sun and moon and a large yin-yang. The inside is decorated with similar symbols, icons, and assorted New Age goods. There is an ankh on the wall, a Stonecutters flag hanging from the ceiling, and a statue of Ganesha on the counter.[39] A small replica of an Egyptian sarcophagus can be seen at the bottom of the screen and faint flute music plays, providing atmosphere.

While Homer's actions in "Homer the Heretic" support the kind of individualistic self-spirituality that Heelas sees at the core of New Age beliefs, Homer does not condone many of New Age's accoutrements. New Age ideas do not appeal to him, but the movement's experimentation and willingness to appropriate ideas from other cultures entices Lisa. This is apparent after they enter Karma-ceuticals and Homer complains about buying a dreamcatcher, calls the owner "hippie lady," and refuses to hear about the store specials, asking if they have something to make Lisa stop complaining. The answer to Lisa's problems is sensory deprivation tanks.

After Homer and Lisa are positioned in the tanks, Karma-ceuticals' owner is visited by repossession workers who empty her store of merchandise. Her defense is that the *I Ching* told her she had six months until bankruptcy. Later, when they are driving away with the goods, one repossession worker holds up a crystal and looks at the other one (whose stomach bulges out over the steering wheel of the truck) and says "Abracadabra. The crystal says your baby shall be a girl." The other man tells him to shut up and throws the crystal out the window.

New Age goods in this episode are merely goods. They are shown to be a waste of money, devoid of any spiritual powers. They are material

Homer and Lisa in "Karma-ceuticals"

objects that can be bought and sold in a store and repossessed when the proprietor cannot make payments. These jokes echo the criticisms of spiritual consumption that have already been discussed and suggest that it is misguided to try to find meaningful experience in material culture that is sold on ideas appropriated from other cultures. Rather than providing a way of accessing meaningful experience in a capitalist economy, *The Simpsons* and *South Park* both share the idea that New Age spiritual goods are a product of late capitalism and its commodification of everything.[40] These jokes are consistent with the view that New Age spirituality is not built on any solid ground and that it is associated with a cash grab.

Conversely, business scholar Nurit Zaidman argues that New Age stores are not just places of business. Many are also "spiritual centers" with designated sacred spaces where spiritual experiences occur away from the main business areas.[41] When Homer and Lisa enter Karma-ceuticals they are faced with a wide variety of items, from dreamcatchers to toothbrushes. Yet, the back room with the sensory deprivation tanks is a stark contrast. There are two tanks (white pods with water in them), hooks on the walls, and a small table with a copy of *New Ager* magazine on it (featuring a man sitting in lotus position). The walls and floor are grey and there is a curtain pulled across the door. In the inner sanctum the idea is to get people into the sensory deprivation tanks where, according to the store owner, "You're about to take a journey into the mind. You may see and experience things that are strange and frightening. But remember, they can't physically harm you—though they may destroy you mentally."

Once inside the sensory deprivation tank, Lisa undergoes a series of hallucinations in which she experiences what it is like to be the family cat, a tree, and journalist Cokie Roberts. She then experiences Homer's life and realizes that she takes his sacrifices to spend time with her for granted. While New Age's material culture has been satirized as ineffective and a waste of money, the reality of spiritual experience that can be gained through participating in commodified spiritual activities is affirmed. Lisa can—and does—have a meaningful, personal, and *real* spiritual experience. The episode's emotional climax comes through the experience of imagining herself as her father. A New Age technique reconciles Lisa and Homer. The core of "spirituality" on which *The Simpsons'* religious satire stands is reaffirmed and is positioned in opposition to *Family Guy* and *South Park*, which distance themselves from spirituality's consumerism.

The irony involved in this example makes it difficult to claim that *The Simpsons* directly criticizes religion's commodification and consumption. On the one hand, we could say that it lampoons the New Age by having Homer refer to Karma-ceuticals' owner as "hippie lady," having her appear to be flaky, and mocking New Age's material culture. Yet, pursuing a healing experience through sensory deprivation *works*. Heelas argues that the pursuit of "experience" is what draws people into the New Age marketplace in the first place.[42] While *The Simpsons* portrays much of that marketplace as ridiculous, Lisa's hallucination in the sensory deprivation tank also validates New Age spiritual pursuits. As in *South Park*, the buying and selling of New Age goods is treated as a scam, but just because somebody is exploited, that does not mean that the individualism at the heart of spirituality cannot find new tools with which to manifest spiritual experiences.

At this point we can see differences emerging between the three programs over their core values. *The Simpsons* prizes individual freedom to seek spiritual fulfillment, whether that comes through joining a new church or going into sensory deprivation. *Family Guy* encourages personal development, but treats religious traditions and consumer spirituality as ineffective and dangerously delusional. *South Park* finds consumer spirituality to be fraudulent and deceptive. Each program bases its satire in part on these values, but they also construct their arguments by drawing upon other discourses that criticize organized religion in the United States.

Rejecting Religion: Atheism, Agnosticism, and Scientific Rationalism

Spirituality's commercialization is dealt with in conflicting ways in these series. Material goods can be seen as corrupting when people can buy, sell, and ultimately discard that which ostensibly gives their lives meaning. The materials and techniques that facilitate spiritual growth are products bound in the logic of production and consumption upon which capitalist economies are built. The individualist spirit celebrated in the episodes "Homer the Heretic" and "The Father, the Son, and the Holy Fonz" is facilitated by consumption, but there is a widespread ignorant familiarity that the price we pay for individual choice is diluted religion. Indeed, Lisa's conversion to Buddhism stands in stark contrast to Homer and Peter's religious seeking. Lisa is presented as a moral character, while Peter and Homer are idiots. By extension, Buddhism is portrayed as a good choice, while Peter and Homer's new churches are failures. *The Simpsons* and *Family Guy* echo criticisms of spirituality that see it as shallow and selfish—a common misconception that religion scholar Siobhan Chandler's and Heelas' research disproves.[43]

While the option to start a spiritual quest apart from a religious institution is presented as a valid choice, there is another avenue available for distancing oneself from religion. People can leave religion altogether or become atheist. Sociologist Jessie Smith demonstrates with a small interview sample that atheism is an *achieved identity* in the United States today.[44] It is an identity adopted through social interaction because theists are so plentiful in America that disbelief in any god requires explanation. Atheists and agnostics are likely to experience a high degree of discrimination in their social lives—although not necessarily in professional settings.[45] Yet, their numbers grow. The 2015 Pew Religious Landscape Survey revealed that 22.8% of Americans identified themselves as "religious nones," a 6.7% increase from their 2008 survey.[46] The category of "religious nones" needs unpacking. Only 3.1% of the total population identifies as atheists, a modest increase of 1.5% since 2007, while another 4% considered themselves agnostic, an increase of 1.6% over the same time.[47] These positions vis-à-vis the dominant Christian traditions in the United States are growing, but still marginal. Atheists and agnostics are also viewed with great suspicion. Standing with the small minority of Americans who say that the growth of nonreligion is a good thing (11% of Americans think the growth is good, 48% say it is bad, 39% say it doesn't matter[48]), *The Simpsons*, *South Park*, and *Family Guy* openly engage with atheism through their humor, which they use to take stands regarding religion's, spirituality's, science's, and especially Christianity's place in the United States.

Family Guy takes the most atheistic and antagonistic approach to religion, which stems from MacFarlane's public atheism. For example, he has said that atheists have to speak out because "There have to be people who are vocal about the advancement of knowledge over faith";[49] and in his 2006 Harvard Class Day Speech he used Stewie's voice and, in imparting wisdom to the graduates, said, "Stay away from the Church. In the battle over science versus religion science offers credible evidence for all the serious claims it makes. The Church says, 'Oh, it's right here in this book. See, the one written by people who thought the sun was magic.' I for one would like to see some proof that there is a god and if you say 'A baby's smile' I'm going to kick you right in the stomach."[50]

In *Family Guy's* most dedicated statement about atheism, Brian comes out as an atheist in "Not All Dogs Go to Heaven." Lois, echoing the majority in the research discussed above, tells Brian that being an atheist is "just about the worst thing a person can be." Yet, Brian persists in his atheism because he does not see any evidence for God. Meg, who has been converted to Christianity by Kirk Cameron (of TV sitcom *Growing Pains* [ABC 1985–1992] fame, and who is now an outspoken evangelical Christian), decides that the only way Meg can get Brian to see the light is to tell the nightly news about Brian's atheism. Brian's picture is displayed on the screen with the caption "Worse than Hitler" beneath it and Mayor Adam West's reaction is that he would rather have a terrorist in town because "At least they believe in a God." Brian thinks that people will be tolerant, but a brick smashes through the window, his Toyota Prius follows, then he is chased by an angry mob, and, worst of all, the local liquor establishments will no longer serve him booze. Desperate, Brian fakes a conversion so that Meg will take him out and he can buy alcohol again, but then she takes him to "Do the Lord's work." They go to a book burning outside a local church where Meg throws copies of naturalist Charles Darwin's *The Evolution of Species* and physicist Stephen Hawking's *A Brief History of Time* onto the fire.

Outraged, Brian convinces Meg that there really is no God in the cruelest display of evidence and logic he can muster, asking her, "If there were a God, would he have put you here on Earth with a flat chest and a fat ass?" Meg whines that she is "made in his image" but Brian is unrelenting, "Really? Would he give you a smoking hot mom like Lois, and then have you grow up looking like Peter?" Meg starts to waver when Brian delivers the final blow in his argument, "And what kind of God would put you in a house where no one respects or cares about you, not even enough to get you a damn mumps shot?!" Meg breaks down crying, asking Brian where the answers come from if there is no God. At this point, Brian turns hopeful as he tells her, "Well, that's all part of the human experience. It's what we're here to find out. And I bet you that the real answer to the nature of our existence is gonna be more unimaginably amazing than we can possibly conceive." *Family Guy* thus mixes the wonder and hope of scientifically based atheism and a direct assault on religion as an institution.

Family Guy is at its best in presenting atheism positively when it uses throw-away jokes rather than extended episodes. The program frequently uses the scientific ignorance of some vocal Christians as proof that scientific atheism is based on better knowledge than Christianity (and, by extension, all other religions). *Family Guy*'s portrayal of Christians in these examples reduces all Christians to a stereotype based on a vocal subgroup of fundamentalist Christians who interpret the Bible literally and hold antagonist positions vis-à-vis other religious groups. Throughout *Family Guy*'s oeuvre this is the default interpretation of Christianity. It is a useful ignorant familiarity for teaching *Family Guy*'s audience what is wrong with Christians and right with those who reject the religious teachings being satirized. For example, in "Airport '07,"

Peter and Brian watch *Carl Sagan's Cosmos Edited for Rednecks* on televi-sion. Sagan's *Cosmos* was an incredibly influential PBS series that aired in the fall of 1980 and brought the astrophysicist's love of science and his expansive cosmic perspective into millions of homes, inspiring scien-tists around the world. McFarlane spearheaded an updating of *Cosmos* for a new generation in 2014, continuing his effort to promote rational thought based on empirical research of the material world. In the red-neck version, Sagan stands before a celestial backdrop and drones, "Just how old is our planet? Scientists believe it is four-" when an overdubbed, nasally voice with a southern accent cuts in "hundreds and hundreds of years old." It continues:

SAGAN
Scientists have determined that the universe was created by a . . .

OVERDUB
God [*Word is drawn out while Sagan continues talking.*]

SAGAN
Big bang. If you look at the bones of a—

OVERDUB
Jesus

SAGAN
—saurus Rex it's clear by the use of carbon dating that—

OVERDUB
Mountain Dew is the best soda ever made.

Within *Family Guy, Cosmos'* statement about science's expansive vision, power, and beauty is incompatible with "rednecks," the derogatory term for white, rural, stupid—and in this case, explicitly Christian—Americans. A similar joke is made in "Excellence in Broadcasting" when Brian joins the Republican Party and has his belief system turned upside down. Praying loudly he intones, "Dear God, who definitely exists, we your people who have been on this planet for 6,000 years and not a second more, wish to thank you for this bounty, and for keeping Congress predominantly white, through Christ our Lord, Amen." Ignorance, racism, bigotry, and Christianity are all tied up in a neat little package that satirizes one of the country's major political parties and its base. Brian is normally the brains of *Family Guy*; inverting his personality to this Christian stereotype is a way of generating institutional dissonance with the atheism at *Family Guy*'s heart.

Family Guy's scientific atheism enables jokes from a position of presumed superior knowledge over American Christians. Jokes from this religious position echo Davies' categorization of marginal groups as stupid when they disagree with the dominant group. *Family Guy* rhetorically claims that there is no God so why believe in something so foolish? Such faith can lead to serious problems. For example, in the episode "Friends of Peter G.," one of *Family Guy*'s more famous "anti-religion" jokes is presented (and repeated online as a "truth about religion"). Attending an Alcoholics Anonymous meeting, Brian states, "people got along just fine for thousands of years without AA. Just as they got along for thousands of years without religion." They cut to a scene that is set in period dress from the turn of the Common Era in which two men are talking to each other:

MAN 1
I like you and have no reason not to.

MAN 2
I like you and have no reason not to.

MAN 3 [ENTERING]
Hey, did you hear about that magic baby that was born in Bethlehem? [*They draw swords and stab each other to death.*]

Subtlety is not a prerequisite for satirists.

Science is an essential tool for *Family Guy*, *The Simpsons*, and *South Park*. Each program employs scientific knowledge to criticize the discourse of religion and public life in the United States. In an episode entitled "Untitled Griffin Family History," Peter explains that the universe was created when God ignited a fart and created the universe, which is constantly expanding across the cosmos from that originating big bang. Then, he explains that evolution took course and we see an "evolution montage" that is familiar to television viewers and includes a time-lapsed sequence of a fish crawling out of water and then evolving into a dinosaur. Suddenly, the montage stops and Peter intones, "Of course, I'm obligated by the State of Kansas to present the church's alternative to the theory of evolution." The theme music from the 1960s sitcom *I Dream of Jeannie* (NBC 1965–1970) starts playing and the blonde-haired, belly-dancing Jeannie shimmies out of the water. Once on land she crosses her arms, nods her head, and various animals, people, objects, Jesus (with an "America #1" giant foam finger), and Santa Claus appear with each subsequent bob.

The Simpsons, South Park, and *Family Guy* have each offered a more sustained criticism of young earth creationism and the Christian-inspired Intelligent Design movement, which has led to numerous court battles over what gets taught in America's high schools. *Family Guy* directly references cases in 1999 and 2005 in Kansas, but *The Simpsons* and *South Park* each aired episodes at the time that another trial was under way. *The Simpsons* episode "The Monkey Suit" criticizes the fight between religion and science in America's biology classrooms, from the 1925 *Tennessee vs. John Scopes* trial (also known as the "Monkey Trial" over the right to teach evolution in school) to the 2005 *Kitzmiller vs. Dover Area School District* (hereafter "Dover trial") decision to ban Intelligent Design in Dover, Pennsylvania.[51] After attending an exhibit at the Springfield Museum of Natural History, which presents creationism as a myth, Flanders convinces the church council to pressure Springfield Elementary to teach alternatives to evolution. Principal Seymour Skinner is blackmailed and creationism is to be taught in all science courses. Lisa is furious, but she still watches the "educational" film, "So You're Calling God a Liar: An Unbiased Comparison of Creationism and Evolution," in which the Bible is "written by our Lord" and Charles Darwin is called a cowardly drunk and shown passionately kissing Satan. Every answer on a test is "God did it." Eventually, the town passes a law stating that only creationism can be taught in schools.

Lisa is arrested after she breaks the law and starts reading from *The Origin of Species*, leading to a parody of the Scopes Trial. Springfield scientist Professor Frink witnesses for the defense, testifying that evolution tells us that God has less power than the Under Secretary of Agriculture. Witnesses for the prosecution include a "Ph.D. in Truthology from Christian Tech" and Ned Flanders. At one point during the trial, the William Jennings Bryan parody, Wallace Brady, holds a baby fawn in an attempt to sway the jury, saying, "Now, Bambi, who started that forest fire that killed your mama? Evolution?!" Eventually Marge turns the tables by giving Homer a bottle of beer in the courtroom. He acts like an ape, proving that Homer is related to the missing link in human evolution. The episode ends on a conciliatory note with Lisa praising the separation of church and state while still respecting Ned's religious beliefs.

This episode and others within *The Simpsons* consistently portray science trumping religion, while allowing for religion's continued, if marginalized, relevance. While Lisa's civil stance at the conclusion of "The Monkey Suit" resembles a good example of this principle, we cannot forget that she just won a trial against creationism. A similar point is made in *The Simpsons* episode "Lisa the Skeptic," which is based around a skeleton that looks like an angel that is found in a construction site. Springfielders debate whether or not it actually is an angel skeleton, leading to a trial after it goes missing. At the trial's conclusion the judge rules, "As for science versus religion, I'm issuing a restraining order. Religion should stay five hundred yards away from science at all times." As a final example, in the episode "НОМЯ," Homer mathematically proves there is no God, causing Flanders to burn Homer's work.

Arguments about religion and science in *The Simpsons*, *South Park*, and *Family Guy* build upon ignorant familiarities and religious conflicts in American society. Neuroscientist Sam Harris' *The End of Faith* started a brief trend of highly publicized anti-religious books that favored an approach to understanding life based on scientific rationality dubbed "New Atheism."[52] Harris and his colleagues contend that religion and rationality cannot coexist and that in order to progress as a species we should do away with religion. Yet, religion persists and science does not have all the answers. *South Park*'s satire of evolutionary biologist Richard Dawkins after his book *The God Delusion* vaulted him to a new level of celebrity for his atheism stresses the tension between good scientific fact and the possibility that there may be something spiritual to the universe.[53] In a two-part arc, "Go God Go" and "Go God Go XII," Ms.

Garrison (formerly Mr. Garrison, but having undergone a sex-change operation) refuses to teach evolution because it is "a hair-brained theory that says I'm a monkey!," even though, as the school counselor Mr. Mackey reminds her, "evolution has been pretty much proven."[54] In "Go God Go" Ms. Garrison explains evolution (with a handy chart showing the progression from aquatic-based life-forms to modern *homo sapiens sapiens*) as follows:

In the beginning we were all fish, swimming around in the water. Then a couple of fish had a retard baby and the retard baby was different so it got to live. So retard fish goes on to make more retard babies and then one day a retard baby fish crawled out of the ocean with its mutant fish hands and it had butt-sex with a squirrel or something and made this, retard frog squirrel. And then that had a retard baby that was a monkey-fish-frog and then this monkey-fish-frog had butt-sex with this monkey and that monkey had another mutant retard baby that screwed another monkey and that made you. So there you go, you're the retarded offspring of five monkeys having butt-sex with a fish squirrel. Congratulations.

This tirade results in Dawkins teaching class in Ms. Garrison's place. They get off to a bad start. For example, after Dawkins admits his atheism, Garrison throws feces in his face because she is acting like a monkey. Over dinner, Dawkins tries to convince the outspoken Garrison to consider atheism, mentioning the Flying Spaghetti Monster—a creation of physics graduate student Bobby Henderson that he posited in an open letter to the Kansas State Board of Education in 2005 as part of a satirical protest against teaching Intelligent Design in schools. On the Internet the meme became an instant hit and has since launched its own parody church and faith, "Pastafarianism."[55] Dawkins' mention of the Flying Spaghetti Monster instantly convinces Garrison to change as she now fully embraces evolution, and the two start dating.

The next day Ms. Garrison tells the children there is no God, but Stan argues that there could be. After all, evolution could be the "how" and not the "why." Ms. Garrison grabs a giant triangle and starts banging it, yelling, "Retard alert! Retard alert class! Do you believe in a flying spaghetti monster too bubble head?" Later, in bed, Dawkins tells Ms. Garrison she might have gone overboard, but she convinces him that with her "balls" and his brains, they could get rid of religion and make the world a better place. Meanwhile, Cartman has frozen himself so that he does not have to wait for the Nintendo Wii to be released, only to find himself unfrozen in the year 2546. In this future everybody is an atheist as people in the past were convinced by Dawkins' ideas about atheism after he married Ms. Garrison. There is still war, however, between the Unified Atheist League, United Atheist Alliance, and Allied Atheist Allegiance (which is comprised of evolved sea otters).

In "Go God Go XII" we learn that the future's atheists are fighting over the answer to "the great question" and take their inspiration from Richard Dawkins' actions in the early twenty-first century. After meeting Ms. Garrison, Dawkins learned that "using logic and reason isn't enough, you have to be a dick to everyone who doesn't think like you." Parker and Stone attack Dawkins' atheism throughout the episode. At one point the "wise one" from the sea otters challenges his fellow otters to stop their plans to attack the human atheists, whom the sea otters consider illogical because the humans chop down trees to eat food off of when they have perfectly good tummies. The otters had learned from "the Great Dawkins" that people who do not use reason cannot be tolerated, but the wise one speaks against this position, saying, "Perhaps the Great Dawkins wasn't so wise. Oh, he was intelligent, but some of the most intelligent otters I've ever known were completely lacking in common sense. Maybe some otters do need to believe in something. Who knows . . . Maybe, just believing in God . . . Makes God exist." After a moment of ponderous silence the otters respond by cheering "Kill the wise one!" in unison.

Cartman, meanwhile, has been trying to return to 2006 since he cannot play the Wii in the future. As the atheist groups battle each other he learns that the great question is what atheists should call themselves and the three factions have been fighting over this question for years. With explosions going off around him, Cartman uses a phone that can dial the past and calls Ms. Garrison. Dawkins is in the middle of having sex with her and answers the phone, but when Cartman tells him that Garrison had a sex-change operation Dawkins is disgusted and leaves. With Ms. Garrison no longer by his side, the future changes and the three factions are at peace with each other since there are no more "isms," which are only for logical people. There is still war, however, as "the stupid

French-Chinese think they have a right to Hawaii!" As the new people of the future plan to send Eric back to the past they deliver the moral of the story, "Tell the people of the past that no one single answer is ever the answer."

These episodes focus on the most controversial scientific theory in contemporary America—Darwinian evolution—and both *The Simpsons* and *South Park* support the theory's acceptance by the scientific community. While professional scientists almost universally accept evolution, evangelical and fundamentalist Christians have a long history of opposing evolution for moral and religious reasons. Executing what philosopher Barbara Forrest (an expert witness for the plaintiffs in the *Kitzmiller* case) and zoologist Paul Gross call a "seduction phenomenon,"[56] proponents of what is now called "Intelligent Design" (ID) are trying to redirect the nation's scientific discourse.[57] Utilizing American sympathies toward having every position heard in public debate, ID proponents question evolution's validity and promote the idea that there is an intelligent designer behind the natural world.[58] However, as ID's critics routinely attest, it has yet to contribute to scientific theory—especially evolutionary biology—with new theories and concepts that can be empirically tested. Furthermore, its main argument from "irreducible complexity"—"a single system composed of several well-matched, interacting parts that contribute to the basic function, wherein the removal of any one of the parts causes the system to effectively cease functioning"[59]—is heavily challenged by refutations from natural scientists.[60] *The Simpsons* explicitly supports the critique of ID when it satirizes Christian arguments against evolution, and *South Park* also supports the scientific community's opposition to ID when it shows Garrison's ignorance of evolution and depicts Dawkins as a logical and rational thinker when it comes to the gradual development of species. Scientific rationality—the empirical testing of evidence and drawing conclusions about the world from observation—is a standard all three programs employ when evaluating religious people and their dogmas. Their approach manifests institutional consonance and moral and cultural boundary reinforcement at its finest.

The Simpsons and *Family Guy* take fairly clear stands against religion in favor of science. *Family Guy*'s atheism is firmly rooted in the conviction that science provides the best explanations for reality. This has become clearer in recent seasons and *Family Guy* has favored outright attacks on religious plausibility, entrenching itself as a bastion of scientific atheism—even if some of its earlier episodes supported spiritual seeking. *The Simpsons* uses scientific rationality to check the religious claims it deems most egregious while still supporting personal spiritual development. Science is a boundary marker in *The Simpsons* between good personal spiritual exploration and bad religious behavior. *South Park* is not as clear in its boundaries. In fact, in the episode "Red Hot Catholic Love" atheists are literally portrayed "spewing crap out their mouths," a sentiment echoed in the fact that while Dawkins might be right about how evolution happens, *South Park* does not put atheism at its center. This marks *South Park* as different from its peers; by exploring three interconnected episodes we can come to a clear understanding of its core values.

Thinking through the Complications with *South Park*

South Park supports scientific rationality, but that does not mean that it denies the existence of something more than the natural world. As "Go God Go" and "Go God Go XII" make clear, the series is open to the existence of something beyond the material world. Stan's statement that evolution might be the how but not the why, and the wise one's assertion that just believing in God might make God exist, speak to the significance *South Park*'s creators place upon creativity. This perspective is highlighted in the series' Imaginationland trilogy of episodes. In "Imaginationland I: Kyle Sucks Cartman's Balls" the boys follow a leprechaun and eventually board a zeppelin with the mayor of Imaginationland, who takes them there. In Imaginationland, "all the wonderful and goofy things that people have made up over the years live together"—including major religious figures such as Joseph Smith, Jr. and Lao Tzu. Unfortunately, upon their arrival an Arabic man yelling "Allah" detonates an explosive vest and causes mass death and destruction in the city. The boys escape on the back of the dragon from the film *Dragonheart*, but their friend Butters is trapped behind.

The episodes shift between our world and Imaginationland. At the first episode's conclusion, the Pentagon acknowledges that Muslim terrorists have hijacked our imaginations, which will soon be running

"The Council of Nine in Imaginationland Part II." Jesus and Wonder Woman have their backs to the viewers.

wild. The military is able to identify Butters as the one character who is not from American folklore or popular culture, but before they can rescue him the terrorists use "Rockety Rocket" to blow up the barrier between the good and evil sides of Imaginationland. In the second episode ("Imaginationland II: The Drying of the Balls"), Butters is taken to Castle Sunshine, where he meets with some of the most powerful good characters our imaginations have conjured—the Council of Nine. Seated in a triangle are such figures as Zeus, Aslan the lion, Luke Skywalker, Wonder Woman, Popeye the sailor, and Jesus.

They inform Butters that he will have to help them to protect Imaginationland if he wants to return home. Meanwhile, the American government has built a secret portal to Imaginationland (parodying the *Stargate* franchise) and, after the evil Manbearpig breaks through, prepares to nuke our imaginations in order to stop them from running wild.

In the third episode ("Imaginationland III: The Moistening of the Scrotum"), the thought of a nuclear attack on our imaginations starts people protesting in the streets. Legally, the military is allowed to carry out the assault because imaginary things are not real. Throughout, the three episodes debate the reality of imaginary things because, if imaginary things are real, Kyle has agreed to suck Cartman's testicles. Kyle does not want to imbibe Eric's scrotum, but once Stan is pulled through the portal and is trapped in Imaginationland, Kyle has to stop the assault to save his friend. As the nuclear warhead is about to be sent through the portal, Kyle breaks into the Pentagon and speaks to everyone who is preparing to launch the attack. He delivers a monologue that encapsulates the criticisms *South Park* has made in these episodes about religion, spirituality, science, and belief:

> It's all real. Think about it. Haven't Luke Skywalker and Santa Claus affected your lives more than most real people in this room? I mean, whether Jesus is real or not, he's had a bigger impact on the world than any of us have. And the same can be said for Bugs Bunny and Superman and Harry Potter. They've changed my life. Changed the way I act on the Earth. Doesn't that make them kind of real? They might be imaginary, but they're more important than most of us here and they're all gonna be around long after we're dead. So in a way, those things are more realer than any of us.

For *South Park*, the social reality of religious figures and ideals is more important than their empirical validity. What matters for *South Park* is that imaginative creativity is used to make the world a better and more meaningful place. It is only when imagination and creativity are twisted for exploitive purposes that they become problems that need to be satirized.

As we have seen, *The Simpsons*, *South Park*, and *Family Guy* satirize a variety of religious traditions and modes of interacting with them outside the traditional Christian Church. When Lisa Simpson went to church, she left for a Buddhist temple. When Homer and Peter went to church, they left to found new ones. When the church came looking for Brian, he fought back. People repeatedly left "religion" to find themselves. They went to the marketplace and found personal fulfillment, or they went to science and found a way of explaining the world that keeps religions—specifically Christianity—at bay. The programs all use their humor to positively depict acts of individualism, advocating critical thinking that leads people away from America's established religious institutions. Their *institutional consonance* is with *deinstitutionalization*. Ironically, that sentence reads as if they are breaking apart an institution. Nothing could be further from the truth. Our working conception of a social institution is that it is a standardized pattern of behavior that exists apart from the individuals who habitually perform according to these standards. Leaving religious traditions, borrowing from disparate faiths, and standing in opposition to religious groups can all thus be conceptualized as acting in an institutionalized pattern of individualism. As we shall see in the next chapters, in *The Simpsons* individualism and religion are governed by ethics, in *South Park* by the ability to be a free and creative individual, and in *Family Guy* by an anti-religious orthodoxy. All other religions are judged from these central moral positions.

2

The Difference Race Makes

Native American Religions, Hinduism, and Judaism

LOVEJOY
He [God] was working in the hearts of your friends and neighbors when they went to your aid, be they Christian, Jew, or miscellaneous.

APU
Hindu, there are 700 million of us.

LOVEJOY
Aww, that's super.
—Reverend Lovejoy in *The Simpsons'* "Homer the Heretic"

Reverend Lovejoy's statement near the end of "Homer the Heretic" exudes ironic ecumenical sentiment. God uses Jews and Hindus for good and that matters more than beliefs. Yet, there is something unsettling about the Jewish Krusty the Clown and the Hindu Apu in *The Simpsons'* world. They are religious, but their religions are not co-opted into the spiritual marketplace like Buddhism is. In *The Simpsons*, these religions are too visceral, too tied to ethnic and racial identities to be anything but the religions of distinct groups of people. It is crucial that characters be identified as Jewish or Indian and that their religion is tied to this bodily distinction. Indeed, one of the unspoken benefits of being a white Christian (as opposed to white and Jewish) in the United States is to embody the cultural norm to which others are compared.[1]

Sociologists Stephen Cornell and Douglas Hartmann find a tension arising between the power to ascribe racial and ethnic identities upon a people and the way that racial or ethnic identity can be asserted at other times by groups through their own agency.[2] Native American religions, Hinduism, and Judaism are each treated in *The Simpsons, South Park,* and *Family Guy*, in part or in whole, through a social stratification of different racial and ethnic groups. For our purposes, race can be defined as "a human group defined by itself or others as distinct by virtue of perceived common physical characteristics that are held to be inherent."[3] This distinction based on physical characteristics is frequently accompanied by assumptions of differences in moral character. Each program reinforces racial stereotypes that start with physical differences and uses them as boundaries to exclude people from the program's centers. Concurrently, when the shows recognize ethnic identity politics, ethnicity becomes a way of determining whether Native Americans, Indians, and Jews will be accepted in their world. This book's definition of ethnicity relies on religious studies scholar Paul Bramadat's definition of an ethnic group as "any significant group of people, typically related through common filiation, or blood, whose members also usually feel a sense of attachment to a particular place, a history, and a culture (including a common language, food, and clothing). . . . its members believe themselves to be related and to owe some degree of loyalty to the main institutions, leaders, history, or symbols of the larger group."[4] Bramadat's framework is useful because it shows the complex cultural elements that a blood and cultural relationship can have in uniting people who *feel* connected. The power to assert connection, as Cornell and Hartmann rightly demonstrate in their work, is unequally divided.[5] Sometimes it is asserted by outsiders, as we will see with Native Americans and their assumed universality when stereotyped; other times the groups themselves can assert their uniqueness, which gives them a special status as "equal but different," as when the shows depict Jewish characters asserting their ethno-religious identities and religious traditions.

The Simpsons, South Park, and *Family Guy* showcase three ways of dealing with religion/race/ethnicity combinations that resist easy appropriation in the spiritual marketplace and defy scientific rationality's interpretation of reality. First, the shows create institutional consonance by appropriating a religious tradition while simultaneously marginalizing the people for whom those beliefs and practices are central to their identity. *The Simpsons'* and *Family Guy's* treatment of Native American religions illustrates this process. Second, as we will see, immigrants are welcomed, but they are kept at arm's length from the center because their religion and ethnicity signify their difference. Apu serves this purpose in *The Simpsons*, allowing the program's creative staff to explore Hinduism without ever having it enter the American mainstream at the program's heart. Third, the programs can welcome a group into their religious centers only if the religion can be modified to the program's core values. Taking Jews as our example, when Jewish characters can meld their Judaism to the program's core values they become like other white characters with different religions. Each program, however, finds it difficult to reconcile some Jewish practices and convictions with their central positions; when they cannot, Jewish caricatures are raised as a way of marking the distinctions between insiders and outsiders. Race and ethnicity, as marks of exclusion, point to a generic "whiteness" at the core of each program which allows for spiritual consumption of different traditions without making the social commitments and sacrifices accompanying membership in ethnic or racial groups.

Ignorant familiarity is used to initiate institutional resonances when evaluating different groups. When those groups are presented positively according to the programs' core values, they are shown to be institutionally consonant. When they are portrayed negatively, they are institutionally dissonant. Each type of resonance accompanies an evaluative framework that mobilizes an assumed stock of knowledge to generate humor that either draws these embodied people closer or pushes them away.

Following One's Spirit Guide: Appropriating Native American Religions

In *The Simpsons*' episode "El Viaje Misterioso de Nuestro Jomer" (The Mysterious Voyage of Homer) Homer undertakes a vision quest after eating extremely spicy peppers at a chili cookoff. This episode is explicitly modeled on debunked anthropologist Carlos Castaneda's writings about his alleged experiences with Yaqui shaman don Juan Matus. Castaneda has been accused of fraudulently presenting fiction as ethnography, but in doing so he tapped into a deep-seated sense among anthropologists and spiritual seekers who argued that his reported experiences express a greater truth about the world.[6] In "El Viaje Misterioso de Nuestro Jomer," Homer hallucinates and finds himself in a mysterious desert with giant butterflies and a constantly changing environment

Homer meets his spirit guide

(e.g., a pool of water turns into a giant rattlesnake). After following a tortoise to a massive pyramid, Homer scales its summit and thinks he has found Marge, but she dissolves into a pile of sand. Homer then encounters his spirit guide, a coyote voiced by Johnny Cash. The coyote tells Homer that he is on a quest for knowledge and gives him advice such as, "The problem, Homer, is that the mind is always chattering away with a thousand thoughts at once" and "Clarity is the path to inner peace." These suggestions could come from any number of New Age books, but when Homer asks, "What should I do? Should I meditate? Should I get rid of all my possessions?" the coyote laughs, "Are you kidding? If anything you should get more possessions. You don't even have a computer."

The coyote's rebuttal embraces both the anti-materialist and the consumerist elements discussed earlier. Some people eschew personal improvement for worldly possessions, but the means for personal growth are found in a competitive economic marketplace that includes a variety of gurus, seminar leaders, and producers of New Age material culture. Homer's discussion with the coyote captures this apparent logical tension and resolves it in a way that reaffirms spirituality's consumption. After gnawing on Homer's leg, the coyote sends him on a journey to find his soul mate. Homer claims it is Marge, the coyote asks if it is, and the rest of the episode involves Homer coming to realize that he was right all along.

Homer's seeking draws upon imagery appropriated from both Native American traditions and a debunked anthropologist to frame a contemporary seeker's story without any consideration of the cultures from which the story is taken.[7] Castaneda's work relates, among other incredible events, his head turning into a crow, a story about how he saw giant moth shadows, and how he was chased by the wind.[8] Despite being proven as a fabrication, Castaneda's work has institutional consonance with the culture of spiritual seeking. *The Simpsons* uses the theme of inner spiritual exploration facilitated by the use of natural hallucinogenics as revelatory (Homer uses a Guatemalan insanity pepper; Castaneda uses a combination of peyote, jimsonweed, and psilocybin). The problem is that *The Simpsons'* creators take Castaneda's creation as a basic truth, treating it as an accurate account of the spiritual insight people assume Native American traditions possess.[9] Castaneda's ideas are not representative of real people. Instead, they allow spiritual seekers who want the supposed benefits of Native spirituality to "play Indian" without being tied into the political, economic, and social realities that are entangled with Native spirituality and religion in practice.

Family Guy further excludes Native Americans from the practice and ownership of their traditions in the episode "The Son Also Draws." In this episode Peter takes a spiritual journey after the Boy Scouts dismiss Chris and Peter insists that the family go to New York City to have him reinstated. Chris is happy he was removed, but Peter ignores his son's wishes. On the way to New York, the Griffins end up at "Geronimo's Palace" where Lois develops a gambling problem and loses the family car. When she informs Peter that all members of the tribe receive some of the casino's profits, he hatches a scheme and declares himself an Indian to the manager, Leonard Cornfeathers—a man with brown skin, wearing a blue three-piece suit and a headband with a feather, who sits behind a large desk. After Peter declares that his ancestor "Jeep Grand

Cherokee" was actually "Chief Grand Cherokee," Cornfeathers goes elsewhere and discusses Peter's status with the elders. They decide to test him with "a really impossible stunt to prove he's the real deal"—a vision quest. Cornfeathers explains to Lois what is expected of Peter as follows:

CORNFEATHERS
A vision quest is a sacred spiritual journey. Your husband must go out in the wilderness without food or water . . .

FRANK (ONE OF THE ELDERS)
Or shoes.

CORNFEATHERS
Yeah. Or shoes. He must remain there until he can communicate with nature. He must hear the wisdom of the rocks and trees. And then, his guiding spirit must appear to him and reveal a great, personal truth. And it's got to be a real vision. We're Indians, we're going to know if he's lying. [*The council of elders all moan ominously and wave their hands as Peter and Lois retreat. After the Griffins leave, they break down laughing.*]

Peter heads into the wilderness with Chris as Lois, Meg, and Stewie await their return at the casino. Six hours later, night has fallen and the men have not returned. Lois questions Cornfeathers about the vision quest's length, but he has no idea. Meanwhile, Peter paces around a fire while Chris sleeps. Peter starts raving, when, over the distant howling of wolves, the following occurs:

VOICE
Hot enough for ya?

PETER
Wa, what?

[*Peter turns around and sees a tree with a mouth.*]

TREE
I said, hot enough for ya?

PETER
Uh, yeah, I guess. Oh my God! I'm communicating with nature. Hey, uh, tree, if one of you falls and there's no one around do you make a noise?

[*The trees argue for a moment because one of them fell and has not stopped complaining. Peter looks dazed and then hears another voice calling him from behind.*]

VOICE
Hey, yo, Griffin!

[*Peter gasps as the clouds in the night sky form into Arthur Fonzarelli.*]

PETER
The Fonz!

FONZI
Ehhhhh! [*Gives Peter two thumbs up.*]

PETER
What are you doing here? Shouldn't you be in the middle of a Tuscadero sandwich?

FONZI
Yeah, but I'm your spiritual guide, see, and I want to lay a little truth on you. Now, Mr. C was like a father to me and he always listened, you know, and Griffin, right now, your son needs you to listen to him. Woah.

PETER
Uh, sure, whatever you say.

The vision helps Chris and Peter reconnect and when they return and Peter tells his story Cornfeathers is furious, yelling, "I want a spiritual vision too. Man, I guess we've lost touch with our noble roots. I mean, this casino's brought our tribe money and prosperity, but what's the price of our souls?" Frank chimes in, "Six million dollars a week." "That's about right," agrees Cornfeathers as he returns the Griffins' car.

Ending on a parody of NBC's "The More You Know" public service announcements that have aired during prime viewing hours since 1989, Stewie calls the Natives "savages" behind their backs before Lois chimes in, "Stewie, that's a terrible thing to say. This one particular tribe has lost their way, but most Native Americans are proud, hardworking people who are true to their spiritual heritage. They are certainly not savages." A star swipes a rainbow over her head with a chime. Lois' point should not be lost on us as this parody speaks to a reality that the episode has just been devoted to systematically undermining. As MacFarlane says in the episode's DVD commentary, this parody is "Just to make horrible, horrible racial comments and then buy them back right afterwards."

Both episodes participate in a larger problem of appropriating Native American religions for white, middle-class spiritual seekers. It is significant that in these examples whites get to experience the vision quest's spiritual insights, a point driven home in *Family Guy* when the Native starts complaining that he wants a spiritual vision too—just not enough to give up the casino's money. Native American scholars have argued that Native spirituality cannot be separated from the local community's reciprocal networks, customs, and politics.[10] However, *The Simpsons'* and *Family Guy's* creators do just this. Homer and Peter do not contribute to any Native American community, but they undertake spiritual quests within the framework of Native American traditions. Appropriating these traditions contributes to a legacy in which Native American communities' insights, practices, and values are treated as something available to everybody without recourse to the community, a key element of Native religious traditions. Returning to Homer's vision—but with an eye toward Peter's as well—even if we believe Castaneda is a fraud, it is a salient fact that many people treat his interpretation of Native spirituality as more real than that practiced by Native Americans. As Lisa remarks in *The Simpsons* episode "Little Big Girl," "Native Americans are a proud people with a noble heritage—a noble heritage that anyone can claim." Although she ends up suffering as a fraud by the episode's end, when we examine Homer's and Peter's mystical journeys there is explicit support for the spiritual appropriation of Native American religious traditions without recourse to the people from whom they are taken. In these examples, when Native religious traditions are decontextualized, commercialized, and individualized, they are treated as part of the spiritual marketplace.

Historian and sociologist of religion Philip Jenkins argues that this commercialization does not delegitimate the religious lives of those who appropriate Native American religions and he contends that Native Americans have benefitted from New Agers who want to draw insight from these traditions, especially in terms of political support for Native legal causes.[11] Yet, Native spirituality's appropriation creates identity issues that shape Natives' lives in ways they cannot control. Religious studies scholar Thomas Parkhill summarizes the "Indian" stereotype's dangers.[12] Although it is positively associated with ecological spirituality it creates a romanticized notion of how Native Americans should, and did, live. The stereotype's reproduction creates expectations that can deprive Native Americans of their dignity and ability to participate fully in society if they fail to meet those standards. Parkhill quotes Smithsonian Institution ethnology curator Rayna Greene, a Cherokee, "I cannot tell you how many times I've gone into a classroom or lectured in front of a group of little children, who are deeply unhappy because I don't wear a costume every day, who think that what the Boy Scouts do is real stuff, real Indian life, and then they want us to live that life. And, when we don't live that life for them, they're brokenhearted."[13]

The positive image of Native Americans is a powerful ignorant familiarity because it burdens real people with unrealistic expectations and roles. It marginalizes them as romantic "noble savages" who live in the countryside being spiritual. Native dreams and aspirations that do not meet appropriators' standards are swept aside by the unequal distribution of the power to define reality. Non-Natives who claim knowledge of Native American religions through reading books, participating in sweat lodges or other ceremonies, and trying to gain insights like Castaneda's through the use of natural hallucinogenic or meditation practices have a disproportionate power to shape Natives' reality. Natives who do not conform to appropriators' expectations generate institutional dissonance and either are labeled "inauthentic" or are considered unimportant. Native communities face a paradox: Without the financial and social capital middle-class spiritual seekers bring in exchange for Native spirituality, Native communities suffer economically and politically.[14] However, when Natives commodify their traditions they change them in such a way that they are no longer tied into the community that gave them meaning. In short, they can either suffer economically, or they can suffer spiritually. Part of that spiritual suffering is that the appropriations like those manifested in programs such as *The Simpsons* and *Family Guy* remain unacknowledged. These mystical journeys are another example of the "spiritual but politically powerless Native" stereotype's acceptance in contemporary American popular culture.

The Other American Indian: Apu Nahasapeemapetilon, Immigration, and Ethnicity

Hinduism is barely mentioned in *Family Guy* and *South Park*, but the multitude of Indian religions that comprise Hinduism are melded into *The Simpsons'* Apu, an ethno-religious stereotype who helps us to unravel some of race, religion, and ethnicity's entanglements. A PhD in computer science, Apu is an immigrant who manages Springfield's Kwik-E-Mart convenience store and lives with his wife, Manjula, and their eight children in a small apartment. He has been associated with Hinduism since the second season's episode "Brush with Greatness" in which he explains that he enrolled in a screenwriting class because "I long to tell the story of an idealistic young Hindu pushed too far by convenience store bandits. I call it 'Hands off my Jerky, Turkey.'" "Homer the Heretic" contains *The Simpsons'* first depiction of Hinduism when Homer asks Apu why he is not in church. Apu replies, "Oh, but I am. I have a shrine to Ganesha, the god of worldly wisdom, located in the employee lounge." The camera pans to the lounge, which features a *murti* (an image that represents the divine, in this case a statue) of Ganesha, the popular elephant-headed Hindu god who removes obstacles and brings luck. Homer tries to offer Ganesha a peanut. Apu, indignant but polite, responds, "Please do not offer my god a peanut." Homer retorts with a rudeness born of a historical hubris that sees Hindu deities not as representatives of an unseen order, but as visible idols unworthy of serious engagement. "No offense, Apu," he says, "but when they were handing out religions you must have been out taking a whiz."

There are two types of jokes about Apu and Hinduism in *The Simpsons*. First, there are jokes based on superficial knowledge of Hindu practices and concepts such as karma, reincarnation, and the Hindu

Homer offers Ganesha a peanut in the employee lounge

pantheon. These jokes emphasize Hinduism's differences from main-stream American religious culture. Second, there are jokes that distinguish Hindus from Christians, casting Hindus in a positive light because they are more tolerant. While religious studies scholars lament general religious ignorance, the fact remains that most viewers, even if they have not learned about Hinduism through study, can find these jokes funny by fitting them into their cognitive framework for understanding different religions, read them through Apu's character, and make sense of them. Superficiality is not inconsequential. The jokes' superficiality speaks to how little one has to know about Hinduism to understand its place in *The Simpsons'* unseen order.

This sort of ignorant familiarity is essential to understanding how depictions of Hinduism in *The Simpsons* generate institutional consonance with the show's central position advocating individualist ethics and spirituality. The jokes are largely based on an "introductory textbook" understanding of Hinduism and of Apu as a "good" person. It is unsurprising that *The Simpsons'* Hinduism jokes repeat a few specific tropes. Ignorant familiarity does not require detailed knowledge and jokes based on Hindu esoterica would be irrelevant to American audiences. Jokes about reincarnation and the polytheist Hindu pantheon, however, establish Apu's difference. For example, in the episode "The Sweetest Apu," Apu contemplates suicide after cheating on Manjula. He has a small reincarnation chart before him and directs our attention along his spiritual path. "Now, let's see what awaits me in the next life. First I was a tiger, a snake, a clod, a goat with a hat, then me . . . Wow! A tapeworm. Then assistant to Lorne Michaels. It's going to be a rough couple of lifetimes."[15] One does not need to know the complex laws of karma and its relationship to rebirth to understand that Apu exists in a religious world different from that of mainstream America and that his actions have cosmic negative consequences.

The Simpsons juxtaposes reincarnation with Christianity's concept of salvation in its "Treehouse of Horror XVI" episode in which Mr. Burns turns his property into a hunting reserve where he kills humans. After Apu is shot, his last words are, "You got me, but I shall be reincarnated." His spirit immediately reincarnates as a rabbit, saying, "Ha ha! You can't kill a Hindu." He is immediately caught in a bear trap and cries, "Help me, Jesus!" This may be a joke on the karmic consequences of Apu's hubris, but it emphasizes the fact that reincarnation and Christian salvation are often seen as incompatible. Calling out to Jesus for salvation is not a part of the Hindu tradition, unlike being reborn as different life-forms. *The Simpsons* mixes and matches from the two traditions for comic effect because people are presumably at least vaguely familiar with the two religions' different understandings of what happens after death.

The Simpsons' best introduction to Hinduism is the episode "Homer and Apu." After selling Homer tainted meat and losing his job, Apu goes to the Simpsons' house to make amends. Upon offering to work off his debt Apu tells Homer he is "selling the concept of karmic realignment." Indignant, Homer replies, "You can't sell that! Karma can only be portioned out by the cosmos!" and slams the door in his face. "He's got me there," Apu concedes. Later in the episode Homer and Apu travel to India so that Apu can ask Kwik-E-Mart's president for his job back. Eventually they ascend a mountain to the world's first convenience store, where they meet the guru-like president and CEO of Kwik-E-Mart International. Designed after the many gurus who have crossed the globe attracting Western followers, the president resembles Maharishi Maheshi

Yogi, Transcendental Meditation's founder, who came to prominence in the West after the Beatles became his followers for a brief period during the 1960s. Seated in the lotus position on a pile of cushions and drinking a squishee, the president bestows answers under a sign that reads "The Master Knows All Except Combination to Safe." The store is designed like an ashram, with Indian architectural motifs such as domed tower silhouettes for doorways mixed with convenience store shelves stocked with goods. Speaking in a soft voice and offering to answer three questions, the president is visually, sonically, and behaviorally a stereotypical guru. When Homer uses all the questions asking variations of "Are you really the president?" Apu is furious, but the president dismisses them with Apu's catchphrase, "Thank you, come again."

"Homer and Apu" references karma and Hinduism's visual culture because these concepts are culturally relevant. Americans have seen images of gurus and know that Hindus believe their actions have cosmic consequences. Gurus are plentiful throughout India and Indian religion has a long history of the divine being revealed through people, places, and things. Harvard religious studies professor Diana Eck explains in her book *Darśan* that Hindus see the sacred through such diverse objects as holy rivers (e.g., the Ganges), people (e.g., gurus and *sannyāsin*, those who have renounced householder status), and murti.[16] Darśan is the gift that Hindus receive from these visual encounters with the divine. Gurus are not only great teachers, they are also *holy* men and women who hold a status beyond just being an instructor, which can lead to great confusion for those unfamiliar with this unseen order. Reincarnation and its determination by one's karma is also misunderstood. Karma is often treated as a celestial score card working on the principle of "what goes around, comes around." The Hindu doctrine of karma encompasses a wide variety of different beliefs, from the "orthodox" version of karma put forth in the *Bhagavad Gita* as selflessly completing one's duty (*dharma*), to the understanding that bad things happen in this life because of actions in past lives, to the basic concept of karma *The Simpsons* uses, but the fact remains that through everyday use Indians are aware of the diversity, breadth, and different understandings of karma, while it is a novel concept in America.[17]

Jokes about the Hindu pantheon also focus superficially on a few well-known deities. Apu's attachment to Ganesha is well established, including when he is seen offering him a bottle of Yoo-Hoo in the episode "Much Apu About Nothing," promising that if Ganesha makes anti-immigrant protestors go away Apu will give him the entire bottle.[18] In this example *The Simpsons* draws upon the phenomenon of "milk miracles" which took place in September 1995 when, for three days, murti of Ganesha and other deities around the world appeared to drink milk offered by devotees.[19] This sacrifice is appropriate because Ganesha is the remover of obstacles, but in other cases when *The Simpsons* uses Ganesha for humorous purposes, the deity's character is not acknowledged or parodied.

The Simpson family has a history of dressing up as Ganesha when they want to influence Apu. In "The Two Mrs. Nahasapeemapetilons," Homer dons a Ganesha costume in an attempt to stop Apu's wedding to Manjula. Walking down the aisle and speaking in a ghostly wail, he flaps his arms and proclaims, "I am the god Ganesha! This wedding angers me! All will die unless it is stopped." Eventually, he is chased up a tree and the wedding continues. In "The Sweetest Apu," Bart, Lisa, and Maggie disguise themselves as Ganesha in an attempt to force Manjula and Apu to reconcile after Apu's affair. Bart, voicing Ganesha, demonstrates his ignorance and, imitating a cinematic vampire, he moans, "I order you to get back together or I'll suck your blood!" While Apu respects Ganesha, *The Simpsons* pays him as much respect as any other god, which is to say very little. However, these depictions also play on general assumptions about gods. That is, they get angry, they can affect people's lives, and they are willing to act on their anger. This ignorant familiarity, combined with culturally relevant intertextual assumptions about gods and their powers, restricts the use of more specific references to devotion to Ganesha because the god is not widely known and worshipped in the United States. Ganesha is a familiar icon, but, as with other Hindu deities (such as in the episode "Kiss Kiss, Bang Bangalore" in which Homer is transferred to India and mistakes himself for a god), his character in *The Simpsons* is usually treated as a generic god.

We can begin to see how the relationship between race, ethnicity, and religion keeps Hinduism out of *The Simpsons'* center through the lack of portrayals of *lived Hinduism*. Apu is clearly an immigrant, marked as different by his skin color (brown), his accent (Indian), and his religion (Hindu). Furthermore, the equation of Hinduism with India and Indianness and its removal from Springfield's larger spiritual marketplace mark it as off limits for appropriation, which was key for bringing Buddhism and Native American religions into *The Simpsons*' centers. Those traditions were acceptable once they were adopted by white spiritual seekers. Part of the reason that Hinduism in *The Simpsons* is pushed away from the marketplace is its transnational ties with India. The program looks to the Indian subcontinent for its Hinduism, although Hinduism is practiced mainly in the home for those Indian immigrants of whom Apu is a caricature. That said, worship in temples is increasing as they are being erected in major urban areas.[20] Apu does not have a religious community. His Hinduism lacks the important ritual traditions that locate Hindus within the world. This is not to say that there are not moments when Hindu rituals are parodied. In "The Two Mrs. Nahasapeemapetilons," Apu's mother comes to Springfield from India and forces Apu to fulfil his obligation to marry Manjula, to whom he was betrothed as a boy. He rides to his wedding on an elephant while Bart prepares a sacred fire by tearing pages from a hymnal and throwing them on the fire. Reverend Lovejoy officiates at the service, but he does not know what he is doing. He admits that he consulted a Hindu website for his information and justifies his officiating as "Christ is Christ," an ecumenical statement that misses the differences between the two religions.[21]

The Simpsons' take on the Hindu wedding is somewhat consistent with real Hindu ceremonies. While a wide variety of wedding traditions exist, if we follow the ritual as performed in Pittsburgh's Sri Venkateswara Temple (one of the first Hindu temples in North America) as recorded in Thomas Tweed and Stephen Prothero's book *Asian Religions in America*, we see some similarities.[22] First, there is the worship of Ganesha. At Sri Venkateswara the bride's parents invite the deity to come and remove any obstacles to the ceremony's smooth procession. In *The Simpsons*, Homer invites himself as Ganesha, circumventing and inverting Hindu tradition with humorous consequences. Homer as Ganesha is an obstacle, missing the god's significance on this occasion. There is also the *pradhana homam*, or worship of Agni, who is represented by the sacred fire. In this, *The Simpsons*' depiction is somewhat closer to reality, with Bart tending the fire. However, a hymnal is not desecrated to sanctify the fire at Sri Vankateswara and, according to the DVD commentary, this was a twist *The Simpsons*' creative team added as a way of signifying that the fire is made sacred. The most accurate depiction of a Hindu wedding ceremony occurs when Apu and Manjula walk around the fire to seal their vows. Called *Sapta Padi*, this moment in the ritual marks a statement before a deity and is an exchange of vows between the married couple. It is also the one element of the wedding *The Simpsons'* team does not satirize. As the episode's emotional climax, the solemnity of marriage is too important to make light of on this occasion.

These examples demonstrate that there are visual elements of Hinduism that a wider audience can access through cultural intertextuality. However, this knowledge is disjointed and superficial, illustrating that for the majority of Americans, any detailed knowledge of Hinduism is unnecessary. They do not practice it themselves, it is not stigmatized like Islam or cults, as we will see, and Hindus have quietly worked their way into different sectors of American culture without trying to change that culture to be more like India's. In other words, most Americans only need an ignorant familiarity of Hinduism to navigate their everyday worlds, and *The Simpsons* uses these basics to generate its humor. People know a little about karma and reincarnation, have seen pictures of Hindu weddings, gurus, and gods, and are not threatened by them. Hinduism exists as one religion among many, but because it is not perceived as a dangerous religion *The Simpsons* does not frame it negatively.

Ignorant familiarities accompany evaluations of Hinduism. Understanding where Hinduism fits in the grand scheme of *The Simpsons'* unseen order is enhanced when Apu and Ned Flanders are juxtaposed. A recurring theme in *The Simpsons* is that religion is acceptable if it is not forced on others, which places Hinduism in a positive light. Consider the following example from the episode "Mona Leaves-a," when Homer goes to the Kwik-E-Mart for solace when his mother dies:

HOMER

Apu, what do you think happens after you die? [. . .] I mean, do you think my mother's out there somewhere? Does she know I feel bad about things I said?

APU

Oh, perhaps she's around us now. She may have already been reincarnated as that newborn baby [*points to a newborn*], or that tiny mouse in the nacho cheese [*a mouse slides down a ladle's handle into the nacho cheese*].

NED
Oh for crying out loud! People aren't mice.

APU
Oh, what a surprise! Joe Jesus Junior's going to set us all straight.

NED
Look Homer, people don't come back as anything, except for our Lord who came back as bread. That's it.

HOMER
That's it. [*Homer sighs, takes his groceries, and leaves the store.*]

APU
What's the thing with your religion? It's a bummer.

NED
Even the sing-alongs?

APU
No, the sing-alongs are ok.

Ned's persistent perpetuation of Christian belief in death's permanence opens the door for Apu to correct him. With the exception of sing-alongs, Apu can find nothing uplifting in the United States' dominant religious tradition. Hinduism, conversely, offers hope. Our loved ones could be in the room with us, they know we are trying to make amends, and there is hope for redemption beyond this life. Here, Hindu concepts such as karmic rebirth and the fact that Apu does not aggressively proselytize offer a hopeful solution to the problem of death, juxtaposed against the negative elements of Ned's Christianity to illustrate how *The Simpsons* positions and evaluates both religions.

While Apu is depicted as a stereotype representing today's ethnoreligious immigrants to America, his religiousness lacks depth. His superficiality lets us know about Hinduism's general acceptance in *The Simpsons*' United States, but also the indifference with which it can be treated. Apu's Hinduism is based on textbook knowledge, is seen positively compared to Christianity, and is easily reducible to a few basic tropes. While this depiction is certainly not representative of Hinduism in America, it focuses our attention on the larger issues ethno-religious groups face in gaining acceptance. That is, they are known only to the extent that their histories and actions impact the lives of white middle-class Americans, and then they are reduced to the bare essentials necessary for navigating those encounters.

But why does *The Simpsons* not appropriate Hinduism like Buddhism and Native American religions? Why is a brown-skinned man with a foreign accent presented as the voice of this religion while white people voice the other traditions? There is no easy answer to this question. Yet, *The Simpsons'* creators' choice makes sense when we look at the lived practice of Hinduism by Indian immigrants in America who are actively reshaping the religious landscape. They are coming to the United States, practicing their religion in their homes, and building temples to center their communities. Indian immigrants are like other religious groups in these regards, but they are still marked by different skin colors, accents, culture, and religion. Apu's Indianness is pertinent as a counter-example to white Christianity. He is Hindu because he is Indian, it is a part of his character, and that is that. Yet, the religion remains untouchable in meaningful ways because it is built into Apu's everyday ethnic practice. It cannot come completely into the program's center because it is unavailable to all and, therefore, not free to be shifted and shaped by the individualist ethic that we see transforming Buddhism and Native American religions in *The Simpsons*. The immigrant is welcomed, but not entirely, because he cannot blend in and be absorbed by the white majority's culture.

What Makes Jews Different?

Apu does not have parallels in *Family Guy* or *South Park*, but *The Simpsons'* Krusty the Clown has his counterparts in *Family Guy's* Mort Goldman and *South Park's* Broflovski family. These characters navigate the Jewish conundrum of being both Jewish and American, and in Kyle's and Mort's cases they exist in worlds that feature explicit anti-Semitism. Across the three programs the question arises as to how Jewish characters are integrated, how they are kept at arm's length, and how anti-Semitism influences the storylines. Similar to the other traditions we have discussed, when Jews embrace individuality and use their Jewish foundations as a springboard for individual exploration, they are depicted positively. When Judaism is characterized as being racially exclusive and unavailable for consumption, it is treated negatively.

Krusty the Clown's Jewishness demonstrates that ethno-religious groups can be welcomed into *The Simpsons'* portrayal of American culture, provided they adopt the individualism, tolerance, and individualist spiritual seeking at the heart of *The Simpsons'* unseen order. Krusty is one of *The Simpsons'* more memorable secondary characters. He is a chain-smoking, hard drinking, gambling, pornography-addicted comic with green hair, white makeup, and a red nose. He consistently produces shoddy merchandise with his likeness, mistreats people, and tells terrible jokes. Krusty is Springfield's foremost children's entertainer and he is also Jewish. In short, he is a complex character who epitomizes a stereotype of professional Jewish entertainers. Krusty's Jewishness provides him with no small amount of angst as he fluctuates between accepting the faith and trying to hide any traces of his ethnicity.

Krusty was not always depicted as Jewish. His Hebraic ancestry was introduced in the season 3 episode, "Like Father, Like Clown." Parodying *The Jazz Singer*,[23] in which the son of a Jewish cantor defies his father to become a jazz singer, this episode tells how Krusty, born Herschel Krustofsky, defied his father, Rabbi Hyman Krustofsky (voiced by the self-professed "ultimate Jew," Jackie Mason), to become a clown. In the second act we learn that Krusty grew up in Springfield's Jewish neighborhood, which is based on New York's Hasidic Jewish neighborhoods. Here Jews dress in ultra-Orthodox fashion (e.g., long robes, beards, earlocks), play chess outdoors, and debate ethical questions. In a flashback sequence we learn that Krusty's father was a rabbi in a long line of rabbis, but young Herschel wanted to make people laugh. His father forbids his becoming a clown, but the comedy bug is too much for Krusty, who got his first laughs impersonating his father in Yeshiva, where he stood before the class and said, "Blah, blah, blah Moses!" Despite his father's efforts, Krusty pursued a career in comedy until one day, at a Talmudic conference in the Catskills, a rabbi sprayed him with a seltzer bottle and Krusty's makeup washed off. His father disowned him for the shame he brought on the family, and they became estranged for twenty years.

Seeing Krusty so disheartened, Bart and Lisa resolve to reunite father and son. Rabbi Krustofsky is still heartbroken after all this time, so the only solution is to appeal to his knowledge, or, as Lisa says, "We're going to hit him where it hurts, right in the Judaica." Two rabbis—Harold Schulweis and Lavi Meier—consulted on the episode so that the following debate between Bart and Rabbi Krustofsky would be as close to an authentic rabbinical exchange as possible. First, Bart corners the rabbi in his office and quotes the Babylonian Talmud: "A child should be pushed aside with the left hand and drawn closer with the right." Bart is sure that he has given a strong religious argument for forgiveness, but the Rabbi counters with the fifth commandment: "Honor thy father and mother, end of story." Lisa then gives Bart some material from Rabbi Simon ben Eleazar, and Bart tracks Rabbi Krustofsky to a sauna where he says, "At all times let a man be supple as a reed and not rigid as a cedar." The rabbi is unimpressed, countering with "the Book of Joshua says 'You shall meditate on the Torah all day and all night.'"[24] Bart cites another Talmudic passage during a circumcision: "Who will bring redemption? The jesters." Krustofsky is not convinced and sends Bart away. It is only with a long-shot quote that Bart convinces the rabbi to change his ways. While they play chess in the park, Bart sighs and quotes a "great man": "The Jews are a swinging bunch of people. I mean, I've heard of persecution, but what they went through is ridiculous. But the great thing is, after thousands of years of waiting and holding on and fighting, they finally made it." Krustofsky is impressed, but cannot identify the "great man" among various religious sources. Bart then reveals that the quote came from Sammy Davis Jr.'s autobiography, *Yes I Can* (Davis is an African-American Jew). The rabbi, broken, laments the lost years and reconciles with Krusty.

This exchange brings Jewish tradition into *The Simpsons*. Although there are humorous elements in the exchange, its significance comes from the fact that Jewish thought is built on continuous argument about the Torah's meaning. Part of a rabbi's job is to offer guidance based on interpreting the Torah, and American Jews are divided between different approaches to the Torah and its interpretation.[25] *The Simpsons* chose this dynamic as the vehicle for its first examination of Judaism. Judaism is introduced through the tensions between popular entertainment's secular seduction and the religious calling to meditate on the Torah all day and all night. Indeed, the struggle to belong and adapt to the American environment while maintaining their ethnic differences has long been a concern for Jews.[26]

American Judaism is diverse, but Krusty is recognizable as a stereotype that marks him as an ethnic, rather than a religious, Jew. That is, he struggles to maintain his identity between the secularized, hard living, sell-out entertainer and the religious tradition to which he belongs by blood.[27] Jewish traditions only matter to Krusty when he faces an identity crisis. While American Jews have struggled with questions regarding the extent to which they should adapt their traditions to American culture, this is not Krusty's struggle. Instead, he wrestles with a problem reminiscent of Will Herberg's analysis in the 1950s, which saw having a religion (Protestant, Catholic, or Jew) as part of possessing an "American" identity.[28] That is, Krusty's ethno-religious identity as a Jew matters when he wants to see himself as complete. In the United States, that often means having a religious identity. Rabbi Krustofsky's denunciation embodies ultra-Orthodox Judaism's defense against modernity's onslaught, as these Jews have tried to preserve their traditions by rejecting modern trends and maintaining the Torah. Yet, while the ultra-Orthodox's numbers grow through high birthrates and modest numbers of converts,[29] Krusty's story is one that echoes the stories of less stringent Jewish denominations that struggle to maintain adherents as Jewish religious practice and belief become less important to younger generations of Jews.

In this light, Krusty can be usefully compared to Kyle Broflovski of *South Park*. Kyle lives morally, tries to practice his faith, and thinks through the big questions in life.[30] Yet, Kyle cannot escape Jewish stereotypes. Kyle's Jewishness is used to explain why he does not have any rhythm and why he cannot play basketball.[31] He faithfully deals with social exclusion, singing that he's "a Jew, a lonely Jew, I'd be merry, but I'm Hebrew on Christmas"[32] as he struggles with being a religious minority in the predominantly white Christian town of South Park. His room has posters of Albert Einstein and "MC Dredel" on the walls and his family decorates their home with Stars of David and menorahs. Kyle is, as philosopher William Devlin notes, the moral voice of the series and is often the character in the early seasons who expounds upon the lesson of the day.[33] Indeed, being Jewish is central to Kyle and his personality, as is being a good human being. As he notes at the end of the episode "Jewbilee" after Kenny has killed himself to release Moses from the Conch Shell of Blind Faith, "It's fine to have your own beliefs and your own traditions, but as soon as you start excluding people from your ways only because of their race you become a separatist, and being a separatist sucks ass."

That Kyle draws attention to exclusion based on race and tries to overcome it reveals an understanding about the racial, ethnic, and religious tensions contemporary American Jews face. Anthropologist Karen Brodkin illustrates that Jewishness was both a racial and ethnic identity that was transformed in the 1950s move from urban neighborhoods to the suburbs. Jews subsequently became culturally associated with postwar whiteness.[34] Kyle's family is stereotypically Jewish, as are their fellow Jews when they make appearances. Episodes such as "Jewbilee," "Ike's Wee Wee," and "The Passion of the Jew" feature other Jews who have large noses, speak with Yiddish accents, and are depicted with some elements of traditional Jewish dress (earlocks are a favorite, and in "Jewbilee" the Jew Scouts' uniforms have earlocks on the hats). Kyle's father, Gerald, is frequently depicted in a yarmulke and works as a lawyer, while his mother, Sheila, stays at home, obsesses over her children, and leads crusades against filthy television. Aside from peppering their language with Yiddish phrases, however, Sheila and Gerald could easily pass as any other "white" character in *South Park*, as can Kyle. The Broflovski's Jewishness is an ethnic identity that can be used to signal that they are different while still being included in society at large. Their Jewishness is not racial because biology is not the factor that separates these Jews from their neighbors.

Krusty and Kyle illustrate sociologist Sylvia Fishman's argument that Jewish and American values have coalesced in the minds of many American Jews.[35] Fishman identifies the specific American liberal values of "free choice, universalism, individualism and pluralism"[36] as the values Jews now find legitimated and incorporated into their Jewish identities.[37] Sociologist Steven Cohen and Judaism scholar Arnold Eisen have further found that a majority of Jews (roughly 60%) are engaged in "moderately affiliated Judaism,"[38] which encompasses a type of "spirituality of seeking"[39] within the confines of traditional Judaism. The self is sovereign over tradition and Jews actively select from the tradition along with their experiences to craft their identities. Drawing on Fishman's and Cohen and Eisen's findings, the modernist problem for Jews is that these moderately affiliated Jews interpret their tradition through an understanding of being Jewish by both blood and choice.[40] In other words, Jews are Jews because they were born Jews, but they are also Jews because they choose to practice the religious tradition that has historically informed that ethnic identity.[41] As historian Jonathan Sarna argues, "the Jewish dilemma, at its core, involves a conflict of loyalties: faith pulls in one direction, America in the other."[42] The question is to what extent one will adhere to Jewish religion or not, a question to which the answer appears to increasingly be "not."[43] Jewish studies scholar Jacob Neusner notes that the Jewish American identity is one that developed after the Second World War around the state of Israel. Specifically, being Jewish in America meant supporting Israel, which in turn preserved the Jewish people, a conceptual development that solidified after the Six-Day War in 1967. After the war, the sense that preserving Israel was essential to Jewish survival became a civil religion uniting American Jews.[44] However, this notion that support for Israel is central to Jewish identity started to change in the 1970s and 1980s as Jewish individualism became more significant for the baby boomer generation. In 2013, the Pew Forum found that fewer than half of all Jews (including fewer than half of religious Jews) found "caring about Israel" to be an essential part of being Jewish. "Remembering the Holocaust" was the most important aspect of Jewish identity, with 73% of all Jews saying it is important.[45] These conflicting tensions help to explain Krusty's struggles as he fluctuates between accepting and resenting his ethnoreligious tradition and Kyle's struggles to be "one of the guys" and still be Jewish. Indeed, as some synagogues adapted to a culture that encouraged spiritual seeking and deemphasized community while helping their members become better individual Jews, people started selecting which practices they wanted to engage in. We see this in *The Simpsons'* treatment of Jewish ritual.[46]

Krusty's adaptations to modernity and his occasional desire to take his faith seriously collide in *The Simpson's* episode, "Today, I Am a Clown." After getting a puppy from the Simpson children, Krusty takes it for a walk in the old Jewish neighborhood. Eventually they find the "Jewish Walk of Fame," which features such notable Jews as Los Angeles

Dodgers pitcher Sandy Koufax, comedian Joan Rivers, children's entertainer and puppeteer Shari Lewis, and her puppet Lamb Chop. Krusty is astounded that he does not have a star and goes to the offices of the "Jewish Walk of Fame: Where the Chosen Get Chosen." While the curator agrees that Krusty should have a star, it turns out that Krusty is not recognized by the Springfield Jewish community as a bar mitzvah because Rabbi Krustofsky was afraid the boy would make a mockery of the ceremony so he never had one. Technically, Krusty is a bar mitzvah—a Jewish adult—and is obligated to follow the commandments, but this understanding of bar mitzvah does not drive the story. Instead, the assumption that he has to have a bar mitzvah ceremony to move him to the new status underlies the episode's humor. When Krusty decides to take his faith seriously, his show gets cancelled because he will not work on the Sabbath and Homer's replacement show becomes a bigger hit. Desperate, Krusty takes his bar mitzvah ceremony to FOX and, cohosted with actor Mr. T, he has an extravagant event, complete with the Beach Boys singing about kosher meal preparation and a performance by the cast of Broadway's *The Lion King*. The ceremony ends not with Krusty reading from the Torah, but with Mr. T strapped to a giant menorah that is spun by Krusty while sparks shoot from its ends. Krusty is a hit again, but, unsurprisingly, his father is disappointed. Ultimately, Krusty decides to have a real bar mitzvah ceremony in a synagogue with a small group of friends.

"Today, I Am a Clown" captures the angst involved in limited religious participation while still trying to maintain an ethno-religious identity. For marginal affiliates, the problem is that they are confronted with a tradition emphasizing practice over belief. Krusty's need for a bar mitzvah ceremony is significant because it is a transition into adulthood; it makes him both a man and a Jew. Without it and the serious commitment it requires, Krusty knows that his identity's religious component is unfulfilled. *The Simpsons* captures the bar mitzvah ceremony's significance, which is a substantial turn for the show because this story arc suggests that there is something important about Judaism's institutionalized traditions. The bar mitzvah ceremony is treated with utmost seriousness, to the point that Krusty feels compelled to have a replacement ceremony because it needs to be held in an "authentic" environment. Willful participation in Jewish ritual fulfills Krusty, suggesting that personal religious pursuits within institutionalized frameworks, without trying to convert others to one's religion, are considered acceptable religious practices in *The Simpsons*' unseen order because they allow for individual spiritual development without infringing on anybody else.

Krusty's religiousness falls somewhere between Cohen's "moderately affiliated" and "peripheral" Judaism.[47] Krusty is not uncommitted to the tradition, but he is not committed enough to participate in regular holidays other than Hanukkah. Krusty's need for religious identity is insufficient to inspire a permanent change in character like Lisa's conversion to Buddhism. Instead, this is the modernist problem of individual identity construction. Krusty understands himself as Jewish and needs the legitimacy that rites of passage provide. However, his individual interests also involve eating pork (and endorsing pork products) (e.g., "Krusty Gets Busted") and in the episode "Today, I Am a Clown" he refers to the 613 *mitzvot* (Jewish commandments) as "all these rules, I feel like I'm in a strip club!" Clearly, Orthodoxy's formal demands are not on Krusty's mind. On the other hand, this puts Krusty's religiosity squarely in the pattern established earlier which takes religion to be a good thing when it provides individual meaning and self-worth, and bad when it prohibits or forecloses individual pursuits. Krusty's commitment makes him a man and a Jew in his eyes, affording him the social recognition he craves, but it does not stop him from indulging in drugs, alcohol, and pork products; mistreating his coworkers; and luxuriating in crass materialism.

Krusty is a Jew both ethnically and religiously, but he walks this path only with his Jewish father. He is an insider in that he indulges his own spiritual development, but an outsider in that he does it through a tradition that is only accessible to people who share his blood. In this sense, he explores his spirituality in a context of low stigmatization, something that cannot be said for Kyle and Mort. Kyle also struggles with how to be a good Jew in the world and he is usually able to navigate his Jewishness and whiteness with relative ease, especially with Stan and Kenny. His Jewishness is, as English scholar Kevin Morefield illustrates, an example of "cool Jewishness" that is unhidden, authentic, and part of Kyle's multifaceted identity.[48] Yet, Kyle has to deal with Cartman's anti-Semitism, which is helpfully compared to *Family Guy*'s use of persistent Jewish stereotypes without a strong counter-example like Kyle.

Jewishness—and by extension Judaism as the religion of Jews—is racialized in *South Park* and *Family Guy* through the caricatures of Kyle's cousin Kyle (Kyle B for our purposes)[49] and Mort Goldman. When we first meet him in the episode "The Entity," Kyle B has a nasally whine, complains about everything, wears large, thick glasses, has a bad haircut, cannot eat beef because of a problem with his intestinal lining, and plans on being an investment banker when he grows up. He is such an obvious stereotype that Kyle pays Cartman $40 not to make fun of Kyle B, a commitment with which he struggles. At the first act's conclusion he cannot contain himself, and when Kyle B starts complaining that the wooden desks give him splinters and about how cold it is in class, Ms. Choksondik (who temporarily replaced Mr. Garrison as the classroom teacher in seasons 4–6) tells him that "concentration is the key to succeeding in my class." Cartman, unable to contain himself any longer, yells out, "Maybe we'll have to send him to concentration camp!"

This reference to the Holocaust draws upon widespread knowledge of Adolf Hitler's final solution for the Jews and the death camps such as Auschwitz where millions were murdered. Hitler's agenda was based upon anti-Semitic ideas that had been circulating in Europe and North America for quite some time and these general sentiments are summarized in perhaps the most infamous collection of anti-Semitic thought, *The Protocols of the Learned Elders of Zion*. Part of the argument against Jews was that they were all greedy (*The Protocols* makes extensive reference to Jewish gold being used to buy and control the world), that they control all media and government, and that they have an active hand in reforming economic structure.[50] *South Park* plays upon this stereotype in "The Entity" when, after learning that Kyle paid $40 to keep Cartman from making fun of him, Kyle B says, "Wow, you think it takes $40 to get people to like me?" Kyle apologizes, but Kyle B continues, "Because I think you really could've done it for about $12.50. I mean, you didn't just start at forty did you? You gotta low-ball these things so you have a place to go." Kyle walks away, dumbfounded.

Later, Kyle admits to Stan that Kyle B is ruining his efforts to make a good name for Jews in South Park, but Kyle's biggest fear is that he will become a stereotype. He tells Stan, "I'm a Jew and he's making me hate Jews." Stan responds, "Dude, a self-hating Jew. You are becoming a stereotype!"[51] On the DVD commentary for "The Entity" Matt Stone (himself Jewish) confesses that Kyle B is based on his own frustrations with how some Jews act and notes that he is "every bad Jewish stereotype put into one." Trey Parker also admits that "These are the kinds of stereotypes about Jews you can't tell on television any more," which is untrue. *South Park* can run this stereotype and attack those Jews who appear different because they are perceived as physically weak, shifty, greedy, and manipulative, by putting them next to a self-hating "cool Jew" like Kyle who shows that some Jews break the mold. Yet, Kyle B gets the last laugh. After numerous attempts to get rid of him (attaching a sled to a bus, putting him in a box and sending him on an airplane, and leaving him in the woods), he leaves after receiving a check for $5 million. Before he departs, though, he calls the boys "hick, redneck jocks" who are "right out of a stereotype catalogue." It is a convenient turning of the tables, but the greedy Jewish stereotype remains intact.

Mort Goldman and his family are equally portrayed as quintessential Jewish stereotypes in *Family Guy*. With their hunched posture, thick glasses, and bucked teeth, the Goldmans are not the physical embodiment of strength. Indeed, in one of Mort's early appearances he bowls a perfect game, causing the local newspaper to run the headline "Local Jew Excels in Sports."[52] *Family Guy* continues using the stereotype of the weak, sickly Jew in season 10's episode "Meg and Quagmire," in which Mort is standing in a room full of shirtless men, one of whom has earlocks and a big grey beard. In his nasally, whiny voice Mort sets the scene for the encounter: "Ok, the first rule of Jewish fight club is if somebody says 'Ow' you stop." One man punches another and the second man says "Ow." Mort ends the confrontation with "Ok, let's eat." Unlike the characters in David Fincher's 1999 film *Fight Club* who mercilessly pound each other into submission as a way of showing masculine dominance, these Jews demonstrate that the *Jewish* male body is weak—an association that is linked to personality. Athleticism is one of the American symbols of strength and dominance and a racial absence of this excellence is part of the ongoing stigmatization of certain racial groups in the United States. Counterexamples of Jewish athletic excellence exist—for example, LA Dodgers pitching great Sandy Koufax and the many Jews serving in the Israeli army—but they are not mentioned here. It is the stereotype of the physically weak, intellectually canny Jew that is important for the ongoing transmission of anti-Semitism because it allows all Jews to be seen as miserly and cunning, but also in need of physical protection from others who can exchange physical security in return for Jewish money.

Jews are popularly conceived in *South Park* and *Family Guy* as "canny" in Christie Davies' terms.[53] Stemming from their supposed ability to manage money with unprecedented excellence, this financial shrewdness is perceived as passing into all other aspects of Jewish life so that we end up with stereotypes about frigid Jewish wives and greedy Jews. Kyle B's ability to invest his money and earn millions of dollars as a young boy who dreams of being an investment banker is one such example. Another example from *South Park* comes in the episode "Two Days Before the Day After Tomorrow" in which Cartman forces Kyle to hand over the bag of gold that all Jews ostensibly wear around their necks. *Family Guy* further encapsulates this stereotype with a cutaway scene to a "Jewish porno" in which two fully dressed Orthodox Jews (one man, one woman) lie next to each other on a bed staring at the ceiling. The man engages in verbal foreplay, saying "I own four apartment buildings." The woman moans approvingly and her eyes narrow. He presses on, "I have central air." She moans again. His *coup de grâce* is to emphasize that he has "a well funded 401K." The woman is totally overtaken at this point and can only exclaim, "Oh! We are gonna have sex at some point!"[54] This stereotype also shapes Mort's actions in the episode "Yug Milaf" when he finds a quarter on the sidewalk, bends over to pick it up, and exclaims, "Oooo, a quarter! I don't care what the doctor found on my nuts, this is a good day!" and in the episode "Burning Down the Bayit" in which he tells Peter that acts of arson to collect insurance money are "all covered in the Torah, right after the chapter on how to write complaint letters that will result in compensatory merchandise."

The greedy Jew stereotype comes to the forefront most clearly in the *Family Guy* episodes "When You Wish Upon a Weinstein" and "Family Goy." In "When You Wish Upon a Weinstein" Peter demonstrates his financial incompetence by purchasing volcano insurance. After Lois rebukes him he heads to the local bar, the Drunken Clam, where he learns that his neighbor Glenn Quagmire has a Jewish stockbroker and their friend Cleveland Brown has a Jewish accountant—and both are flush with cash. Peter can draw only one conclusion: "So you're saying I need a Jewish guy to handle my money." Cleveland corrects Peter's reductionism, saying, "not every Jewish person is good with money." To which

Peter replies, "Well, yeah, I guess not the retarded ones, but why would you even say that? For shock value? Sheesh Cleveland, there's edgy and there's offensive. Good day, sir." Peter's statement establishes a classic comedian's defense against critics who call their jokes offensive and racist. In this case, *Family Guy* invites a definition of being "edgy" and "only joking" instead of hateful. The implication is that he was saying something shocking to elicit a laugh and not speaking his real intentions. But, in the next scene Peter sings to the tune of Disney's "When You Wish Upon a Star" at the windowsill after hearing Lois beg her mother for money:

> Nothing else has worked so far,
> So I'll wish upon a star,
> Wondrous dancing speck of light,
> I need a Jew.

[*As he sings the stars in the sky arrange themselves into a six-pointed star constellation. Then Peter starts walking down the street.*]

> Lois makes me take the rap,
> Because our chequebook looks like crap.
> Since I can't give her a slap,
> I need a Jew.
> Where to find,
> A "Baum" or "Stein" or "Stine"
> To teach me how to whine and do my taxes.

[*At this point a giant spaceship lands, turns into a dreidel upon which Peter climbs, it blasts him into space, and then Peter slides down a giant menorah which turns into a menorah constellation. Peter looks at the sky as he reenters his house.*]

> Though by many they're abhorred,
> Hebrew people I've adored.
> Even though they killed my lord/I don't think they killed my lord,[55]
> I need a Jew.

[*Peter falls asleep at the windowsill and the next morning there is a knock on the door. The man introduces himself as Max Weinstein, says his car broke down, and asks to use Peter's phone. Peter looks to the ceiling and sings.*]

Now my troubles are all through,
I have a Jew.

Max is an accountant who helps Peter recover his money, after which Peter becomes enamored of his new Jewish friend. Peter's ignorance, however, causes him to spew stereotypes. Max tries to educate Peter, but Peter decides that the best thing he can do is have Chris turn Jewish so that he can become successful. Against Lois' wishes, Peter and Chris head to the temple where Peter tries to convince the rabbi to make Chris a bar mitzvah, even offering to buy a ceremony. "You can't just buy a bar mitzvah!" replies the rabbi, "It requires a lot of study." Peter, undeterred, responds with "Well, can't we just skip that part? I mean, come on, if Chris knew how to study he wouldn't need to become Jewish in the first place, right?" Peter ends up taking Chris to Las Vegas to the "Bar Bar Bar Mitzvah" Synagogue. When Lois learns of this, she races to Vegas, where she stops the ceremony because Chris is doing it for all the wrong reasons. Unfortunately for her, everybody in the synagogue thinks she is a Jew stopping a bar mitzvah ceremony and a fight breaks out. The Griffins run out of the synagogue, Lois fights off the angry Jews with a Star of David, and they leave Las Vegas as Peter apologizes for trying to convert Chris to Judaism. Lois reminds him that a person's religion is no guarantee of success and Peter agrees.

"When You Wish Upon a Weinstein" concludes season 3 and was the last episode FOX had ordered when they first cancelled *Family Guy*. FOX did not originally air it because its content was considered too anti-Semitic, but the episode debuted on Cartoon Network in syndication in 2004 and FOX aired it after starting production on new *Family Guy* episodes. At the time it was originally pulled, the *Family Guy* staff was incensed because they had been making fun of every other ethnic group and did not see the harm in lampooning Jews as well. Furthermore, the episode's writer, Ricky Blitt, and some of the voice actors and guest stars were Jewish.[56] This defense of having some members of the group in question doing the offending is often used as a buffer against charges of racism. Indeed, being an insider in a racial, ethnic, or gender group is widely accepted as a license to say slanderous things without being called a bigot. *Family Guy*'s narrative structure in "When You Wish Upon a Weinstein" is also important because Peter is presented as a well-meaning idiot who needs to learn his lesson rather than as a hateful anti-Semite. Jewish money handling is not a sign of corruption here, it is a blessing that this idiot desperately needs. While the stereotype persists, *Family Guy* could defend itself by saying that Peter is the idiot and that he is the problem here, not Jews.

Even though "When You Wish Upon a Weinstein" was originally withheld, "Family Goy" contains much more defined anti-Semitism. After Lois has a benign lump removed from her breast, the doctor checks her family history and we learn that her mother is Jewish. "Wow, breast cancer's starting to look pretty good," Peter responds. The second act starts with Lois' mother explaining that she concealed her Jewish identity so that her husband, Carl Pewterschmitt, could get into country clubs. Lois is stunned and questions what she thought she knew about her family: "So grandma Hebrewberg is actually Jewish?" "Yes," replies her mother, "When she moved to America, her family changed their name. It was originally Hebrewbergmoneygrabber. That makes you Jewish, Lois, and your children too."

This information overwhelms Lois so she contacts Max to learn what to do. Brian, indignant, says that she should do nothing, and Max agrees. Before Lois can settle into a period of quietly contemplating this revelation, Peter bursts into the room, yelling "Shalom, Jews" and wearing a giant Star of David pendant, a yarmulke, and a prayer shawl.

He also has glistening chest hair which he claims came with the Star and has changed his name to a "Hebrew" name that sounds like coughing up phlegm. Max cautions Peter that becoming Jewish is a long practice of spiritual education and good works and Lois argues that she does not want to make a big deal out of her heritage. Peter, however, insists, saying, "Leave it to a Jew to take all the fun out of being a Jew. Now, listen up. I like the hat and I like the scarf, so we're doing this."

The family then starts exploring what it means to be Jewish, which includes a trip to the synagogue where Peter shouts out "I'm Jewish! Yeah! Holocaust! We're number one!" and a visit to the local Jewish school where, after learning about Hanukkah, Stewie quips, "How long before we play 'pin the eviction notice on the black guy's door?'" When the teacher asks if there are any questions, Stewie inquires, "What are you going to do when Jesus comes back and puts a boot up your ass?" He is won over by the eight days of presents and becomes

Peter presents himself as Jewish in "Family Goy"

an athletic hero at the school for kicking a soccer ball a few inches in gym class.

Peter's acceptance of Judaism fades after his Catholic father's ghost visits him in the night. Reminded of his heritage, Peter becomes abusive and tries to get rid of the "Jewish curse" in his house. He puts a crass anti-Semitic stamp on his new position when he says, "Jews are gross Lois. It's the only religion with the word 'ew' in it." The next morning when Lois wakes up she finds herself strapped to a cross made out of Stewie's crib and Peter runs in, yelling, "How do you like it, huh? How do you like it?" Lois eventually heads to her parents' house to get away from Peter's harassment, where she admits, "I don't really care about being Jewish, or even Christian for that matter. I just want to be a good person on my own." The central tenet of *Family Guy's* perspective on religion—reject religion, be good—is upheld in this simple statement.

The episode's climax is a Passover Seder that Peter, drunk and dressed as the Easter bunny, interrupts. After Peter sleeps off some of the drunkenness, he and Lois argue until Peter says that he can't be with somebody who "doesn't believe in Jesus," which prompts Jesus to appear. Jesus then explains that he is Jewish and proves it by arguing that a 9% tip on $200 is "$18, which is fair." Peter is astounded as this confirms Jesus' Jewishness for him. Jesus mitigates Peter's confusion, saying that Judaism and Catholicism are similar and that the Last Supper was a Seder. After Peter and Lois reconcile, Peter asks Jesus which religion the Griffins should be. Jesus replies, "Six of one, they're all complete crap."

Jesus' sentiments cap an episode referencing Jewish greed, the longstanding Christian accusation that they are responsible for Jesus' death based in Matthew 27:25, and the weak-bodied stereotype. Unlike "When You Wish Upon a Weinstein," "Family Goy" serves up Jewish stereotypes with no other purpose than to offend and to establish Judaism as but another religion that can be rejected for being "complete crap." The racial element only emphasizes *Family Guy*'s rejection of Jewish tenets. As a religion that is of "a people," if the religion is "complete crap" so are those who are part of the religion by blood, hence the numerous attacks on Jews as weak and manipulative.

Keeping *Family Guy*'s anti-Semitism in mind, there may be no stronger counter to the Jewish stereotype than Kyle's interactions with Eric Cartman in *South Park*'s episode "The Passion of the Jew." This episode originally aired on March 31, 2004 amid concerns that Mel Gibson's *The Passion of the Christ* would spark new waves of anti-Semitic hatred. Cartman has been an anti-Semite throughout *South Park*'s history. In the episode "Mr. Hankey, the Christmas Poo" he tells Kyle that Jews cannot eat Christmas snow (and has the local police officer confirm that it is against the law); in another case he stops Kyle from being "the tough one" in their boyband, Fingerbang, because Jews are not tough;[57] he blames Jews for war in the Middle East;[58] and in the episode "It's Christmas in Canada" the Canadian government takes Kyle's adopted brother, Ike, back to the great white north and Cartman says, "I didn't want to say this Kyle, but maybe this is what your family gets for being Jewish at Christmas." In later seasons Cartman tells Stan that "I know you think that he's your best friend, but Kyle is a Jew rat. He has his Jew ethics, while he hoards his greedy Jew gold, and he will Jew you out if you tell him about this [destroying a beaver dam and flooding a nearby town]."[59] In the episode "Lice Capades," when Ms. Garrison tries to gently discuss the problem of lice in the school, Cartman misinterprets this, saying "Ahhhh yes, you mean the Jew problem [*points to Kyle*]. Good, good,

I'm glad we're finally going to do something about it." In the episode "Le Petit Tourette," Cartman fakes having Tourette Syndrome so that he can slander Jews on national television and even calls Sheila a "Jew bitch" to her face because she thinks he has a serious medical condition. In season 16 he has trouble remembering if his security password is "Kyle is a dirty, no-good Jew" or "Kyle is a no-good, lying Jew" in the episode "Insecurity," and he creates a phony cryptozoological creature, the "Jew-pacabra," that preys on children during Passover and whose mating call is "There is no Christ!"[60]

South Park has clearly used anti-Semitism as a source of jokes and dramatic tension over the years. Yet, Cartman's anti-Semitism echoes anti-Semitic currents in American culture, and to illustrate this we turn to the episode "The Passion of the Jew." In this episode Kyle declares that Cartman knows nothing about Jews, but Cartman, quoting Mel Gibson via his blockbuster *The Passion of the Christ*,[61] claims that "Jews are the devil." Kyle denies this, but Cartman, having seen *The Passion* thirty-four times, not only assures Kyle that it is true, he repeats the story of Barabas from the Christian scriptures (Mk 15:6; Mt 27:15; Lk 23:17; Jn 18:39) and declares that the Jews laughed about killing Jesus. When Kyle continues protesting, Cartman presses his point saying, "You know what it is? You're scared. You're scared of the truth. You don't want that movie to show you just how bad the Jews are, and why everyone hates you." When Kyle says that people don't hate the Jews, Cartman notes the $300 million domestic box office gross and that the film was the highest grossing film of all time. Kyle watches the film and is traumatized. He leaves the theater and tells Cartman that Cartman was right. Cartman, overjoyed, sends prayers of thanks to Mel Gibson for his blessings, guidance, and strength in his room that night.

Later, Kyle dreams that he is one of the Jews condemning Jesus to death and even sticks a spear into Jesus' side. He laughs maniacally throughout the vision, but wakes up screaming. Traumatized by the cinematic depiction of Jesus' death, Kyle struggles with his Jewishness. Meanwhile, Cartman dresses up as Hitler and holds rallies for the local Christians who think that the film is an accurate depiction of Jesus' suffering and want to share the gospel message. Cartman, however, thinks that the film is about "the horror and filthiness of the common Jew." At his first *Passion* meeting, Cartman suggests not talking about the message aloud, so he starts making references to "what needs to be done" and "the cleansing." The humor in this scene is built upon the fact that "what needs to be done" and "the cleansing" can be taken by Christians as euphemisms for helping people convert and reform their lives and not, as Cartman intends, as a reference to the Holocaust.

Kyle continues to struggle with guilt and visits the local Catholic priest, Fr. Maxi. Asking the priest if God sent Jesus to die or if Jesus "kind of got [screwed] over," he confesses that he "can't live with the guilt anymore. Because, even if Jesus wasn't really the Son of God, he was still a nice guy and he didn't deserve what happened to him in Mel Gibson's movie. I . . . I can't sleep at night." Maxi suggests that atonement is what Kyle needs, and Kyle runs off with a new idea in his head.

Cartman, meanwhile, has grown his group of *Passion* lovers and starts them marching in support of the film. The people are enthralled and as they march down the street, Cartman has them chant German anti-Semitic slogans. As he leads them around town, Kyle tells the members of his synagogue that the Jews should take some responsibility for Jesus' death. The congregation is, understandably, outraged, but just after the Rabbi calms them down the Christians march outside, chanting their anti-Semitic slogans.[62] The Jews and Christians meet in front of the local theater, but Mel Gibson shows up and everybody considers him crazy and loses interest in *The Passion*. Kyle, without ever actually dealing with the anti-Semitic angst of the Christ-Killer claim, says, "I feel so much better about being Jewish now that I see that Mel Gibson is just a big wacko douche."

"The Passion of the Jew" draws upon the long-standing stigma of Jews as Christ-Killers, tainted by blood and the cause of all humanity's suffering. While it is dismissed in this episode because it came from "a big wacko douche," it never really dies in *South Park* when Cartman's bigotry can be used as a foil for humor.[63] Indeed, as we can see from these examples, Cartman is a constant source of stereotypes that remind us just what Kyle has to be a "cool Jew" against. Taking the ongoing presence of anti-Semitic stereotypes in *South Park* and *Family Guy* into consideration, each program's anti-Semitism identifies Jews as not fully "white," which is the implicit racial category for inclusion and, as such, keeps Jews and their religious traditions from being adopted into the normative frameworks for acceptable religion. Kyle's cool Judaism complicates the anti-Semitic exclusion in *South Park*, but Carman's anti-Semitism—which is not always conclusively defeated—keeps the program's response to Jewish inclusiveness ambiguous. In many ways, this is in keeping with *South Park*'s creative individualism at the core of its unseen order. For *South Park*, the question is not whether or not Judaism is to be included; it is *how Kyle lives as a Jew* that becomes the basis for evaluating the tradition. In both *South Park* and *Family Guy*, however, Jewish characters are attacked and ridiculed because they *are* Jews, not because *they choose to be*. So long as the idea of individual choice remains at the forefront of all three programs' unseen orders, whether it is practice in the case of *The Simpsons*, belief in *Family Guy*, or creativity in *South Park*, any tradition that is heavily invested in what you are racially and ethnically will pose problems that must be resolved.

The Exclusionary Power of Race and Religion

People's lives are built on what they, and others, think about what their bodies signify. Religions, as institutions that arise around beliefs in an unseen order and that guide our harmonious adjustment to them, have a profound influence on how every*body* is understood. Each program has shown how it struggles with the complications that race and ethnicity introduce in everyday life. In *The Simpsons*, ethnicity and race are obstacles to bringing non-whites into the program's religious center when religious practice is not divorced from communal grounding. In the case of Native American religions, the removal is total as there are no Native American characters practicing their traditions, and it is partial in the cases of Apu and Krusty, who have minimal—if any—connection to a living body of fellow practitioners. Krusty's and Apu's religious traditions are there to guide them when needed, but otherwise the traditions can be put aside. This is similar to the way that spirituality, Buddhism, and science are useful guides at the center of *The Simpsons'* unseen order, but spirituality, Buddhism, and science were ostensibly available to every*body*. The bodies of Native Americans, Indians, and Jews complicate the appropriation of spiritual practices that are at the heart of *The Simpsons'* model of individual spirituality.

By the same token, *South Park* emphasizes individual cool Judaism in Kyle as a way of showing that the Jewish tradition can offer a solid grounding for personal growth, but that this choice must be his and the failures of other Jews and their bodies are obstacles to be overcome. Kyle B's nasally whine, Cartman's anti-Semitism, Kyle's wrestling with the legacies of anti-Semitism, and the basic problem of being Jewish in a world dominated by Christians stand as challenges that Kyle navigates with differing degrees of success. As we have seen, it is through individual creativity and thoughtful reflection against these challenges that Kyle is able to be a good Jew and a good American too. Of all the programs, Kyle's ethnicity is the least problematic for *South Park* because of the program's emphasis on individual creativity. At the same time, Kyle's individual responses are shaped by a social world that marks him as different and, by definition, excluded. His inclusion comes through navigating both tradition and the wider social world, embodying the contemporary American Jewish struggle.

Finally, *Family Guy* attacks Jews as Jews because, by "Family Goy's" time, the program had firmly entrenched its anti-religion stance. The navigations that Krusty and Kyle can take, finding personal purpose in their religious traditions even as those traditions are not seen as part of the cultural mainstream, are not available to Jews in *Family Guy*. As Jesus says in "Family Goy," Judaism, like all other religions, is "complete crap." Without ideas, traditions, or ethics to fall back on, the religious elements disintegrate into assaults on Jewish bodies and stereotypes about Jewish wealth. Religion must be attacked, and the ethnic and racial elements sustained by that tradition are also targeted.

In *The Simpsons*, *South Park*, and *Family Guy*, race and its relationship to religious traditions present problems for the implicitly white, individualist, rationalist individual that is upheld as an ideal. These programs each present a particular vision of who constitutes an ideal American and what constitutes ideal American religion. In light of these standards, a people's religion that is at the core of their ethnic and racial identities may be a barrier to inclusion. This fact of intertwined religious and ethnic identities speaks to broader cultural struggles with diversity. How should Native Americans and their religious traditions be seen in the cultural landscape? *The Simpsons* and *Family Guy* suggest that their religious traditions are fair game for anybody who wants to take the practices for personal gain and profit, a stance that violates the communal spirit within which those traditions were originally cultivated. How should Americans incorporate immigrants with different religious traditions? *The Simpsons* suggests that they should be invited to stay, but that their religion is foreign and not a part of the cultural mainstream and should be kept at arm's length. What does it mean to be Jewish in the United States? For Krusty and Kyle it is a chance to build their personal understanding of a meaningful life upon a tradition that is theirs by blood. For Cartman and *Family Guy,* Judaism and Jews are never completely welcomed into their visions of a good, unseen order. For them, the religiousness that is part of Jewish identity is a reason to heap scorn upon Jews.

Despite the three programs' open support for individual spiritual seeking and creativity, when the traditions that people seek are tied to ethnic and racial identities, they are considered problematic and not part of the programs' cores. To think about race and ethnicity and their links to religious practice is to conceive of religion in the United States as an unseen order that is more than just an ideology available to anybody. Instead, these religions are accompanied by a responsibility to others who are bound together as a people through the tradition. Thinking about religion like this puts religion back into the community in a deep way that individual seeking does not acknowledge and challenges the ideas at each program's core. Hence, these religions are kept at arm's length. Race and ethnicity are not the only reasons a tradition can be excluded. We now turn to Christianity, its American legacy, and the religious claims that drive so many Americans' behaviors.

3

American Christianity, Part 1

Backwards Neighbors[1]

BART
What religion are you?

HOMER
You know, the one with all the well-meaning rules that never work out in real life. Uh, um, Christianity![2]

Homer's statement helps us to understand Christianity's place in *The Simpsons*, but although millions of Americans call themselves Christians, we should remember that there is no such thing as American Christianity. There are numerous American *Christianities* and they offer *The Simpsons*, *South Park*, and *Family Guy* a plethora of material. From devout evangelicals to ethnic stereotype Catholics and indifferent mainline Protestants, American Christians have provided the programs with numerous stock characters and historical moments to satirize. A recurring theme in all three programs is an evaluation of Christians as stupid and dangerous. The meaning of stupidity, in this context, draws on Davies' formulation of the term as: "a general and universal quality and has come to include and to refer particularly to an inability to understand and cope with those technical aspects of the modern world that are common to most countries rather than simply to a lack of understanding of local customs, practices, or forms of speech."[3] Stupidity is taken as an inherent quality of groups that are seen as marginal and incapable of joining the core. Christian beliefs and behaviors are portrayed in these series as revealing an underlying stupidity in the tradition that can lead to dangerous behavior because Christians are seen as unable to cope with the core values of individual spiritual seeking within a context of scientific rationality in *The Simpsons*, personal creativity in *South Park*, and scientific atheism in *Family Guy*. Christianity is never welcomed into any of the programs' cores, but its contributions to American culture are available as tools for criticizing those who believe in any of the Christianities that are practiced in the United States.

To examine what positions Christians as stupid in the programs' unseen orders, we consider how depicting major Christian symbols—God, Jesus, and the Bible—is a commentary on the plausibility structures that make these entities relevant in American public and private life. We also examine how *The Simpsons* portrays Christianity as increasingly irrelevant and unable to connect with everyday people in the form of Reverend Timothy Lovejoy, while the depiction of Ned Flanders demonstrates that when Christianity becomes politically relevant it becomes dangerous. Understanding Christians' influence in setting the terms for debate about religious freedom in the United States is key to comprehending how they are handled. The politics of religious diversity are frequently shaped by Christians acting in their own interests in the public sphere. These actions and interests frequently clash with the three programs' creators' values. Their portrayals of Christianity are shaped by their responses to what they see as the failure of all "those well-meaning rules that don't work out in real life."

Studying Christianity in the United States is a complex challenge for anybody. Religious traditions are intensely creative and incredibly productive. Scholars can specialize in theology, liturgy, polity, lived religion, and a denomination's history, but in these endeavors we become aware of our limitations. The lives, institutional twists, denominational differences, and regional variations that comprise Christian life in the United States are varied, pluralistic, and deeply rooted into numerous local, regional, national, and international cultures. From Episcopalians and Presbyterians to Methodists, African American churches, and numerous evangelical Protestant traditions, the United States has always had a flourishing diversity of Christianities, and part of American religious life has been an ongoing competition among Christians for their neighbors' souls.[4] This diversity has birthed not only a wide variety of American theologies, but also a generic understanding of Christianity, a common stock of knowledge that people can reference before bringing their own theological twists to the discussion.

This generic knowledge about Christians is a significant part of sociologist Will Herberg's argument in *Protestant, Catholic, Jew*—that one needs to be a member of one of these three religious traditions to be a fully participating American.[5] Protestants and Catholics, however, are the numerically dominant groups, with roughly 70% of the country identifying as some kind of Christian.[6] For those who are engaged in public discourse, it is impossible to comprehend American politics without an understanding of how the United States has restructured itself around conservative and liberal identities within the churches since World War II.[7] Without a concern for an unseen order based in God's laws, legislative battles about marriage, abortion, media content, contraception, sexual education, welfare, and prayer in public schools make no sense. Politically active Christians who want to see their unseen orders legislated clash with *The Simpsons'*, *South Park's*, and *Family Guy's* creators and their unseen orders because these programs treat the sacredness of freedom of speech, freedom of religion, and the individual's autonomy in seeking their own path as antithetical to the goals of politically engaged Christians. In the United States, God-talk flavors the national discourse and numerous religious and political figures claim to know what God wants—marshalling support and financial gain from millions of devout believers. For *The Simpsons, South Park*, and *Family Guy*, the hypocrisies between what Christians do and their claims about what is good are low-hanging fruit that they can pick at any time to both assault those they see as threats and simultaneously reinforce their own unseen orders. It is, therefore, useful to look at the three programs' depictions of God, Jesus, and the Bible to understand their critical approach to Christianity.

God: A Class Act All the Way?

"Homer the Heretic" not only depicts God for the first time in *The Simpsons*, but also discusses his character. After Homer dreams about God, he informs his family that God told him that missing church is acceptable. Intrigued, Bart asks his father what God is like and Homer replies, "Perfect teeth. Nice smell. A class act all the way." This depiction is contrasted with God's portrayal in Homer's explanation for why his house almost burned down: "God is vengeful." These characteristics of class and vengeance have been noted before, but how should we approach God's frequent appearances in *The Simpsons*?[8] A significant portion of

Simpsons jokes about God could be considered as mocking God and the way Christians talk about him. For example, when the family watches a biblical epic parody about Noah in the episode "Das Bus," Bart proclaims, "God is so in your face." Homer responds, "Yeah, he's my favorite fictional character." Furthermore, in the episode "Homer Loves Flanders," Homer prays for tickets to the big football game. Ned, having won tickets in a radio contest, arrives at the front door and offers to take Homer with him. Slamming the door in Ned's face, Homer looks toward the ceiling and asks "Why do you mock me, O Lord!" Homer mistakes a waffle Bart threw on the ceiling for God, and after Marge peels it off, Homer catches it, saying, "I know I shouldn't eat thee but . . ." He then takes a big bite and drools, "Sacrilicious." Last, in the Halloween episode "Treehouse of Horror XIV," God, depicted as a beam of light, chases Homer. After Homer crosses railroad tracks before God can catch him, God mutters, "I am too old and too rich for this," before letting Homer escape, bringing God's omniscience and omnipotence into question. God is as open to ridicule and mockery as any character in *The Simpsons*.

While sometimes *The Simpsons'* portrayals of God are mocking, others are serious, and Jamey Heit expresses this best when he writes, "God thus comes to reflect cultural values rather than embody traditional notions of who God is. . . . The critical point here is that Homer fails to recognize the theologically inconsistent image he offers."[9] Heit has a good point in that *The Simpsons'* portrayal of God reflects cultural values, but his argument misses a significant issue: Homer's many misconceptions about God mirror different ways American Protestants have depicted God. To rebut Heit, God *always* reflects cultural values.[10] Traditional notions of God are cultural values that have become sedimented over time. Why should *The Simpsons'* representations of God adhere to traditional standards or be theologically consistent? None of the program's creators' and owners' vested interests—entertainment, cultural subversion, or profit—are concerned with upholding Christian orthodoxy. *The Simpsons* mines contrasting images of God in the biblical and American traditions for humorous material, and in so doing it suggests that God transitions between grace and vengeance, and that keeping him satisfied is in everybody's best interest.

God is also frequently featured in *Family Guy*. God's character is a bearded old man whose sense of humor and interests make him less

God aims a sniper rifle at Meg's head

a benevolent, caring deity than a wise-cracking, annoyed, and lustful old man who appears when characters invoke his name through casual swearing. A good example comes from the episode "Fifteen Minutes of Shame" when Meg, embarrassed, says, "Oh God, kill me now." A red dot from a laser scope on God's sniper rifle appears on Meg's forehead, but before he can pull the trigger God's phone rings. He answers and, using his best "pick-up" voice, exclaims, "Cheryl."

Family Guy's God is a player. This depiction can seem unsettling to some viewers because of American squeamishness about sex and religion. God, as holy, is kept at arm's length from sex talk, even as God is brought into discussions about regulating sex. It is almost impossible to understand American discussions about sex and marriage without an understanding of conservative Christian theologies about what God wants in sexual relationships. In the episode "Blind Ambition" God emerges as a pick-up artist in Quahog. Standing in a bowling alley he hits on a woman using his cosmic powers, saying "Hey, want to see what I can do? Check it out. Ready? Beer, glass, now watch this?" God then turns his back on the woman and has the beer pour itself into the glass. He turns back and says, "Oh, hey, I guess I'll go over here for a minute" before singing to himself. Then, feigning surprise, he turns back to the glass and says, "Oh, holy crap! That's still pouring itself. Oh wow! That's amazing. I've never seen anyone do that!" He then leans in toward the woman and asks, "You want to go out later?"

God's sexual proclivities are also used in jokes that feature Jesus. In "Blind Ambition" God lights a woman on fire in a bar with his "magic fingers" and yells "Jesus Christ!" Jesus runs in and asks "What?" God urgently instructs him, "Get the Escalade, we're out of here!" In another scene, Jesus calls God because things are not working out between him and Joseph. Their conversation is as follows:

JESUS
Hey dad, uh it's me. Listen, things here aren't working out any more and I was just, I was wondering if I could come live with you and Janet for a while.

GOD
Oh, wow kiddo, you know I'd love that but I don't know if now is the best time. Maybe next year, ok? I'll see you Friday night. Oh, tell your mother I sent the check. [*Turns to his blonde girlfriend.*] So where were we?

JANET
Right about here. [*Holds up a condom.*]

GOD
Awwww . . . Come on baby, it's my birthday.

JANET
No.[11]

Family Guy frequently lampoons everyday discourse about God, showing what it would be like if God actually responded to simple utterances. In the episode "One if by Clam, Two if by Sea" Peter utters,

"Oh, thank you God" which prompts God to reply, "Don't mention it" while riding off on a horse. Another time Peter watches a plastic bag floating on the wind and exclaims, "Look it's dancing with me. It's like there's this incredibly benevolent force that wants me to know there's no reason to be afraid. Sometimes there's so much beauty in the world it makes my heart burst." The scene shifts to God standing on a cloud and he yells, "It's just some trash blowing in the wind. Do you have any idea how complicated your circulatory system is?"[12] In "Partial Terms of Endearment," Peter learns that Lois had a sexual encounter with another woman. He excitedly exclaims, "No way, my wife messed around with another chick?! Thank you God!" The scene shifts to God standing on a cloud, where he says, "Don't mention it Peter." God gives a thumbs up, the frame freezes, and captioning kicks in with a women's chorus singing "God, he knows what turns you on." When it comes to creating things in the world, one of *Family Guy*'s cutaway scenes comes after Quagmire says that Asians are smart because "that's just the way God made them." The scene shifts to God standing in a board room in front of a covered display. He says, "Gentlemen, I give you the Asian" before removing the cover to display an Asian man with glasses in red underwear. The members of the board "oooo" as God explains his new creation, "Compact, hairless, and fiercely intelligent. Penises, while tiny, are extremely efficient. We're projecting 10 billion within five years. Also, there will be different varieties that will all hate each other for some reason."[13] Finally, in the episode "3 Acts of God," Peter, Joe, Cleveland, and Quagmire go in search of God to convince him to stop helping athletes beat the New England Patriots. God agrees, but only if the players can get notoriously taciturn football coach Bill Belichick to smile because God is upset that, after all he has done for Belichick, he has not received a simple smile in return.

These jokes rely on a rich history of Americans claiming that God fluctuates between benevolence and vengeance. First we will explore portraits of God as a vengeful god. Perhaps the most famous American sermon, Puritan Jonathan Edwards' "Sinners in the Hands of an Angry God," explains that "God is a great deal more angry with great numbers that are now on earth: yea, doubtless, with many that are now in this congregation, who it may be are at ease, than he is with many of those who are now in the flames of hell," and "The God that holds you over the pit of hell, much as one holds a spider, or some loathsome insect over the fire, abhors you, and is dreadfully provoked."[14] Edwards' wrathful depiction of God was not unique. His contemporary George Whitfield warned, "O obstinate sinner, whoever thou art, he [God] will by no means spare thee."[15] The Second Great Awakening's leading voice, Charles Grandison Finney, urged the churches to take a proper moral stand, opposing slavery and promoting temperance because "God cannot sustain this free and blessed country, which we love and pray for, unless the church will take right ground."[16] These wrathful proclamations about God continue to the present day, frequently featuring in radical political sermons against liberal political actions. For example, on September 13, 2001, former Moral Majority leader and fundamentalist televangelist Jerry Falwell claimed on his colleague Pat Robertson's *700 Club* TV program that God withdrew his protection from America on September 11, 2001 because of the actions of the American Civil Liberties Union, pagans, homosexuals, and abortionists.

While Falwell and Robertson do not represent all Americans, the fact remains that one cannot live in the United States without hearing ongoing debates about God, what he is angry about, and the punishment in store for sinners. According to the 2012 General Social Survey, 75% of Americans believe in God.[17] Among believers, however, there are also significant divides in how God is understood, which generally correlate with political positions. While the majority of Christians conceive of God as a loving, caring, and compassionate entity, conservative Christians in particular also associate God with power and judgment.[18] This matters because people's concepts of God affect how they solve problems, including social issues such as abortion and capital punishment.[19] In America's polarized political environment, contrasting opinions about God emphasize religio-political divisions. While American Protestants, who make up 46.5% of American adults, can agree that God is a loving entity, conservatives are leaders in characterizing God as punitive.[20]

Like *Family Guy*, *The Simpsons* is aware of this tradition of God's vengeance and frequently references God's anger for humorous purposes. In the episode "I Married Marge," Marge tells Homer that she thinks the song "You Light Up My Life" is about God. Homer responds, "Oh, well, he's always happy. No, wait, he's always mad." In another episode, "Mr. Plow," Homer and his best friend Barney Gumble start competing snow

removal businesses. At the episode's conclusion they decide to work together, prompting Homer to proclaim, "When two best friends work
together, not even God himself can stop them." God's voice then echoes
from overhead, "Oh no?" and a ray of light melts the snow, ruining
their business. In an episode entitled "Pray Anything," Homer becomes
FCOS's proprietor after suing the church. He throws a huge housewarming party at which numerous sins—including gambling, drunkenness,
blasphemy, and idolatry—are committed. Storm clouds gather over the
church and Marge, fearing for everybody's safety, warns him, "Aren't
you afraid you might be incurring God's wrath?" Homer nonchalantly
replies, "Eh, God's cool," to which Marge says, "See, I don't know he is.
In the Bible he's always smiting and turning people into salt." Shortly
thereafter, a bolt from the heavens electrocutes Homer and the town
almost floods in an act of God's vengeance. Only pleas from the Buddha
and Kentucky Fried Chicken's founder, Colonel Sanders (who feeds God
popcorn chicken), calm the deity. Marge has a point—the biblical God
has a violent record. Marge references Genesis 19:26, in which God turns
Lot's wife into salt because she looked back at Sodom and Gomorrah.
The Simpsons has also referenced the story of Noah in Genesis 6–9, in
which God killed all but eight people in a giant flood because people
were not following God's commands.[21]

In the Halloween episode "Treehouse of Horror XVIII," *The Simpsons* parodies the contemporary "hell house" phenomenon, in which
evangelical Christians depict punishments for people's sins on earth in
a Halloween spectacle. The documentary *Hell House* chronicles Cedar
Hill, Texas' Trinity Church members' careful planning and sincerity in
creating a phenomenon that reflects their unseen order.[22] In *Hell House*,
rape victims kill themselves, homosexuals die of AIDS, and only a girl
who took an abortion pill and bleeds over a hospital gurney before calling out to Jesus is saved. The rest are condemned to eternal punishment
and torture. *The Simpsons* summarizes its creators' position on God's relationship with hell and hell houses, which are designed to scare people
into believing, when Ned prays, "Please Lord, grant me the power to
psychologically torture them into loving you." He then turns into the
devil, illustrates how the seven deadly sins are present in Springfield,
and shows the children hell, which is based on Hieronymous Bosch's
depiction in "The Garden of Earthly Delights." In *The Simpsons*' ver-

sion, Principal Skinner's head and shoulders are now a building in the middle of a lake of fire, into which people jump from a hole in the back of his head. Apu is chased up a tree and poked with pitchforks while protesting that he is Hindu, and Mr. Burns has been turned into a toadlike creature, although he insists he regrets nothing. Terrified, Bart, Lisa, Milhouse, and the local bully Nelson Muntz all swear they will never commit the deadly sins and Ned is satisfied that the children are scared straight.

Vengeance and cruelty are cultural traits attributed to God by various Christians and commentators. Drawing from scripture to determine God's animosity toward homosexuals (Lev 18:22; Rom 1:26–32), condemnation of adultery and sexual immorality (e.g., Ex 20:14; Prov 6:32; Mt 5:27–28; 1 Cor 6:9–10, 18–20; Gal 5:19–21), and the granting of eternal salvation for those who choose Jesus as a personal savior, while damning those who do not (e.g., Jn 3:16, 10:9, 11:25, 14:6; Acts 4:2; Rom 6, 10:9–10; 1 Tim 2:4–5; Rev 3:20), are part of the unseen order conservative American Protestants emphasize when missionizing others. Only by accepting Jesus' death on the cross as redemption for their personal sins do conservative Christians think people go to heaven. Emphasizing God as a cosmic bully may seem cold and harsh to some, but scaring nonbelievers into what these Christians see as ethical behavior is congruent with their lived religious realities, and they see it as an act of love. This is the God that Stewie identifies with in the *Family Guy* episode "Holy Crap" when he reads the Bible and says "I rather like this God fellow. He's very theatrical, you know. A pestilence here and a plague there. Omnipotence! Gotta get me some of that, hmm?" or, as Chef explains to Stan in *South Park*'s episode "Kenny Dies," "If you want to make a baby cry, first you give it a lollypop. Then you take it away. If you never gave it a lollypop to begin with it wouldn't have nothing to cry about. That's like God, who gives us life and love and health just so he can tear it all away and make us cry so he can drink the sweet milk of our tears. You see, it's our tears Stan that gives God his great power." Another time, after Cartman does not get to keep the Humancentipad in "Humancentipad" he yells at the sky, "What is this, some kind of sick prank? I get the greatest thing ever and just to have it taken away? Why did you do this to me God? The next time you're gonna get my hopes up could you please take me to a Grease Monkey? Because I like to get lubed up before I get

FUCKED! Huh?! Some lube would be nice, or at least a courtesy lick God! How about a little courtesy lick God next time you decide to fuck me!" Cartman then gets struck by lightning. In all three programs God is portrayed as vengeful and distributes his justice at will.

That said, *The Simpsons* offers varied portrayals of God and he is not always a wrathful deity. Some depictions draw upon the American liberal Protestant tradition that sees God as benevolent. While conservative Christian voices about God may be the loudest and the most sensational, American liberals have a long history of invoking God for their causes.[23] The influential Unitarian Universalist William Ellery Channing wrote that Christianity's essence lay in "The elevation of men above the imperfections, temptations, sins, sufferings, of the present state, to a diviner being,—this is the great purpose of God, revealed and accomplished by Jesus Christ."[24] Some nineteenth- and twentieth-century reformers shared Channing's sentiments about human elevation. They also saw Jesus' example as revealing a loving God, often seeing him as a divine person in the Christian Trinity.[25] Finney's advice to revivalists included ensuring sinners accepted Christ's atonement, which would both satisfy God and lead them to new ethical practices for the social good.[26] One of the social gospel's major proponents, Walter Rauschenbusch, argued that Christ's goal was to bring about a moral realignment that would lead to a better society based on equality, justice, and sharing property.[27] Here God commands a great society in which contemporary social ills are cured through moral changes and altruistic decision making. Today, liberal evangelical pastor and social activist Jim Wallis writes that poverty is the foremost biblical concern and that we should adjust our social policies toward its alleviation (regardless of political affiliation).[28] Positioning himself between conservative calls for personal ethics and liberal requests for increased funding, Wallis makes his stand in Matthew 25:31–46, in which Jesus separates the saved from the condemned based on how they treated the impoverished and persecuted. For him, "This judgment is not about right doctrine or good theology, not about personal piety or sexual ethics, not about church leadership or about success in ministry. It's about how we treated the most vulnerable people in our society, whom Jesus calls 'the least of these.' Jesus is, in effect, saying, I'll know how much you love me by how you treat them."[29] Like Rauschenbusch generations before him, Wallis found that biblical

Christianity calls him to a greater love for the least privileged Americans. God, through Jesus, calls people toward repentance and greater social purpose. He blesses those who adhere to his commandments and directs society toward an ultimate good. If God punishes, he also rewards and finds joy in those who adhere to his commandments.

This sentiment is found in some depictions in *The Simpsons*. God frequently helps those who call upon him while living according to his commandments. Of all the characters, it is Ned and his family who benefit the most from God's favor. In the episode "A Star is Burns," the Flanders family films a re-enactment of the story of Moses in the rushes. After the youngest son, Todd, is placed in a basket and carried away by the river's current, Ned prays, "Flanders to God! Flanders to God! Get off your cloud and save my Todd." A bolt of lightning knocks over a tree which stops the basket. In "Homer the Heretic," when the fire from the Simpsons' home moves to the Flanders', a raincloud appears over their house, puts out the fire, and then a rainbow appears. Similarly, in the episode entitled "Team Homer," Ned's bowling team "The Holy Rollers" competes against Homer's "Pin Pals." After Ned rolls a spare, Homer taunts him: "God boy couldn't get a strike." Ned looks upwards and says, "It's me, Ned." Then the pin falls over and the ball returner jolts Homer with electricity.

Heit takes exception to this last example, arguing that "to suggest that God will help Ned during a bowling game characterizes prayer in a way that belittles God. If God truly cares about knocking down Ned's bowling pins, one would have a difficult time explaining why God does not seem to care about other, more serious problems in Springfield."[30] Cultural studies scholar Matthew Henry responds, "I interpret the many examples of God immediately responding to Ned's prayers as moments of absurdity on the show, and thus candidates for satire, not sincerity. The highly exaggerated way in which Flanders's faith is portrayed is an indication that the writers are satirizing the presumption that, through prayer, one has the power to effect immediate change in one's physical environment."[31] Henry's assessment nicely encapsulates how *The Simpsons* satirizes the idea that one can pray and change the physical environment. His interpretation, however, does not exhaust all explanations, as this event can also be read as God helping those he favors and punishing their enemies. While Henry interprets all prayer in *The Simpsons* as satirizing fundamentalist preachers who claim to affect the natural world through prayer, he misses much of the spiritual depth that prayer in the program offers and ignores the breadth of religious behaviors such as prayer and proselytizing being satirized. After all, prayer is not a foreign concept to Americans.[32] Indeed, God is an active character in all three programs, but when we link God to the second person of the Christian trinity—Jesus—we start to see just how human this God is.

Jesus: Between God and Human

If God exists in the three series as a real character who enacts vengeance upon his creation, then Jesus and the Bible are also venues for understanding God and Christianity. Jesus is a particularly useful character for the programs' creators because his status as both God and human is used as an effective foil for satirizing Christian claims about Jesus' power and influence in American life. Indeed, in the United States there are a variety of interpretations of Jesus, and his body has been inscribed with multiple constituencies' racial/ethnic, class, and gender concerns.[33] Aside from the politics of physically associating oneself with the bodily Jesus, there are also expressions about Jesus as the Christ, a savior for all humankind, provided people say, believe, and do certain things depending on the religious group one consults. *South Park* and *Family Guy* have used Jesus to harshly criticize right-wing uses of Jesus and to comment on Jesus' humanity as a way of criticizing Christian hubris. In their critical examination of Jesus and race, historians Edward Blum and Paul Harvey summarize *South Park*'s episode "Damien," which features a boxing match between the massive, red-skinned, yellow-horned Satan and the frail, white, brown-haired Jesus.

Befitting their extended survey of Jesus' body throughout American history, they write:

> *South Park* showed his [Jesus'] image and body as malleable. Small and white in real life, television advertising altered him to look more muscular. The boxing announcer rhetorically rendered him Hispanic when pronouncing his name and then associated blackness with the red devil. Cheered as a tough guy by the townspeople, Jesus was then called "gay"

Jesus and Satan square off in *South Park*'s "Damien"

in whispers to criticize his masculinity. Geographically, Jesus lived in the American West, and hell was located in the American South. The black chef worried about his mother's love for the white Jesus while trying to save him for the mostly white community. . . . Many have chuckled at sacrilegious shows like *South Park* because Christ failed in many ways to solve the nation's racial problems.[34]

Indeed, the many Jesuses who have populated American physical and mental landscapes have not solved America's racial problems, but Blum and Harvey do not give credence to the many ways in which Jesus jokes have helped people to navigate a life between everyday demands and Christian salvations that are tied to ethical and personal reform. Individuality, being an essential aspect of each program's evaluative criteria, is often at odds with the *requirement* that we conform to an unseen order. Jokes about Jesus resonate with institutional dissonance to alert their audience to an ignorant familiarity's presence and a moral boundary that will be restored. While people are free to choose to be religious, when religious leaders and organizations start claiming that Jesus wants people to do something, Jesus jokes enable people to resist and criticize their motives while also reflecting on the values and ethics Jesus preached according to the canonical gospels.

South Park's early episodes, in which Jesus is a recurring character, allow us a glimpse into how Parker and Stone navigate these tensions. Jesus often succumbs to the pressure of being the messiah and son of God. During *South Park*'s early years Jesus hosted the "Jesus and Friends" talk show on local television, where he answers callers' most pressing questions. The tensions between Jesus' humanity and divinity can be seen in the first season's episode "Death," when Stan calls Jesus after his grandfather starts pressuring Stan to help him commit suicide:

STAN
Jesus?

JESUS
Yes my son?

STAN
Jesus, is it ok to kill somebody if they ask you to because they're in a lot of pain? You know, like assisted suicide, is that ok?

JESUS
My son—

STAN
Yes?

JESUS
I'm not touching that with a 60-foot pole [*Jesus hangs up*].

STAN
God damn it.

JESUS
I heard that.[35]

As both god and man Jesus is caught between the difficult moral dilemma euthanasia poses (and that he will not use his divine authority to resolve) and his omniscience as both the son of God and God incarnate. This tension consistently arises for Jesus, and in the episode "Are You There God? It's Me, Jesus" he tries to win people's affection after they pressure him to do something big for the coming of the millennium. After visiting God in heaven, Jesus decides that the best way to accomplish this goal is by staging a Rod Stewart comeback, but when the aging rocker can only poop his pants, the townspeople prepare to crucify Jesus a second time. It is only when Jesus realizes that life is about overcoming obstacles that God shows himself and the townspeople change their minds about crucifying Jesus.

Jesus' insecurities never quite leave him in *South Park*, as may be seen in the season 16 episode "A Scause for Applause." The episode parodies cyclist Lance Armstrong's fall from grace in 2012 after a federal investigation into his use of performance-enhancing drugs while he was winning the Tour de France and his amassing of a personal fortune while building an image around being drug free and accomplishing his athletic feats through talent and hard work.[36] Jesus is found with the performance-enhancing drug Human Growth Hormone (HGH) in his blood at the time of crucifixion (through tests on the Shroud of Turin) and experts claim Jesus "Did not suffer for our sins. He was, in fact, very high." Priests start removing Jesus from the historical record and people have their WWJD (What Would Jesus Do?) bracelets removed at the drug store, which parodies the betrayal those who wore the yellow "Livestrong" bracelets for Armstrong's cancer foundation felt. Everybody in South Park feels stupid for believing in Jesus, whose miracles were only possible because of HGH, but Stan still wears his bracelet. Everybody starts attacking Stan because, they say, Jesus lied saying that he performed his miracles when they were the result of HGH, but Stan stands his ground and starts the "Stanground" movement, marked with a brown wristband, until it is revealed that he did at one point remove his WWJD bracelet, which negates his credibility. Afterward, Stan breaks into the home of the scientist who discredited him and Jesus, where he meets Jesus. While they both deny lying (which they obviously did), they decide to start a new cause and go to the Dr. Seuss–inspired "scause" factory, where they create new bracelets. The "Scause Seller" eventually goes to South Park and sells wristbands until the town is out of money before moving on to the next place, but Stan's and Jesus' reputations are still spoiled. As they try to think of the next thing to do, Stan asks "What would Jesus do?" Jesus then takes HGH, goes on a rampage destroying the scause factory, and proceeds with this message:

> Thank you, my children. We've been through a lot. We got caught up in scauses . . . that didn't mean squat. They turned my message away from the teachings it hid and made it about me and the things that I did. Which, of course, I didn't do. And even if I did use performance enhancing drugs, so did all the other prophets. But I didn't. So what have we learned, from this great wristband theft? Maybe, that when stripped of our scauses, only causes are left. And causes shouldn't be worn on our wrists with a sneer, let's keep our causes where they belong, which is right here. [*Folds his hands over his heart.*] On t-shirts! [*Opens his robes to a "Free Pussy Riot" t-shirt.*] Free Pussy Riot![37]

Jesus is always depicted in *South Park* as a scrawny man who has to contend with the fact that his miracles are considered less than stellar, such as in the episode "Super Best Friends" in which his multiplying of the loaves and fishes cannot compete with magician David Blane's "miracles." He struggles to deal with his legacy. He wants to be loved and adored, but is a frail, weak man who is mostly ignored. In the early seasons he gets into a basic cable ratings war with Stan's Uncle Jimbo and his Vietnam veteran friend Ned's show "Huntin' and Killin'," which leads him to turn "Jesus and Pals" into a daytime talk show of Jerry Springer proportions. He also ends the first Christmas episode singing "Happy Birthday" to himself since nobody can remember the reason for the season.[38] *South Park*'s Jesus is a combination of confused prophet who wants to be loved and the biblical miracle worker. Parker and Stone leave Jesus with his cosmic powers, but temper and control them through his physical and emotional frailty. This Jesus stands opposite to the loving, friendly Jesus who welcomes believers to his bosom while simultaneously slaying unbelievers during the apocalypse. Instead, he is God incarnate who just wants to be loved.

Family Guy shares a similar stereotypical portrayal of Jesus, although that series is far more willing to attack his miracle work. In the episode

"Brian Wallows and Peter's Swallows" Peter justifies growing a beard by saying, "Now, now Lois. It's time I joined the ranks of great men with beards. Why do you think Jesus Christ was so popular? Because of all them magic tricks?" and in "Stu & Stewie's Excellent Adventure" Stewie's future self explains that he time-traveled "back to visit Jesus Christ. Turns out his abilities might have been exaggerated a bit." Then the scene shifts to Jesus wowing an adoring crowd with simple finger tricks. *Family Guy*'s most sustained interrogation of Jesus as both man and God is the episode "I Dream of Jesus" in which Peter meets Jesus in a record store.[39] After mistaking Jesus' presence as the second coming, Jesus explains that he checks in every hundred years or so, but that he has not been identified for 2000 years. Peter invites Jesus over to dinner and when Jesus is eating with the Griffins he informs them that "one of you will betray me . . . Just kidding!" Peter then points at him and laughs, saying, "He's doing that thing he did in the storybook." Meg then asks Jesus to finish the story he was telling, and Jesus expounds upon the Passion narrative: "So there I was, they'd just beaten me senseless, stuck thorns in my head, nailed me to a piece of wood, shoved a sponge full of vinegar in my mouth and killed me. *Then* they put me in a hole with a rock in front of it for two whole days, and come Sunday, bam, I rise from the dead." Peter chuckles, "Okay, that sounds like a nutty weekend, but I can top it." The conversation continues until Brian steps in and says, "All right, I'll be the one to say it. How do we know you're really Jesus? Can you perform miracles?" Jesus then turns everybody's dinner into sundaes. Next, Peter asks Jesus to do him a favor, whispers in his ear, and Lois' breasts expand until they burst out of her shirt and knock over her sundae. In the next scene, Peter introduces Jesus to President George W. Bush after the latter claims that even though the American people turned against the war, he answers to Jesus. Peter then brings Jesus on stage and Jesus says, "I heard what you were saying. You know nothing of my work. How you ever got to be president of anything is totally amazing." Peter looks into the camera and says, "Boy, wouldn't it be great if life were like this?"

Together, Peter and Jesus agree that it is time for Jesus to reveal himself to the world; after Jesus walks on water to retrieve a dollar in the town square, people recognize the Christ's return. After appearing on *The Tonight Show* with Jay Leno, Jesus' star continues to rise and eventually he presents an award at the MTV movie awards with the Pussycat Dolls. Jesus then gets into a limo with his posse and shrugs off Peter, who wants Jesus to remember who his friends are despite the fame. Jesus is eventually arrested after being found in Mary Kate Olsen's apartment, "face down and unconscious." After the police revive him he is taken to prison and calls Peter to bail him out. Facing a bedraggled Jesus in lock-up, Peter launches into a lecture, "Jesus Christ, look at you. You had it all—money, fame, eternal life—and you blew it! You let it all go to your head!" Jesus remorsefully responds, "I know, Peter. I guess it turns out I'm just as human as anyone else." Jesus decides that he needs to go because "This world's not ready for me yet, and I'm not ready for it. I don't know. Maybe I'll try coming back in another thousand years, when I'm a little more mature."

South Park and Family Guy use extended episodes about Jesus to play up his humanity without discounting the miraculous powers attributed to him. This approach allows them to criticize Christians and their claims about Jesus. Jesus looks less like a divine figure in these examples than a figure whom people adapt to their needs as they navigate this world.[40] Jesus in South Park and Family Guy is white, a miracle worker, and a victim of American celebrity culture. His miraculous powers are downplayed in favor of his ethical vision, a depiction that echoes the central positions of both programs. This is not the Jesus of John 14:6, the "way, and the truth, and the life. No one comes to the father except through me" (NRSV) or the miracle worker who healed the sick and cast out demons. Instead, South Park's and Family Guy's Jesus is similar to the Jesus of Matthew 5–7 and Luke 6:17–49. This Jesus is a preacher on a mountain or in a field who speaks in parables and pithy sayings that, like primitive jokes, spin incongruity into profound ethical insights. Just like the comedians behind the programs who have to deal with fame and fortune and with being treated as great social critics, the Jesus who is credited with these famous sermons told people in the Roman Empire to be meek because the meek will inherit the earth and that peacemakers will be called the children of God. Confusion over Jesus' message has, perhaps ironically, perhaps purposefully, confounded people to the present day, and South Park and Family Guy take the irony in Jesus' message to a new level by showing just how difficult it is to live in the modern world and practice what you preach. Jesus, in taking HGH or succumbing to phony friends, has to balance being a supernatural force, prophet, and, to use Stephen Prothero's term, an American icon.[41] By dismissing the miracles as a fun source for jokes, these programs satirize the plausibility structures supporting the claims that Jesus is watching over you, judging you, or providing you salvation due to your belief in him (or, in *South Park*'s case Jesus is watching you when he wants to, but will not offer you help with any problem as big as euthanasia). *The Simpsons'* jokes about Jesus are much in the same vein, but Jesus has never been a character who interacts with the Simpsons the way that God does. Indeed, while Jesus can appear in fantasy jokes, he is largely absent from *The Simpsons'* world. They do occasionally take a stab at Christians and their claims, such as when Lisa explains that the "Mound Builders" (a group of unknown Native Americans) "worshiped turtles as well badgers, snakes, and other animals," and Bart responds, "Thank God we've come to our senses and worship a carpenter who lived 2000 years ago,"[42] which largely repeats *South Park*'s and *Family Guy*'s patterns.

Portrayals of God and Jesus in the three programs show the flexible interpretations that structure America's Christians' lives. Since each show values scientific rationality, however, the inherent logical flaws surrounding miracle claims and threats that a vengeful God will punish those who do not adhere to Christian unseen orders are used as ignorant familiarities to make jokes based in institutional dissonance. By emphasizing God's and Jesus' humanity, these programs show us how these divine figures are human projections of American aspirations and are open to critique as such. Blum and Harvey are not quite right to argue that these jokes are "a sign not of less faith in God but of a dwindling trust that the people could right the nation's social wrongs—with or without Christ's aid."[43] Rather, they are a sign that if God is unpredictable, then the Jesus who is supposed to mediate on our behalf is as confused as the rest of us and puts his stock not in supernatural powers, but in rational ethics which do not require him to be special. There is little hope in Jesus as Christ in these programs. As Prothero argues, "the cultural authority of Jesus has been used to promote the Christian tradition. But it has also been used to reform and subvert it, both from within and without, by Americans who see the man from Nazareth as a nondoctrinal, nondenominational, non-Christian. . . . All drew sharp distinctions between the religion *of* Jesus and the religion *about* Jesus, and all used the former to attack the latter."[44] So it is in *The Simpsons, South Park,* and *Family Guy.* To further understand fights about God's and Jesus' divinity, we turn to how the Bible is represented in the three programs.

The Bible: A Bunch of Stories and Not God's Word

According to the 2012 General Social Survey, 31% of Americans view the Bible as the literal word of God, 45.3% see it as the inspired (but not necessarily literal) word of God, and 20.9% see the Bible as "an ancient book of fables, legends, history and moral precepts recorded by man."[45] The Barna Group's 2014 "State of the Bible Report," conducted for the National Bible Society, found that 79% of Americans found the Bible to be a sacred text, with the next closest text being the Qu'ran at 12%. Eighty-eight percent of American homes also contain at least one Bible, with the average household having 4.7 Bibles.[46] This collection of texts from the ancient Near East inspires religious fervor throughout the United States in ways that our three programs find fascinating and problematic. All three shows have parodied biblical stories, most notably *The Simpsons* episode "Simpsons Bible Stories" which features *Simpsons* versions of the Garden of Eden, the exodus, and David and Goliath; nativity stories in *The Simpsons*' "Simpsons Christmas Stories" and *Family Guy*'s episode "Jesus, Mary, and Joseph!" *South Park*'s episode "Jewpacabra" even features a retelling of the tenth plague (death of the firstborn son).[47] These parodies are interesting, but as we have already seen in our discussions of God and Jesus, what is significant about these biblical representations is the way that people use the Bible to advance and justify their own agendas. Even as these three programs criticize others' interpretations of the Bible, they are also engaged in debating the Bible's place in American culture and with it, God and Jesus' legitimacy as forces to be taken seriously.

Biblical authority is widely considered to be sacred in the United States. For example, recurring political issues such as displaying the Ten Commandments in courtrooms speak to the Bible's authority, even if people do not necessarily know the Ten Commandments.[48] According to the American Bible Society, 37% of Americans read their Bible at least once a week and 45% read it at least once a month.[49] Views on what the Bible contains and teaches, however, appear inconsistent, although it is understandable that people answering the surveys might have difficulty answering, say, whether or not the Bible strongly discourages war (28% of respondents thought this).[50] If you read the book of Judges with its brutal assaults against the Israelites' enemies and compare it to Jesus' commandment to turn the other cheek in Matthew 5:39, then the question of whether or not the Bible strongly discourages war can become less one of biblical literacy than of situational interpretation, in which different texts are drawn together to make a case that is significantly more complicated than an answer for a quantitative survey. That said, if we return to the Pew Forum's Religious Knowledge Survey's findings, we can safely say that Americans are largely ignorant of biblical content.[51] This general ignorance, combined with the high esteem in which the Bible is held, demonstrates the text's sacredness. It is set apart and treated as special, but ignorant familiarity helps to maintain this sacredness. So long as the book is sacred and used as a sign of authority, then its power remains.

Ignorant familiarity and its relationship to power are fodder for jokes in the three series as they criticize belief in the Bible without knowing its context. In the *Family Guy* episode "Internal Affairs," Lois and Peter argue after Peter encourages his friend Joe to have an affair. When Peter tries to end the fight by declaring, "Look Lois, it's in the Bible!" she replies, "What's in the Bible?" Peter, baffled, stammers, "I, I don't know. Doesn't that always cover it somehow?" Peter uses ignorant familiarity about the Bible's sacred authority to try to win, but he is disarmed by Lois' refusal to accept his argument's basic premise. That Peter did not know an actual verse or story to support his argument shows that Lois called his bluff. *Family Guy* then emphasizes the point that some people will use the Bible to justify their arguments, regardless of whether or not invoking the Bible is valid.

The Simpsons has also used the juxtaposition between relying on the Bible's authority while being ignorant of its content as a foil for humor. In one case, Homer tells Lisa, "If the Bible has taught us nothing else (and it hasn't) it's that girls should stick to girl sports, such as hot oil wrestling, foxy boxing, and such and such,"[52] or when they composed such jokes as these:

HOMER
You'd think that wouldn't ya but, you see Lisa, your mother has this crazy idea that gambling is wrong. Even though they say it's ok in the Bible.

LISA
Really? Where?

HOMER
Eeeehhhh. . . . Somewhere in the back.[53]

. . .

MARGE
I know we didn't ask for this Homer, but doesn't the Bible say "Whatsoever you do to the least of my brothers, that you do unto me"?

HOMER
Yes, but doesn't the Bible also say "Thou shalt not take . . . moochers into thy . . . hut"?[54]

. . .

MARGE
Maybe I should apply for that job.

HOMER
Forget it Marge, we already live together, we shouldn't work together. As the Bible says, "Thou shalt not horn in on thy husband's . . . racket."

MARGE
Where does the Bible say racket?

HOMER
It's in there.[55]

In each case, just like Peter, Homer tries to use the Bible's symbolic authority to win an argument without knowing anything about its content. Ultimately, he ends up looking like a fool and the Bible's authority becomes the butt of the joke.

The Simpsons also inverts the Bible's moral authority in "Midnight Towboy." Bart and Milhouse are sitting in Bart's room, carefully cutting words out of a Bible with a penknife. Taking the word "whore" from Revelations 17, Bart exclaims "Got one!" before posting it on a bulletin board in his room that also has "ass," "hell," "damn," and "Leviticus" pinned. Bart proudly continues, "We can say these swears any time we want because they're in the Bible." Milhouse counters, "I don't think Leviticus is a swear" before Bart silences him with, "Shut the hell up you damn ass whore." In this case, instead of being a model for good behavior, the Bible supplies Bart with language many adults would consider inappropriate and immoral for children to use.

Jamey Heit correctly acknowledges that in *The Simpsons*, biblical interpretation is less a matter of biblical literacy than it is a way of appealing to the Bible's cultural authority: "The show characterizes Christians in a way that problematizes the task of interpretation. Quite simply, many Christians are, to some extent, ignorant or self-serving when it comes to interpreting the Bible as an authoritative text in a particular cultural context."[56] He argues further that "the Bible becomes a way to enforce one's own beliefs in a particular situation rather than providing sincere moral guidelines."[57] In both *The Simpsons* and *Family Guy* the Bible's cultural authority matters more than its content. This is important because the Bible's morals that each program finds valuable can be extracted from the Christian tradition and made general and humanistic. Good behavior is not reliant on adhering to Christianity, but by staying true to principles located within oneself. At the same time, the authority Christians assign to the Bible is mocked as being an invalid argument. Mixing ignorance with misplaced authority is a recipe for being mocked as stupid. The above examples demonstrate how *The Simpsons* and *Family Guy* erect barriers against the supposed sacredness of a specific text within a religious tradition as a way of stopping the public imposition of this faith on others. Biblical literacy would help if *The Simpsons* and *Family Guy* were arguing biblical interpretation. In these cases, however, they are desacralizing the Bible itself, making it a collection of stories and not the word of God that three-quarters of Americans think it is. They are inverting the authority vested in the ignorant familiarity of biblical authority. Those who appeal to the Bible's authority now appear stupid and ignorant of the Bible's content, a not insignificant political move in a country in which the Bible is invoked as a justification for a wide range of social policies. By revealing the paucity of knowledge justifying widespread biblical authority as the foundation for moral conduct, the three programs' portrayals of the Bible, God, and Jesus are intertwined. All three programs leave the individual question of ethics to the viewer, but they desacralize the authority ascribed to God, Jesus, and the Bible in American public life. The Bible is a book of stories, Jesus is a confused human being, and God is a vengeful old man who is sometimes on your side. This desacralization of widespread Christian assumptions about the unseen order to the universe carries over to the three programs' treatment of religious institutions. Two examples from *The Simpsons* illustrate how morals can come from Christianity, but that attempts to share the unseen order supporting those morals are a danger to others.

The Symbols in Practice: Reverend Lovejoy

Reverend Timothy Lovejoy is a fantastic satiric ideal type. Dressed in clerical blacks with a white collar, standing behind a plain pulpit in a large urban church with faux stained-glass windows and ample parking, he delivers sermons on topics that are tangential to his congregation's interests. When the need arises he leads Springfield's charge for moral hygiene, but he would rather play with his model trains. It is impossible to tell what denomination he belongs to, although in later seasons we learn that he is a member of "the Western branch of Reformed Presbylutheranism."[58] Like the minister, Dr. Matthew Collins, in the 1953 version of *The War of the Worlds*,[59] who is also dressed in clerical blacks and collar, "audiences are left free to map onto his character any tradition they choose."[60]

However, mainline Protestantism's liberal elements are absent in Lovejoy's preaching, making him a more conservative caricature than he would be were he representing mainline Protestantism's liberal theological developments which emphasize critical historical thinking, a social ethic based on Jesus' teachings, and a postmillennial view of the world that encourages the betterment of human beings through social improvement.[61]

The first observation to be made about FCOS is that its pews are full on Sunday, which Pinsky notes "is, in part, a plot device."[62] Just because

Lovejoy preaches in his generic clerical garb in "Homer the Heretic"

people are in the pews does not mean they are particularly pious. Church is treated as a chore on *The Simpsons*, literally topping Homer's chores list in *The Simpsons Movie*.[63] Furthermore, in the episode "In Marge We Trust," Lisa pronounces that the time right after church is the best time of the week because "it's the longest possible time before more church!" In the Simpson family, it is Marge who insists that church is important for teaching morals and guiding people in their daily lives.[64] For the others, church is boring and irrelevant. Homer constantly falls asleep during the service,[65] listens to football games on a portable radio,[66] and makes noise with his motorcycle's engine during the service, causing Lovejoy to give up and cut his sermon short.[67] Bart's irreverent attitude extends to both the service, during which he distributes Iron Butterfly's "In-A-Gadda-Da-Vida" as the hymn "In the Garden of Eden" by I. Ron Butterfly[68] and plays with troll dolls[69] and video games,[70] and to Sunday school, where he pesters the teacher about whether or not severed limbs will be waiting for you in heaven (the answer is "yes"),[71] and he gets excited to learn about hell[72] and why God causes train wrecks.[73] When he returns to Sunday school after being banned, the teacher announces, "but Bart, we banned you from Sunday school. You were happy. We were happy. Everybody was happy—particularly the hamster." When Bart claims he has changed his ways the teacher accepts him back, noting that the Bible teaches forgiveness. Her efforts at teaching are futile though, as the students give her confused looks when she says that the prodigal son has returned.[74] Prothero's claims about American biblical ignorance are exemplified in FCOS's Sunday school and in the church, where people are present but do not care enough to invest their energy in learning about Christianity. Springfielders are in the pews not because it is congruent with their character (Marge and Ned Flanders exempted), but because this is a good setting for jokes.

This indifference leads us to the problem of declining attendance, a major concern for contemporary mainline churches.[75] While FCOS is apparently not suffering an attendance problem, it is stricken with apathy. For sociologists Roger Finke and Rodney Stark, mainline denominations decline because they uphold cultural norms without causing members to invest time, money, and identity in the organization.[76] There is little to distinguish the religion from the culture at large so people do not bother attending. For Finke and Stark, religions that demand significant investment of this world's resources in exchange for benefits in the next are more likely to succeed than those that do not.[77] *The Simpsons* suggests that while FCOS does not demand much of its members, it is the religion's content and otherworldly character that cause people to leave.

FOCS is a church that does not reflect upon Christian doctrine, nor does it have regular rituals that engage people's minds, hearts, and bodies. The Eucharist is rarely referenced, and when it is, it is either to make a joke about the wine's alcoholic content[78] or about transubstantiation.[79]

Lovejoy's sermons are all the members have. Occasionally, Lovejoy preaches passionately, usually when he is mad about something Homer has done. In the episode "The Telltale Head," he attacks sports gambling, calling it the eighth deadly sin, while Homer listens to the football game on headphones. In "Homer the Heretic," he warns people to honor the Sabbath in a sermon advertised as "When Homer Met Satan." However, Lovejoy's usual sermons are drab and irrelevant. That people fall asleep during them or while he reads through the entire Bible on a hot Easter Sunday is part of Lovejoy's problem.[80] His sermons miss any contributions Christian teachings could make to people's lives. In the episode "The Springfield Files," an "alien" (actually Mr. Burns) is spotted in Springfield, prompting Lovejoy to preach, "I remember another gentle visitor from the heavens. He came in peace, and then died only to come back to life. And his name was . . . E. T. the extraterrestrial. I love that little guy." In the episode "Bart's Girlfriend," Marge tells Bart that he has to go to church to learn morals and how to treat others. The scene shifts to Lovejoy mid-sermon where he says, "And with flaming swords, the Aromites did pierce the eyes of their fellow men and did feast on what flowed forth. Among whom also we all once conducted ourselves in the lusts of our flesh [*his voice trails off*]." This content subverts Marge's goal and suggests that Lovejoy's emphasis is counter-intuitive to the values Christians claim as their own. Finally, Lovejoy comes across as defeated by the tradition. In the episode "Faith Off," he begins his sermon, "In his letter to the Corinthians, Paul instructed them to send ten copies to the Thessalonians and the Ephesians. But the Ephesians broke the chain, and were punished by the . . ." at which point Bart interrupts him, snoring. Lovejoy holds up the Bible and says, "Hey, I'm doing the best with the material I have." Bart, who recently attended a revival meeting, argues, "But church can be fun!" When the parishioners laugh, he protests, "No, really, it can be a crazy party with clouds and lasers and miracles! . . . A real preacher knows how to bring the Bible alive through music, and dancing, and Tae-Bo!"[81] When Bart starts dancing in the aisles, a dejected Lovejoy rolls his eyes and mutters "Never give them an opening." Bart is able to recognize the fact that religion can be made interesting if properly communicated—communication at which Lovejoy clearly fails. Lovejoy's sermons direct our attention to the fact that in *The Simpsons*, mainline Christianity has failed to captivate its adherents' hearts and minds, suggesting that contemporary preaching is largely boring or irrelevant in people's lives.

Lovejoy can also be interpreted through the lens of internal strife within mainline denominations. As historian William Hutchison illustrates, the modernist impulse in American Protestantism led progressive Christians to try to adapt Christianity to the times.[82] In the late nineteenth and early twentieth centuries, this meant rejecting established creeds and doctrines that were not deemed useful in elevating humans to their fullest potential in modern society. The progressives' focus was on improving conditions in this life as a way of showing God's love, and using human knowledge to achieve the kingdom of God on Earth. However, Lovejoy not only fails to inspire his congregation, he is also fairly staunch when it comes to moral issues. While he appears leading moral crusades against lewd behavior,[83] science,[84] and Krusty the Clown,[85] his most controversial (or, depending on one's perspective, conventional) moral stand comes in the season 16 episode "There's Something About Marrying" in which he opposes same-sex marriage. When it comes to moral affairs in the United States, Lovejoy holds what can be seen as a conventionally conservative Christian position.

American Christianities cover all political positions in the United States, but the harsher, more judgmental picture of God is currently favored more by conservative Christians than mainliners. Vocal Christians who mobilize politically against what they perceive as sins, but *The Simpsons* views as personal choice (such as lewd behavior and same-sex relationships), tend to be more on the conservative end of the spectrum. As they are politically opposed to *The Simpsons'* worldview, their religious justifications are satirized as well. Lovejoy represents a tension in mainline Protestantism between traditional moral standards and an expanding view of acceptance for non-heterosexual couples and liberal politics. In *The Simpsons'* world, traditional institutions and authority are problematic and the program is inherently suspicious of them. Reverend Lovejoy's portrayal in these examples is a criticism of preachers who politicize Christianity; it speaks to the program's distaste for the ways in which conservative Christian morals affect American public policy.

Lovejoy's personal problems also affect his ability to minister effectively. Like other clergy members, he constantly worries about finances.

He borrows the local library's copy of the Bible every week because he cannot afford one himself.[86] In the episode "Bart Sells His Soul," when Milhouse asks Bart what the world's religions have to gain by lying about the soul's existence, the scene cuts to Reverend Lovejoy pouring money from the collection plates into a coin sorter. Furthermore, in the episode "The Joy of Sect," Lovejoy denounces the new religious movement "The Movementarians," saying, "This so called 'new religion' is nothing but a pack of weird rituals and chants designed to take away the money of fools. Let us say the Lord's Prayer forty times, but first let's pass the collection plate." Lovejoy's church is just as greedy as any new religion, a point that is reinforced in the episode "Viva Ned Flanders" in which Lovejoy explains tithing to his congregation: "And once again, tithing is 10% off the top. That's gross income, not net. Please people, don't force us to audit." Heit correctly notes that Lovejoy's financial concerns reflect ministers' realities across the United States. They are overworked and underpaid because people do not financially support their religious institutions,[87] but these jokes point to the history of unscrupulous pastors exploiting their congregations for financial gain.

Lovejoy's ennui stems from the fact that he originally came to Springfield to help others, but he has since become overworked by Ned Flanders' constant questions about applying Christianity to the smallest details of his life. Yet, the reverend often comes through for people when called upon. This is illustrated in the episode "In Marge We Trust" when Marge volunteers at the church. When people start calling the reverend for advice, she notices that he dismisses them. For example, Lovejoy tells Principal Skinner to read his Bible for guidance after a fight with his mother. When Skinner asks about a specific passage, Lovejoy responds, "Oh, it's all good." Marge then asks him what had happened to his passion and Lovejoy explains that over the years Ned has asked him so many inane questions that eventually he stopped caring about people. Marge then takes over the reverend's advising role, which leads him to feel that he has lost his flock. Walking into the church he looks at the stained glass windows of saints dying gruesome deaths and experiences a vision in which they talk to him, asking him what he has done to inspire faith. When Lovejoy says that he had the church vestibule recarpeted, one of the saints looks at him and complains, "I've appeared in over eight thousand visions, and that is the lamest reply I've ever heard." After Lovejoy protests, the saint silences him, saying, "You're just lucky God isn't here." Meanwhile, Marge excels at Lovejoy's job as advisor until she gives Ned some bad advice, and he needs to be rescued from baboons at the local zoo by Lovejoy. Lovejoy also comes through for his congregation at the end of the episode "Pray Anything." Lovejoy returns to Springfield after leaving because Homer won the deed to the church in a lawsuit and turned FCOS into the Simpsons' home. Homer's housewarming party has caused massive flooding, and the entire town huddles fearfully atop the church. Lovejoy appears just in time, prays for forgiveness, and the rain stops. Even if Lovejoy represents Christianity's failed theology, greed, and general irrelevancy in many *Simpsons* jokes, when he is needed, Lovejoy selflessly looks after the people he serves.

Although Lovejoy is often a caricature for organized Christianity's failures, he is a complex character who wants to thrive professionally and encourage people. It is in those moments when he embodies love and courage in Christianity's name, and leaves his bigotry and judgmentalism behind, that he is applauded. Heit accurately assesses Lovejoy's Christian leadership: "He accomplishes more than simply re-carpeting the vestibule. He is inconsistent and cynical, to be sure, but he shows that he is capable of making himself and the church he represents relevant to a town that will turn its back on its faith. Springfield's parishioners will fall away, neglect the demands their faith places upon them, do their best to avoid their fiduciary obligation to the church, but their pastor will trudge along, even at a low hourly wage."[88] These are the acceptable Christian elements for *The Simpsons*, leaving the boring sermons, irrelevant scriptural references, and conservative bigotry for their scorn. But Lovejoy is not the only Christian caricature in *The Simpsons*. Ned Flanders provides a nuanced interpretation of American evangelicalism and raises more questions about what is acceptable and damnable in *The Simpsons'* unseen order.

Ned Flanders as Evangelical Satire

Ned Flanders is widely known as an evangelical caricature who reflects both positive and negative aspects of American evangelicalism.[89] The dark side of evangelicalism is projected through Ned's political work as a moral watchdog and his goal of returning the country to "the America of yesteryear that only exists in the brains of us Republicans."[90] Ned attempts to bring his fellow citizens into line with his unseen order through public action dedicated to moral reform on issues such as homosexuality, abortion rights, prayer in public schools, and media content. He actively promotes an alternative unseen order rooted in conservative Christianity's biblical literalism and morality. *The Simpsons*' satirical gaze focuses on these evangelical characteristics. Satires of Ned's public moral action are balanced by his personal Christian morality, which suggests that he also represents Christianity's moral aspects that *The Simpsons* portrays as valuable. This assessment complicates Flanders' character, moving him away from being a purely negative American evangelical caricature and making him into a plausible representative of evangelical values.

Ned's evangelicalism has deep roots in American culture. Today's evangelicals stand upon a rich and colorful history that stretches back to the First Great Awakening. Evangelicalism had a strong public presence during the nineteenth century, but with increased questions about biblical inerrancy introduced through German higher biblical criticism, intellectual skeptics influenced by Darwinism, and the fundamentalist retraction from the mainline Protestant denominations after the Scopes trial in 1925, conservative evangelicals withdrew from the American mainstream into their own isolated communities and abandoned the world to its sinful nature.[91] However, this isolation did not last long, as less conservative evangelicals began actively engaging the culture at large in the early 1940s, starting with the National Association of Evangelicals' (NAE) founding in St. Louis in 1942 to combat the liberal Federal Council of Churches. After a lull in political engagement into the 1960s, evangelicals were drawn back into the public square because of church and state issues regarding prayer in public schools and the 1973 landmark *Roe v. Wade* decision legalizing abortion. Ronald Reagan's election in 1980 marked a new high point for conservative religion's political influence, a phenomenon repeated when George W. Bush took the presidency in 2000 and 2004 with strong conservative Christian support. Evangelicals were also known through highly visible public preachers and televangelists, including Billy Graham, Jerry Falwell, Pat Robertson, and Jim Bakker.[92] Evangelicalism is a diverse religious subculture, with members spanning the political spectrum from conservative to liberal,[93] and different studies categorize varying groups under the mantle of "evangelical" (e.g., "conservative" Protestants, Fundamentalists, and Pentecostals can all be lumped under this rubric[94]). Ned most closely resembles historian Randall Balmer's broad description of evangelicals, which includes Pentecostals, Fundamentalists, and other conservative Protestants, making for the widest range of possible jokes coming from the mouth of one character—an ironic choice on *The Simpsons'* creators' part since Balmer aptly demonstrates the movement's internal diversity.[95] Ned embodies those subcultural elements within evangelicalism that combine right-wing politics with a sincere desire to live as Christians.

Ned's dark side can be seen in his overprotective parenting and his role in Springfield's moral watchdog groups. He is not only a moral exemplar, but is what sociologist Howard Becker described as a "moral crusader"—a person who works to enact changes he or she believes will improve others' lives.[96] In the episode "You Kent Always Say What You Want," Ned writes an email to his online compatriots after hearing local newsman Kent Brockman swearing on television. When his sons Rod and Todd ask what he's doing, Ned replies, "Imploring people I never met to pressure a government with better things to do to punish a man who meant no harm for something that nobody even saw!"[97] Another time, Ned tells Homer that he spent his whole morning blacking out the words "gosh" and "darn" in *Hardy Boys* novels.[98] He also argues that "our courts aren't fit to keep children in line. The only thing they're good for is telling women what to do with their bodies."[99] He scares Bart by wearing finger shears (visually referencing *Nightmare on Elm Street*'s Freddy Krueger), telling him to say his prayers because the schools can't force him like they should.[100] Furthermore, he reassures his children that Harry Potter and his friends will go to hell for practicing witchcraft,[101] but he allows them to watch "Gravey and Jobriath," in which a young man, Gravey, is making a pipe bomb to blow up Planned Parenthood.[102] Parodying the Lutheran Church of America's popular *Davey and Goliath* Claymation cartoon from the 1960s and 1970s, *The Simpsons* takes *Davey and Goliath*'s association with Christian teachings of love, forgiveness, and tolerance and inverts it, suggesting that evangelicals share abortion clinic bombers' moral self-righteousness and willingness to use violence to achieve their ends. In an extended sequence on the DVD version of this episode, Ned refuses to explain Planned Parenthood to the boys because he is busy writing down doctors' names being listed on the screen.

These examples reference the moral boundaries various evangelical groups use to differentiate themselves from other groups in American culture. References to courts controlling women's bodies and attacks on Planned Parenthood recall the evangelical anti-abortion lobby of the late twentieth century and today, which saw sit-ins at abortion clinics and the harassment of women seeking abortions. In some cases, doctors were murdered and properties burned. Anti-abortion has become a significant issue in evangelicalism's symbolic boundaries and is a litmus test for political support.[103]

Abortion decisions are not the only legal issues evangelicals have challenged. When Ned complains that the schools cannot force Bart to pray, he references 1962's *Engel v. Vitale*, 1963's *Abington School District v. Schempp*, and 1971's *Lemon v. Kurtzman* U.S. Supreme Court decisions banning school board–drafted prayers and prohibiting the promotion of religion in public schools. These are contentious decisions and evangelicals continually seek ways to circumvent them.[104] As we saw earlier, Ned's quote about the America of yesteryear only exists in the minds of Republicans. As school prayer and anti-abortion are popularly associated with evangelical support for the Republican Party, it comes as little surprise that *The Simpsons* would use its evangelical character to satirize the Republican Party's base's religio-politics, because these issues are seen as antithetical to the secularism *The Simpsons* generally endorses. Flanders' political evangelicalism encroaches on one of *The Simpsons*' core values, individualism. Changing laws and public policy so that people are unable to access legal services because of somebody else's religious views is institutionally dissonant with *The Simpsons*' sacred values of everybody being free to seek their own spiritual path. As such, these evangelical actions are satirically attacked through Ned.

The Flanders home and family are also portrayed as caricatures of American evangelicals. Their house is filled with pictures of God and Jesus, Ned has an extensive collection of Bibles, and the boys play games such as "Christian Clue," "Good Samaritan," and "Billy Graham's Bible Blaster."[105] An episode entitled "Home Sweet Homediddly-Dum-Doodily" emphasizes the Flanders' differences with the Simpsons. After

the Simpson children have been placed in the Flanders' protective cus-
tody, Lisa characterizes the disparity as, "It seems like our house, but
everything's got a creepy Pat Booneish quality to it." Instead of watching television, the Flanders play "Bombardment of Bible Questions" to
relax. While Ned and his wife Maude (who died in season 11's episode
"Alone Again Natura-Diddly") are caring parents, they are presented as
the wrong custodians for Bart and Lisa.[106] This is made readily apparent
in the bombardment scene when, asking questions from the Vulgate of
Saint Jerome, Ned questions the children about their biblical knowledge:

NED
Come on, this one's easy.

LISA
We give up.

NED
Well, guess! Book of Revelations, fire-breathing lion's head, tail made out of
snakes. Who else could it be?

BART
Jesus?

NED
[*Yelling*] Je . . . Jes . . . don't you kids know anything? The serpent of Re-
haboam? [*Bart and Lisa stare blankly*] The well of Zohassadar? [*More blank
stares*] The bridal feast of Beth Chadruharazzeb?

When Maude says that these are the things the children should have
learned in baptism class, Lisa acknowledges that they were never baptized. After Ned faints and recovers, he decides to take the children to
the Springfield River and baptize them for the good of their immortal
souls. Once Homer and Marge discover this, they come and rescue the
children. The Flanders are loving and caring, but far too entrenched
in fundamentalist conceptions of family values for *The Simpsons*.
Emphasizing Rod and Todd's sheltered lives suggests that the Flanders
have built a barrier to the outside world, protecting themselves with

evangelical trappings. Their unseen order is exclusive and strong enough to prevent neighboring forces from penetrating.

Ned is not always a moral crusader. He can also be a model of compassion, generosity, and neighborliness. Indeed, Ned is important in the way that he embodies the ideal type of a kind, caring Christian—even if that type becomes corrupted by his moralizing and Christian exclusiveness. Throughout the series we see Ned practice neighborly love, even though Homer is one of the most obnoxious characters anyone could ever imagine having as a neighbor.

In season 5's episode "Homer Loves Flanders," Ned and Homer briefly befriend each other after Ned generously invites Homer to a football game, buys him snacks, and offers him the game ball. Homer's friendship, however, quickly becomes overbearing. Ned wants to be a good neighbor, but ends up lying to Homer to get some time with his family. Eventually, as he tries to escape from Homer, Ned is stopped by the police. The church bus passes him and everybody judges Ned while praising Homer's good works. Dejected, embarrassed, and angry, Ned is eventually redeemed after Homer declares that Ned is the most caring person he knows. Homer reminds us that if everybody were like Ned Flanders, "there'd be no need for heaven, we'd already be there." Similar sentiments can be seen in the episode "Home Away From Homer," in which Ned moves away after Homer humiliates him. Homer tracks him down, begging him to come back because the new neighbor is not nearly as gracious with Homer's failings as Ned has been. Finally, in the episode "No Loan Again, Naturally," Ned becomes the Simpsons' landlord, eventually evicting the Simpsons after they continue wrecking the house. Yet when two new tenants are about to move in, Ned has a change of heart. Explaining why he allows the Simpsons to return, he says, "Well, the people who lived here before weren't always the best neighbors, but I love 'em. And you can't be a saint unless you live among the lepers." Despite its criticism of conservative Christian politics, *The Simpsons* thus promotes Christian charity as valuable. These individual acts of charity are rooted in a consistent Christian worldview and are consistent with *The Simpsons'* moral boundaries because Ned is using his religion to be a good person and is not trying to force anybody else to change. The space for making personal decisions about spiritual development is preserved and a way of being a Christian within that space is put forth as socially beneficial.

Ned takes his Christian charity seriously. He helps financially when strangers are in need.[107] When Homer and Bart think they have contracted leprosy, he pays to send them to a first-class leper colony on Hawaii's Molokai Island, famous for the work of Fr. Damien of Molokai, who dedicated his life to improving conditions at the leper colony there.[108] He does charity work in a variety of episodes, including feeding the homeless and planting a tree at the seniors' center.[109] Indeed, Ned's willingness to extend a helping hand makes him an easy foil for Homer's abuse, but evangelicalism's ethical vision of loving others and doing the right thing persists in the face of Homer's torments. Ned legitimates Christianity's ethical side. While the institutional and culture warrior elements of Ned's character are decried by *The Simpsons*, his faith is affirmed as ethical.

Ned has two major crises of faith that reveal his spiritual depth. In the episode "Hurricane Neddy," a hurricane destroys the family house while nothing happens to the Simpsons'. The Flanders take shelter at FCOS, where the sign in front reads, "God Welcomes His Victims." Echoing the biblical story of Job, Ned wonders if he is being punished. Lovejoy's response is far from comforting. "Ooh . . . short answer yes with an if, long answer no with a but. Uh, if you need additional solace by the way I've got a copy of something or other by Art Linkletter in my office." Lovejoy's ambivalence forces Ned to find answers for himself. That night he climbs into the sanctuary and prays, "Why me, Lord? I've always been nice to people, I don't drink or dance or swear. I've even kept kosher just to be on the safe side. I've done everything the Bible says, even the stuff that contradicts the other stuff! What more could I do? I feel like I'm coming apart here! I want to yell out but I just can't dang-diddly-do-dang-do-damn-diddly-darn do it! I . . . I . . . [*sighs*]." Unlike Job, who receives an audience with God and is rewarded for his faith in the face of hardship, Ned's prayer is never answered and *The Simpsons* uses a long camera shot to show his isolation.

His actions call into question Turner's claim that "in the Flanders home, spirituality often appears to be fragile and other-worldly—couched in antiquated language, in need of constant protection from the rough-and-tumble of everyday life."[110] Instead, religion's institutional concepts—the rules, dogmas, and rituals—have driven Ned toward a moral life. While he does not receive any consolation for his family's suf-

Ned's isolation in his moment of need in "Hurricane Neddy"

fering, religion frames his question of "why do I deserve this?" and gives Ned's life meaning even if the answers he receives are unsatisfactory. It is exemplary of a deep faith developed within religion. Ned's fundamentalism is satirized when it drives his political actions, but it also provides a framework for meaningful spiritual experience despite its cultural baggage. Understanding Flanders' value for *The Simpsons'* satire requires seeing past caricatures. *The Simpsons'* creative team takes what it deems positive traits from different religions and then shows how those traits can fruitfully enrich a character's life.

Ned's other major crisis comes in the episode "Alone Again, Natura-Diddly," when Maude dies. Grieving her loss, he prays, "Lord I've never questioned you, but I've been wondering if your decision to take Maude was, well . . . wrong. [*Hastily*] Unless this is part of your divine plan. [*Groaning*] Just give me some kind of sign. Anything. [*Nothing happens*] And after all that church chocolate I bought, which by the way was gritty and had that white stuff on it! Well I've had it!" The next morning he threatens not to go to church, but cannot follow through. When he arrives he walks into a performance by the Christian rock band Covenant, and lead singer Rachel Jordan's lyrics convince him that putting his faith in God will carry him through this dark time. Unlike the last time, Ned's prayers are indirectly answered, with the church and Christianity facilitating his healing. While *The Simpsons* has not spared Ned's politics, parenting, or preachiness, the program's creators demonstrate that they recognize that evangelicals can find meaningful answers to difficult problems in their religious traditions through the way that Ned copes with pain.

Christians between Stupidity and Danger

Ned and Lovejoy are but two caricatures from the three programs, but their complexity helps us to see that in *The Simpsons*, stupidity and danger are narrowly separated. Much of Ned's evangelism skirts the boundary between being stupid and being dangerous. There is a good reason for the thin line between stupid but not dangerous and dangerous religious practice. Once the programs have so thoroughly struck chords of institutional dissonance regarding God's, Jesus', and the Bible's sacredness, then the institutions that are built upon them are either benignly stupid or extremely dangerous because they run the risk of violating what is held as good and moral in the programs' worlds by adhering to that which the programs consider stupid. When Christians explicitly try to reshape society so that the seen order reflects one of many Christian perspectives and threatens a program's moral center, then Christian actions become grounds for vicious counterattacks. It is to this topic that we now turn.

4

American Christianity, Part 2

American Christianities as Dangerous Threats[1]

The climax of *South Park*'s episode "Bloody Mary" is like a train wreck in slow motion. Pope Benedict XVI travels to a tiny Colorado town to confirm whether the local statue of the Virgin Mary, which has been "bleeding out its ass," is a miracle. As he inspects this link between the transcendent and the mundane, we hear a loud farting sound and the statue gushes blood onto his face.

To say that watching the Virgin Mary "shit blood on the Pope," as Parker and Stone describe the event on the episode's DVD commentary, is shocking is an understatement. In this moment the program's scatological humor, religious criticism, and boundary pushing coalesce into a single shot.

It was also labeled a vicious act of blasphemy and powerful Catholics used it to take action against the show.[2]

By now, *South Park*'s blasphemy is unsurprising, and it has developed through a long and vicious history of treating the Catholic Church and other Christian traditions as both stupid and dangerous. Indeed, *The Simpsons*, *South Park*, and *Family Guy* all criticize Christians as stupid—in the sense of being unable to adapt to the modern world's intellectual standards—and dangerous—especially in their attempts to control others. In the three programs' eyes, exploiting others is Christianity's greatest failure, and they spare no expense ridiculing conservative Christian sexual ethics, persecution, and censorship.

Threatening Missionary Positions

The Simpsons, *South Park*, and *Family Guy* all embrace individual choice and freedom as core values. They view Christian missionaries as dangerous, and missionary activities have been explicitly satirized

The Virgin Mary "Shits blood on the Pope" in *South Park*'s "Bloody Mary"

in *Family Guy*'s episodes "Holy Crap" and "The Father, the Son, and the Holy Fonz," in *The Simpsons'* episodes "Missionary: Impossible" and "Faith Off," and in *South Park*'s episodes "Starvin Marvin in Space" and ". . . Probably." When Christians deliberately try to convert others through force or shame in these episodes their attempts fall short, exposing Christianity's dangers. Missionary efforts are treated as failures because they are attempts to force individuals to adopt an unseen order that the programs typically portray as stupid. The Great Commission in Matthew 28:19–20 ("Go therefore and make disciples of all nations, baptizing them in the name of the Father and of the Son and of the Holy Spirit, teaching them to observe all that I have commanded you" [NRSV]) and its popular manifestations in contemporary America are the foundations for what makes Christians dangerous in the worldviews of these shows and thus appropriate targets for satire and ridicule.

In creating their jokes the programs engage with a deep stock of cultural knowledge in the United States. American Christianity has been profoundly shaped by figures who have enthusiastically engaged audiences from the colonial period to the present day. From Jonathan Edwards' efforts during the First Great Awakening to the revivals that led to upstate New York being known as the "Burned Over District" in the early nineteenth century, to charismatic revivalists such as Dwight L. Moody, Billy Sunday, and Billy Graham, to large para-church organizations such as the Promise Keepers and contemporary religious entertainers, there have always been people who traveled from town to town to bring the message of Jesus' love and salvation in an entertaining package that engaged the heart and sometimes the mind. Billy Sunday was a former professional baseball player who mimicked plays while working his stage, and major revivalists from Moody to Graham have featured choirs and gospel music prominently during their revivals. Revivalism's legacy as popular culture, entertainment, and evangelism has impacted evangelical popular culture. It is impossible to conceive of evangelical popular culture without acknowledging that for centuries Americans have been getting together to hear charismatic speakers, sing with dedicated gospel choirs, listen to amazing soloists, and be redeemed by the Holy Spirit.[3] Evangelical entertainment is entertainment with a sacred purpose.

The Great Commission has long inspired Christian missionaries to spread their versions of the gospel. Evangelism is a major concern for all three programs because, Reverend Lovejoy and Ned Flanders in *The Simpsons* excepted, Christians are rarely featured as dynamic main characters. Rather, guest characters or single-episode "religion" plots that feature a main character parodying some aspect of Christianity serve as the primary vehicles for commenting on Christianity. In some cases the goal of the episode is to point out Christian beliefs' stupidity. Yet, Christian organizations and traditions wield considerable power in American society and they challenge the three programs' underlying ideologies. Missionary work and revivalism—which connect belief and behavior—are treated as dangerous because they are perceived to lead people to a competing, incorrect unseen order. So long as Christians leave other people's beliefs unassailed, the programs generally treat them as stupid. When they try to change people's religious beliefs they are treated as dangerous.

The individual choice of spiritual seeking is sacrosanct for *The Simpsons* and *South Park* and, provided that beliefs are not being forced on others, it is acceptable in *Family Guy*'s atheist space. But Christianity's sexual ethics and belief in God's laws as the basis for an unseen order are viewed by all three shows as wrongheaded. The three programs resolve institutional dissonance by attacking evangelists' efforts.

Family Guy's episode "Holy Crap" introduces Peter's father, Francis Griffin, an old New England Irish Catholic with a vicious hatred of any tradition not resembling his Catholicism. Early on, the Griffins attend Francis' retirement party, where we hear his take on the world: "At mass this morning it occurred to me that I may never see any of your faces again. I just want to say that Jesus loves you. But in my eyes, you're a bunch of sinners and slackers who forced a hard-working old man to retire. So you can take this shiny watch and shove it." Later, Francis reads Bible stories to Stewie that describe God casting pagans and sinners into the fiery bowels of hell, which prompts Stewie's episode-long fascination with the Bible's more violent stories, and he terrifies Chris when the boy takes too long in the bathroom. In a standard joke about misunderstanding the situation, Francis says he knows what Chris is doing in there and that if Chris ever does it again he will go to hell. Even though Chris may think he is alone, God is watching. The implication is that Chris was masturbating, but he was just using the toilet. Chris concludes that "I'm a sinner and God's a pervert." Francis again mixes shame and fear with Meg when he learns that the boy next door, Kevin, walked her home. Calling her a harlot, he says that God will strike her sinful heart with leprosy. Francis also shames Peter after Peter gets him a job at the toy factory. Peter is soon fired for talking back to Francis and the old man says that if he has a problem he should go and confess his sins. We see the emotional damage Francis does to Peter when Lois asks how Peter could accept his father's condemnation and Peter resigns himself to the idea that he is going to hell. While Lois tries to convince him he is wrong, Peter will only accept Francis' recognition, which he gains when he takes the Pope to the toy factory and has his holiness tell Francis that he has raised a good son. The two Griffin men are reconciled—after they both admit that they love, but do not like, each other.

Francis' return in "The Father, the Son, and the Holy Fonz" continues satirizing Francis' missionizing and shows it driving Peter to search for a new religion. Francis comes to the Griffins' house for his birthday dinner and asks Lois when Stewie will be baptized. Lois asks why this matters and Francis explains that it is "Because I love this family and I don't want my grandson to burn in hell." When Brian challenges Francis on baptism and its relationship to salvation, Francis warns him, "Watch that kind of talk or you'll get your heathen head smacked." "Oh, that's very Christian. 'Believe what I say or I'll hurt you,'" Brian replies. "Now you're getting it," Francis retorts as he knocks Brian to the floor with a Bible. As we saw earlier, Francis' belligerence inspires Peter to his find own religion. Of course, Francis is intolerant and he calls Peter's religion "an abomination." He complains that he had told Peter to find real religion and that "What I saw today wasn't real religion. It was just a bunch of sheep, singing songs and listening to ridiculous tall tales." Even though Francis eventually accepts Peter's new church, the humor he inspires is rooted in a stereotype of uncouth Christians who think they know everything. Francis embodies a Catholic stereotype that is willing to stand firm on who and what constitutes a Catholic.[4] For Francis, *extra Ecclesiam nulla salus*—outside the Church there is no salvation.[5]

Francis' evangelism is rooted in his staunch belief that he is right and his religion is real. Francis is employed as a bad model in *Family Guy's* unseen order precisely because *he is wrong and worships something fake.* Yet, he persists and his dogma ruins others' lives. He stands as a prime example of the problem of Christian missionaries in the three programs. In their use of Francis it is not his Catholicism that is at issue. The distinctions between Catholic and Protestant missionaries across the programs are not emphasized because doctrinal nuances are not the source of humor. Self-assurance mixed with hypocrisy characterizes the portrayals of missionaries and the programs are ecumenical when satirizing Christian stupidity as dangerous. Protestant missionaries in *The Simpsons* and *South Park* are used in similar ways to *Family Guy's* use of Francis. The willingness to forcefully attack others for not sharing one's beliefs is treated as common across Christians and it is the self-assured belief in Christian unseen orders that the programs portray as dangerous.

The Simpsons and *South Park* both satirize American foreign missionary work. In the episode "Missionary: Impossible," Homer finds himself in trouble with PBS and asks Reverend Lovejoy to hide him. Lovejoy smuggles him onto a Christian Relief plane headed for Micro-Asia. There is a problem because, as Homer says, "I'm no missionary. I don't even believe in Jebus!" Upon arriving on the tropical island Homer sees half-dressed, brown-skinned natives before the two departing missionaries, Craig and Amy, welcome him. While leaving, Craig explains the situation: "We taught them some English and ridiculed away most of their beliefs." Homer, of course, is indifferent about missionizing. When he sees young women wearing dresses he asks, "Where are all the shirtless girls you see in geographical magazines?" Q'Toktok, a local, explains that "Craig and Amy gave us the gift of shame." Craig and Amy were also digging a well and building a chapel and it is later implied that they were constructing an immunization clinic, but those activities hold little interest for Homer. Upon learning that there is no television, couches, or beer on the island he falls to the ground and wails "Oh God, oh God, oh God" which the natives imitate. This joke draws on the notion that Craig and Amy preached a Christianity based in shame.

Homer eventually tries to become a serious missionary and teaches the natives about religion. When he announces this intent, the people show him that they have imbibed the Christian message that they will be punished for their sins by falling to the ground and wailing "Oh God" again. Homer, misunderstanding their actions, says, "Please, please, that's not necessary. I'm just God's messenger." Then, holding up a Bible, he declares, "And lo, what a wondrous message it is. Like this, from the book of p-salms. 'God will shatter the heads of his enemies, the hairy crown of those who walk in their guilty ways, that you may bathe your feet in blood.'⁶ As true today as it was when it was written." He takes questions from the crowd and is faced with inquiries such as which religion is the right one (Homer is only certain it is not the Unitarians) and "If the Lord is all powerful, why does he care whether we worship him or not?" Homer's answer: "It's because God is powerful, but also insecure— like Barbara Streisand before James Brolin." At this point Homer gives up and admits he is no missionary, but he wants to help. His assessment of the village's situation, however, speaks to Homer's more base impulses: "You don't need a well, or a chapel, or an immunization center. What you need's a little razzle-dazzle." They build a casino.

The casino leads to an outbreak of drunken violence, with one islander, Ak, asking Homer, "How can Ace be one and eleven? Huh? What kind of god would allow that?" Homer has another change of heart and begins building the chapel. After it is built, he starts ringing the bell in the steeple, proclaiming that he is doing God's work, but that causes an earthquake that splits the earth. Before he is immolated, the escapade ends and the scene shifts to a FOX fund-raiser that parodies the PBS fund-raiser Homer had fled.

Homer's work mimics and mocks the Christian missionary tension of bringing the message to people while allowing it to be translated into the vernacular, which can in a subtle way shift Christian teachings to meet the cultural idioms of those receiving the message.[7] Homer is not really a missionary, but he stands on Craig and Amy's foundation. The people are terrified, they have been given shame, and they have no idea how to respond to scripture except to prostrate themselves and writhe. Yet, there is much to the island's context that draws upon ignorant familiarity about missionaries and mission work. Sociologist Robert Wuthnow notes that the estimated $3.7 billion American congregations are said to spend annually on mission work is likely an underestimate because that figure does not include materials and volunteer labor.[8] Hundreds of thousands of Christians sign up for short-term mission trips each year and travel internationally while mixing humanitarian aid and evangelism.[9] When missionaries also do international relief work their positive social justice labor stands side-by-side with their evangelizing. In *The Simpsons*, Craig and Amy's digging wells and building an immunization clinic are coupled with ridiculing away people's beliefs.

South Park's episode "Starvin' Marvin in Space" tackles the problem of missionaries with misplaced priorities. The episode starts with an alien from the planet Marklar (where every noun is "marklar") landing on Earth and being eaten by lions. The scene then shifts to a dilapidated Ethiopian village where people live in tiny shacks, but there is a big church that is staffed by missionaries who teach the people that "reading Bible plus accepting Jesus equals food."

Satirizing missionaries as extorting religious adherence from the poor and suffering drives the narrative. Marvin, an emaciated African child who was introduced in the prior episode, "Starvin' Marvin," is willing to read his Bible, but not in English, which the missionary refers to as "God's language." When he leaves she asks if he is going back to his life of sin and warns him that unless he and his people accept Jesus they will be doomed to an eternity in hell. Walking outside, Marvin is incensed as he passes people moaning in agony. The missionaries could feed them,

A missionary explains that "reading Bible plus accepting Jesus equals food" in *South Park*'s "Starvin' Marvin' in Space"

but are too busy preaching to help them materially. As he crosses a hill, he encounters and commandeers the Marklar's ship. He flies around the world, asking if other nations will adopt his people, but missionaries are present in each one, causing Marvin to depart in disgust.

Meanwhile the CIA tries to track Marvin and they torture Stan, Kyle, Cartman, and Kenny until the boys reveal that they originally met Marvin after Sally Struthers' charity sent him to them. The boys go home and turn on the Christian Broadcasting Network to find Pat Robertson explaining that the network needs money to help others. This scene offers a caricature of televangelism and preachers asking for money on television. On the DVD commentary Parker and Stone acknowledge that they wanted to mock Robertson's "smug little laugh" and the fact that he is always talking about building something huge. The fact that Robertson's 700 Club is based around monthly donations sounds like a scam to them. *South Park* demonstrates the missionaries' moral failures by linking them to Robertson's greed about halfway through the episode. The missionaries are always shown withholding food in favor of giving people crosses or hounding people to confess sins while reciting scripture. Marvin travels to Marklar and gets permission to return with the Ethiopians. Upon his return to Earth, the local missionary asks if the Marklar have heard the word of Christ. "No, never. It's perfect." Cartman replies. The missionary leaves to ensure that the gospel will be spread and soon Robertson is asking for funding to build "an interstellar cruiser. Now, this spaceship will be able to travel through a wormhole and deliver the message and glory of Jesus Christ to those godless aliens. Send your money now! Amen."

Once Marvin manages to get his people into space, the "Missionary 600" starts blasting them with their lasers and telling them to turn back. The missionaries soon discover that their lasers are not powerful enough. This realization engenders an arms race with Robertson asking for donations to upgrade the spaceship. Eventually, the missionaries, the Ethiopians, the boys, and the CIA with Sally Struthers (designed as Jabba the Hutt from *Star Wars*) arrive on Marklar, where Kyle's final speech insinuates that the missionaries are just using the Ethiopians and will only try to change the Marklars' beliefs. When the chief Marklar sends the missionaries away, one says, "But you will all burn forever in eternal hellfire." "Yes, that's nice. Thank you for stopping by," the Marklar replies.

The humor and satire in "Starvin' Marvin in Space" rely on the premise that Christianity's claims are stupid and that attaching humanitarian aid to ideological acceptance and ethical reformation taints the aid's moral goodness. Telling people that accepting Christ equals food highlights this problematic link. Good people would just offer food, hence Marvin's leaving the mission and other Ethiopians rolling their eyes at the missionaries who offer them crosses and Christian names instead of nutrition. Hounding people who want to live healthy lives in peace across the galaxy shows a religious zeal that highlights the hypocrisy of saying you want to help people but then withhold the basic elements of their survival. Making human life contingent on accepting your ideology is an abuse of power in *South Park*. Attaching material sustenance to conversion becomes even more sinister when material support is funneled through a televangelist who is willing to invest in weaponry to chase down potential converts instead of investing in their basic essentials.

Francis Griffin, Homer, and the missionaries in "Starvin' Marvin" are satirical because they reference the idea that forceful attempts to change a person's beliefs to Christianity are morally wrong, especially if you use violence or withhold life's basic essentials. Francis' behavior emphasizes *Family Guy*'s broad dislike of religious proselytization, especially in his willingness to override Lois' wishes or use violence against Brian because he thinks he is correct. "Missionary: Impossible" highlights the ongoing association in *The Simpsons* between shame and Christianity, with Christians serving as sources of unnecessary guilt even if they do some positive things like digging wells and building immunization clinics. The missionaries in "Starvin' Marvin in Space" are unaware of their role in replicating the problems of Ethiopian poverty and are willing to use extreme poverty conditions to press their religion on others. In each program the institutional dissonance comes from using force to make people change their beliefs. This dissonance requires resolution because it violates the sacredness the programs associate with individual choice in religious practice. It is one thing to believe, it is another to share that faith with high costs attached.

Revivalism as the Link between Missionaries and Popular Culture

South Park's caricature of Pat Robertson reminds us that missionary activities are both domestic and international affairs. Throughout the nation's history, there have been evangelists who have used technology to inspire as many people as possible to convert not only to believing in Jesus as the Christ, but also to reforming behaviors to a conservative moral standard. Historian Michael McClymond defines revivalism as "a spiritual movement within Christianity that calls individuals to make a self-conscious decision to repent of sin and believe the gospel, and thereby seeks to bring them an assurance of being in a right or proper relationship with God, and integrate them into a community with other like-minded individuals."[10] For McClymond, revivals bring people into a relationship with God through personal choice. That is, they come as individuals who are impelled to reform themselves and be redeemed and revived by Jesus' sacrificial death and the Holy Spirit's power. This personal reform should lead to affirming one's standing before God as

Brother Faith works the crowd in "Faith Off"

redeemed. The redeemed Christian is then integrated back into the community as somebody who is rehabilitated. Converts often demonstrate their transformation by committing to behaviors deemed appropriate in conservative Christian circles, such as abstaining from alcohol and drugs, having sex only within a heterosexual marriage, and supporting the existing social order.[11] Yet, revivalism's history is also part of American popular culture's history. Revivals are not just places of personal religious conversion, they are traveling spectacles. People traveled to the events, met new people, and enjoyed the revival's pageantry, from enthusiastic preaching to new music and dramatic sketches. Each program treats Christianity's combination with fun, entertainment, and celebrity as something dangerous to be mocked.

In *The Simpsons*, the classic American tent revival takes place at Brother Faith's Revival in the episode "Faith Off." Brother Faith is an African American in a white suit who performs on stage in front of a giant cross decorated with bright lights. He has smoke, lights, and a choir, and he works the crowd.

He gets the Springfielders excited about religion, even though they know they are far from pious. His singing and dancing wow the crowd and Bart is convinced that Brother Faith dances "better than Jesus him-self." Brother Faith conducts faith healings, striking Springfielders who are afflicted, for example he says "The power of faith compels you!" be-fore manipulating Cletus the slack-jawed yokel's arm. Bart, enthralled by the performance, assists Brother Faith and helps to remove a bucket that was superglued to Homer's head while proclaiming "I have the power!"

Afterwards, Bart asks Brother Faith how he really removed the bucket and Brother Faith assures Bart that he performed the healing. Brother Faith is convinced that God gave Bart the power, but Bart counters that with, "Really, hmm. I would think he would want to limit my power." Faith chuckles to himself before having the following conversation:

BROTHER FAITH
When I was your age I was a hell-raiser too. My slingshot was my cross, but I saw the light and I changed my wicked ways.

BART
I figure I'll go for the life of sin followed by the presto-change-o deathbed repentance.

BROTHER FAITH
[*To himself*] Wow, that's a good angle, [*to Bart*] but that's not God's angle. Why not spend your life helping people instead? Then you're also covered in case of sudden death.

BART
Full coverage? Hmmm . . .

At school the next day Bart heals Ralph Wiggum by striking him in the forehead, releasing his milk money—and his milk—from his nose. This success inspires Bart to hold a revival as Brother Bart, where he sings about how he has changed his ways and invites people up to "tes-tify" while he performs faith healings. Then Bart "heals" Milhouse by throwing away his glasses, which lands his best friend in the hospital. Bart realizes that he lacks healing power. Throughout the rest of the episode Bart refuses to perform healings until the episode's climac-tic moment when he tries to heal Springfield University's star football player. Springfield University wins the game, but Bart's healing days are over.

In "Faith Off" *The Simpsons* uses an ignorant familiarity rooted in a suspicion of the revival tradition and its charismatic healers, fantastic claims, and famous frauds. Bart thinks he heals Milhouse but causes his best friend to almost die. Yet, people across the world claim that they can heal people through the power of the Holy Spirit and make money from donations willing believers provide to support these ministries. The implication from *The Simpsons* is that faith healers are frauds with an entertaining show that lures people in and risks their health. *South Park* uses this stereotype of corrupt revivalists who are using Christian entertainment and faith healing to lead people astray in their faith and health, and adds the criticism that revivalists are performing for greed, not faith, in the episodes "Do the Handicapped go to Hell?" and "Probably."[12] In "Do the Handicapped go to Hell?" the boys attend Sunday school classes after the local Catholic priest, Maxi, tells them that their disabled friend Timmy is going to hell since he cannot confess his sins—the only thing he can say is his name. Once there, they mock the sacraments of confession and the Eucharist. These foundational Catholic rituals are stripped of their sacredness and removed from the theological context that frames them as mediations of God's grace. The Eucharist's logic is mocked when the children ask if Jesus was made out of crackers, and they summarize the Church's path to salvation as "if you don't confess all your sins and you don't eat crackers and drink wine then you're going to hell, period!" Instead of coming to love Jesus and his sacrifice for their sins, the children are scared into confessing their sins, fearing that if they die without confessing they will go to hell. The children start to live in a dualistic world in which any sin is potentially a one-way ticket to hell. The episode concludes within this framework of personal piety. At the episode's climax the boys find Maxi having sex with a woman in the confessional. Maxi's sexual failure leads the boys to doubt that he can guide them to salvation. They eventually leave the church and start a televangelist-inspired revival in "Probably."

"Probably" starts with Cartman dressed in a suit, preaching in a Southern accent on a stage in the schoolyard, and telling everybody that they must be saved because the Lord will smite sinners and send them to hell. When Ms. Cartman tries to get him to stop, Stan and Kyle ascend the stage, with Stan asking, "What purpose does school have? The Bible says the only goal in this life is to praise God and get into heaven." Kyle backs him up, saying, "Yeah, this life is short. The afterlife is forever!" The adults try to get the kids back into school, but Cartman continues his Southern televangelist revivalist style, falling on his knees, waving his arms, swinging his Bible, and preaching, "[*in his normal voice*] Many of you knew Kenny McCormick. He was a playful, school-going eight-year-old, and then yesterday [*switches to his vigorous Southern accent*] he was smacked down by the Lord! God bitch-slapped him right to the fiery depths of hell. So when will you go? Tomorrow? Ten years? Does it matter? No, because unless you give this life to the Lord this life belongs to Satan." Cartman sounds like many revivalists in American history as he echoes a centuries-old Protestant message. Yet, in *South Park* style, Cartman's preaching immediately leads to materialistic motives as Kyle brings forth a church design that mimics Garden Grove, California's Crystal Cathedral, which was home to televangelist Robert Schuller and known as a sign of excess, while Cartman preaches: "But we cannot worship God in that church where the priest of sin resides, so we will build a new church with crystal walls, a ceiling eighty feet high, and a slide that connects this part meah to this part meah. Who will help us?" The children all volunteer and construction begins.

The children build the church from scrap lumber and soon Kenny calls Cartman from Mexico. The boys, however, think that he is in hell and demand details, which Cartman works into his sermon at the new church. Cartman's performance is amplified when one child's parents come to take her home, but a loose board falls and kills the father. Convinced that God and not shoddy carpentry has decided the man's fate, Cartman leads everybody in prayer as upbeat organ music plays in the background. After seeing a televangelist perform a faith healing, Cartman mimics him. His performance gets more and more enthusiastic and South Park's children become ever more engaged in his services until he gets a "message from God" that "each and every one of you is to walk up to this stage and give me one dollar. So I want everyone to feel the love of God by coming up here and putting a dollar in the box." Stan and Kyle question Cartman's motives and their suspicions are confirmed when they find a shirtless Cartman backstage rolling in money and proclaiming, "It actually worked!" The church and revival were all part of Cartman's plan to raise $10 million. He is foiled when the local nun, Sister Anne, brings Jesus to the church and Jesus tells the children to go home because "God doesn't want you to spend all your time being afraid of hell or praising his name. God wants you to spend your time helping others and living a good, happy life. That's how you live for him!"

Jesus' message to live a good life and step away from religious services echoes across the revivalism episodes from *South Park* and *The Simpsons* and resonates with each program's core values. Revivals, with their emphasis on finding purity, faith healing, and extravagant performances, are contrasted with the personal spiritual seeking at *The Simpsons*' core and individual creativity at *South Park*'s center. The revivalist's power and motivation for convicting the audience to align themselves with a Christian unseen order is desacralized in these episodes by portraying revivalists as fraudulent healers or greedy showmen. While Brother Faith is portrayed as honest, Bart's faith-healing failures enable *The Simpsons* to argue that one's trust should be in doctors and not religious figures. Cartman's revival also features phony healings, but is a total charade that transparently becomes about his personal greed once Jesus arrives to stop the proceedings. Cartman is dangerous because he uses fear to elicit a change in people's behavior and fraudulently take their money. The message is clear from both series: Steer clear of revivalists if you want to have a strong personal spiritual path.

Of God, Mammon, and Christian Sexual Ethics

The combination of Christians, popular culture, and commercialism is treated as a dangerous recipe in all three sitcoms. Revivalism combines domestic missionary work with an entertaining package to encourage people to be saved or re-dedicate their lives to Jesus, but missionary work does not always have to be explicit. It can also be attached to entertainment. Earlier we saw religious consumerism in the New Age market, noting that while the programs mocked the selling of spirituality and sometimes saw it as dangerously stupid, in *The Simpsons* selling spirituality could lead to positive results. Christian popular culture and its commercial trappings inspire mixed reactions—especially when Christian popular culture's purpose becomes the appropriation of popular culture for missionizing. The programs present consumerism as a double-edged sword for Christianity. On the one hand, consumerism is depicted as cheapening Christianity's moral value, while on the other it enables missionizing efforts as people are deceived into Christianity with comfort and glamour. In either case, consumerism highlights Christians' dangerous stupidity. When Christian missionizing is equated with religio-political missionizing, it is treated as what critical pedagogical theorists Shirley R. Steinberg and Joe L. Kincheloe call "Christotainment," the combination of literalist readings of Christian scriptures within American populist conservativism.[13]

The Simpsons has satirized Christian popular culture for years. The episode "I'm Going to Praiseland" satirizes Christian theme parks. After Maude's death, Ned finds her sketchbook with illustrations for the Praiseland amusement park. He implements her dream and eventually builds a place where "faith and devotion are the wildest thrill rides of all." There is just one problem—the rides are boring. "King David's Wild Ride" is a roller coaster that takes children into the chamber where a giant, robotic King David says he wrote his 150 psalms. He then reads the psalms to the screaming children who cannot escape. There is also a "Whack-A-Satan" without a mallet because you can stop Satan with your faith, and a souvenir stand selling jellybean Noah's arks that are not filled with two of every flavor, but are "all the same—plain." Were it not for a leaking gas line that gives people hallucinations of heaven, nobody would come.[14] Ned has also sold religious trading cards as a way of teaching kids about religion,[15] attended a church fund-raiser with a "Whack-a-Moses" game and the "Tunnel of Abstinence,"[16] and indicated that he likes the Christian AC/DC cover band AD/BC, who sing "Kindly Deeds Done For Free."[17] FCOS hosts the "Cross-games" which, instead of being a Christian alternative to the X-games, is actually a "Gathering of American Messengers for Evangelical Sports," where SPORTS stands for "Strict Parental Oversight Rather Than Sports."[18] Last, in "Pulpit Friction" a temporary pastor references films such as *Meet the Parents*, demonstrates that an episode of *Californication* (Showtime 2007–2014) illustrates Jesus' teachings, and claims that what the Bible teaches is to love others. He aims to make religion fun and proves it by making Homer his deacon which drives out Lovejoy. Only after Bart unleashes a plague of frogs does Lovejoy return, quoting Psalm 23 and putting the frogs to sleep. These examples illustrate the central tension between stupidity and danger as depicted in *The*

Simpsons. While kitschiness keeps the popular culture from being too dangerous, it has a dark side when it is used to win over stupid people. Its overt religiousness disarms its dangerous aspects because people can easily turn away from such a blatant display of religious ideology. Only Flanders routinely uses Christian popular culture to cultivate his Christianity, and when the Springfielders fall for a pastor who is too in tune with popular culture, Lovejoy saves them.

South Park and *Family Guy* also tackle Christian popular culture's dangerous evangelicalism. *South Park's* episode "Christian Rock Hard" depicts the Christian market's dangers by satirizing Contemporary Christian Music (CCM). Inspired by greed, Cartman tries to convince Stan, Kyle, and Kenny to join him in making Christian music because "It's the easiest, crappiest music in the world, right? If we just play songs about how much we love Jesus, all the Christians will buy our crap." The others reject Cartman's idea and he hurries away after betting Kyle that he can make a platinum album first by starting a Christian band. He recruits Butters on drums and the local African American kid, Token, on bass, but when he tells them they are making a Christian album, Token gets up to leave. Cartman convinces him to stay by expounding on market analysis: "Christians have a built-in audience of over 180 million Americans. If each one of them buys just one of our albums at $12.95 that would be . . ." "$2,331,000,000," Butters replies. Cartman envisions what it takes to reach this market while defacing sheet music to Bruce Howell's "Needing You":[19] "All we have to do to make Christian songs is take regular old songs and add Jesus stuff to them. See? All we have to do is cross out words like 'baby' and 'darling' and replace them with Jesus." (*The Simpsons* made the same joke about interchanging baby and Jesus in the "I'm Going to Praiseland" episode.) Cartman then sings the new lyrics, "I need you in my life, Jesus. I can't live without you, Jesus. And I just want to feel you deep inside me, Jesus."

Cartman's lyrics echo evangelical concerns about having Jesus and the spirit living within your heart, reflecting language used in romantic and sexual contexts.[20] Cartman's unthreatening, loving language is amplified by the band's new visuals once they are christened Faith+1. After leading Token and Butters down to the ocean shore and positioning them appropriately, Cartman, dressed in a brown jacket, blue shirt, with a giant cross necklace and his hair combed, explains that "The key

The "inspirational" cover of Faith+1's new album in *South Park*'s "Christian Rock Hard"

to a hot selling Christian rock album is a flashy, inspirational album cover." The result visually associates the band with Christian worship. Butters and Token are placed in the background and Cartman is front and center with his head tilted skyward, eyes closed, arms raised, a huge cross around his neck, and his hands wide in a posture that millions of Christians adopt in their services every week.

Soon, Faith+1's performance at Christfest lands them a meeting with Faith Records, whose executives are ready to sign Faith+1, but they have some problems with the lyrics because they sound like "it appears that you are actually in love with Christ." The implication is that Cartman has a homoerotic fixation on Jesus, but he turns the table on the executives, using evangelical rhetoric about the relationship one needs to have with Jesus to corner them and get the band signed: "Well, what are you saying? That you don't really love Christ?" When the executive starts protesting, Cartman presses his point, "Well, what's the difference? You love Christ, you're in love with Christ? I mean, what the heck is this?" The band gets signed and we see a promotional commercial advertising the album and songs like "I Wasn't Born Again Yesterday," another song with the lyrics "I want to get down on my knees and start pleasing Jesus. I want to feel his salvation all over my face," and "The Body of Christ" which features the lyrics, "The body of Christ, sleek swimmer's body all muscled up and toned. The body of Christ, oh what a body I wish I could call it my own." By this point the music's homoerotic overtones have been driven home and the album sells a million copies. Cartman's plan disintegrates when he learns that Christians do not award platinum albums, they give awards in gold, frankincense, and myrrh. Cartman, who realizes that he cannot beat Kyle in his bet, starts swearing, "God damnit!" and "F*** Jesus" (in season 7 "fuck" was censored), and his audience and bandmates leave.

In this episode Stan tells Cartman that he doesn't know anything about Christianity. Cartman replies with a statement laced with ignorant familiarity: "I know enough to exploit it," and he goes on to exploit Christians through a superficial knowledge of evangelical discourse about the relationships one has with God and Jesus. As a musical category defined by its lyrics, CCM reflects the larger evangelical culture and, as such, is ripe for two major criticisms. First, it does not serve a missionizing purpose and is only there to stop Christians from encountering ideas from outside the subculture. Second, it is part of Christotainment and builds cultural walls around evangelical subcultural groups who force their religion on others. Sociologists Jay Howard and John Streck make the first point in *Apostles of Rock*, as they demonstrate that the CCM art world is built around supporting evangelical conceptions of Christianity. Specifically, "the fundamental unifying force for evangelicals is their common association with the sentimental trappings of the faith: feelings of acceptance, of familiarity, and, often, of superiority relative to non-Christians. For better or worse, it is in the service of this master that contemporary Christian music has most frequently been employed."[21] This is not to say that some musicians do not honestly attempt to evangelize through their music and performances.[22] Rather, CCM is a product of an evangelical subculture that cares deeply about its politics vis-à-vis the outside world. Sexual ethics are one of evangelicalism's key moral boundaries.[23]

DeLashmutt and Hancock argue that this episode is prophetic, stating that "Their [Parker and Stone's] caricature, while hyperbolic, is not far off. The underlying danger they bring to the fore is the tendency of religion to numb practitioners into uncritical, thoughtless automatons."[24] Those thoughtless automatons are oblivious to the way that their sacred patterns for sexual behavior are being inverted in Cartman's lyrics. Christians in "Christian Rock Hard" are stupid, but they are also dangerous because there are so many of them who cannot see past the surface depictions of Christianity to the underlying assault on their sexual ethics. The inability to think for oneself is a moral failure in *South Park*, and those who cannot think for themselves, but who try to make everybody else think and act according to their unseen order, are attacked for overstepping their right to shape social life. "Christian Rock Hard" shares a common pattern for assaulting Christian sexual ethics in the three programs because it draws upon the dichotomy of presenting Christians as not understanding what is at stake in their sexual politics while attacking them for trying to enforce their unseen order on others. Sexual purity, in which the only sexual behaviors God sanctions are between one man and one woman in marriage, is a widely known conservative Christian value in the United States.[25] Codified in laws such as the Defense of Marriage Act and in federal support for abstinence-only sexual education in the nation's schools, this standard is violated by sexual behavior outside of marriage, with homosexuality carrying additional stigma as evangelicals traditionally see it as unnatural.[26] "Christian Rock Hard" draws our attention to how Christians use consumerism to promote their unseen orders, which oppose other approaches to sexual behavior. *The Simpsons*, *South Park*, and *Family Guy* each value individual-seeking above all else. Their sexual politics conform to an individualistic vision of seeking sexual gratification. Thus, moral and religious restrictions against legal sexual behavior are treated as dangerous institutional dissonances.[27]

Sociologist and theologian Gordon Lynch's concept of hierarchies of sacred forms helps to explain why the incongruities between evangelical language about worshipful submission and love of God and the programs' sexual freedom idioms facilitate satire. Hierarchies of sacred forms exist when sacred forms are culturally arranged so that one dominates the others. When this happens subjugated sacred forms still circulate, but the dominant form sets the interpretive agenda.[28] The interpretations of ideal types based in ignorant familiarity we have analyzed facilitate a system of stratifying and classifying religions across the programs. Those classifications are put to use in the sexual-political sphere to illustrate Christianity's dangers. The programs use blatant parodies and outright attacks on purity culture, anti-homosexual politics, and the Catholic Church to forward an argument that conservative Christian sexual ethics are wrong and dangerous when introduced as political legitimations for shaping sexual behavior.

For example, *South Park* and *Family Guy* parody the evangelical abstinence organization Silver Ring Thing (SRT) for its role in pushing evangelical purity culture in schools. SRT made headlines in 2005 after the ACLU filed a lawsuit against the Department of Health and Human Services to strip SRT of federal funding because it had been holding abstinence crusades in schools across the United States and had received federal grants in excess of $1 million.[29] SRT remains active, promoting abstinence before marriage and using language that codes premarital sex as a source of shame and "brokenness" in individuals. For example, "SRT has recognized that behavior change comes through heart change—that the guilt and pain of sexual immorality presents an open door for the Gospel."[30] It also promotes the idea that people who have had extramarital sex are broken and seen as less desirable human beings in its educational video "Bare Essentials Abstinence/Purity Series: Session 1—Dealing With Temptation."[31] Historian of religion Sara Moslener writes that the movement has incorporated countercultural language and presents itself as both media savvy and revolutionary, inspiring young Christians to resist the extramarital sex that SRT leaders and other evangelicals see throughout American culture.[32] Yet, as sociologist Mark Regnerus has shown, abstinence pledges are largely ineffective at stopping sex before marriage. The pledges do lead to different behaviors, as pledgers do delay sexual behavior's onset and have fewer sexual partners over their lifetimes. Moreover, their partners are less likely to cheat and they are more likely than the general public to wait until marriage.[33] Yet, roughly 88% of pledgers will have premarital sex.[34] Regnerus summarizes his findings, writing, "The abstinence pledge movement is the symbolic resistance of evangelical Protestant youth. It is the small but determined force to which a significant minority of these youth claims allegiance, even while they are increasingly sneaking across enemy lines."[35] SRT's hipness and commercialism provide an

open target for satire, especially in light of evangelical pledgers' hypocrisy. *Family Guy* and *South Park* turn the conservative countercultural
sentiment inspiring evangelicals to launch abstinence campaigns into
jokes about evangelicals being stupid, greedy, politically manipulative,
devious, and ignorant about human sexuality.

In *Family Guy*'s episode "Prick Up Your Ears," Lois starts teaching a
sex education class at the high school and is fired for instructing students
in condom use. Instead, the school recruits Reverend Jerry Kirkwood
and the Opal Ring Crusade from the First Evangelical Church. Kirkwood's presentation is hokey; he tells the students to "put their walk-
mans down and listen up" and there is a deep voice-over from God that
says "uh-oh" when Jerry says he is going to talk about sex, but Kirkwood
adds "and why they shouldn't be having it." "That is boss!" God replies.
The Opal Ring players perform a skit about driving to "make-out point"
and freeze after the male character asks the girl if she wants to go all the
way. When Jerry asks what he did wrong, the boy next to Meg answers
that they were going to have sex without being married and Jerry agrees
with him. Jerry then goes on to explain that even though sex is fun, you
cannot have it until you are married even if you use a condom because
"not only do condoms fail 100% of the time, they're also majorly unsafe.
Hey, you wouldn't put a plastic bag over your grandmother's head would
you?" The stunned teenagers are given opal rings to show their commitment to abstinence before marriage. Jerry's final pitch, "Who wants to be
joyful? Who wants to be pure? Who wants to be abstinent?" reverberates
with SRT rhetoric and Quahog's teenagers are converted.

Soon the teens are reading and distributing frightening and misin-
forming literature about sex. For example, Meg gives Peter "The Truth
About Sex" from which he reads, "If you have sex, your penis will fall off
and land in another dimension populated entirely by dogs who will eat
it." Later he informs Lois that the pamphlet says that "Sex turns straight
people gay and turns gays into Mexicans. Everyone goes down a notch."
That warning does not stop Meg from having sex with her new boy-
friend, Doug, but they end up "doing it in the ear." After Lois catches
Meg the younger Griffin explains that "it doesn't count. We're still pure
in the eyes of the Lord." Ear sex becomes a thing at school until Lois
interrupts one of Jerry's assemblies, when he tells students that "if you

have sex, you're automatically in al-Qaeda," and she says it is fine if they have sex provided they use a condom.

Jerry is an extreme parody of Christianity's dangers. He gains the teenagers' trust by superficially relating to them and then provides false information to push his Christianity. The Opal Ring Crusade's materials are so outrageous that they call all evangelical abstinence-only literature into question. A moral boundary has been crossed and exaggerations such as condoms failing all the time and one's penis falling into another dimension strike loud notes of institutional dissonance with *Family Guy*'s core values of atheism, scientific rationality, and personal spiritual pursuits. As previously discussed, *Family Guy* frequently uses conservative Christians as a foil for jokes that contrast Christian stupidity with scientific rationality. Jerry shows the logical extent of *Family Guy*'s disdain for conservative Christianity and explicitly recommends removing evangelical abstinence crusades from public schools.

There are other dangers associated with combining Christianity, popular culture, and sexual ethics. In *South Park*'s "The Ring," the Jonas Brothers (a Disney band who are known for their explicit Christianity) are silver ring advocates. Yet, Disney's profits—not the religious message—are their motivation. When the brothers resist promoting the rings at their concerts, "the Boss" (Mickey Mouse) explains why the rings are so vital to the group's success and image: "You have to wear the purity rings because that's how we can sell sex to little girls, ha-ha. See, if we make the posters with little girls reaching for your junk, then you have to wear purity rings or else Disney company looks bad, ha-ha." After lead singer Joe Jonas says they do not want to sell sex to little girls and refuses to perform, Mickey beats him.

After a series of events that lead to Stan, Kyle, and Cartman being interrogated by a chainsaw-wielding Mickey Mouse backstage at the Red Rocks Amphitheatre before a Jonas Brothers concert, the Jonas Brothers come to a realization after Kyle claims that Kenny's purity ring is killing him:

JOE JONAS
You see? We were right about the purity rings! A nice Christian symbol can't be used for profit gains.

KEVIN JONAS
We've all angered God.

MICKEY MOUSE
[*Walks up to the boys while still wielding the chainsaw*] You think God is in control here, ha-ha? I am in control! I've been in control since the '50s in case you haven't noticed, ha-ha! [*Throws away the chainsaw and points at the Jonas Brothers*] You three faggots are going onstage and [*points at Stan, Cartman, and Kyle*] you three faggots aren't going to stop me! Nobody is ruining this event, ha-ha! I've worked too long and too hard to have anybody fuck this up! [*Kyle pushes up a volume control so that the crowd can hear Mickey.*] Where would you be without me Jonas Brothers, ha-ha? Your music sucks and you know it, ha-ha! It's because you make little girls' 'ginies [*vaginas*] tickle! And when little girls' 'ginies tickle, I make money, ha-ha! And that's because little girls are fucking stupid, ha-ha! And the purity rings make it ok to do whatever I want, ha-ha! Even the Christians are too fucking stupid to figure out I'm selling sex to their daughters! I've made billions off of Christian ignorance for decades now, ha-ha! And do you know why? Because Christians are fucking retarded, ha-ha! They believe in a talking dead guy, ha-ha!

Everybody now knows Mickey's plan, they leave the concert, and he grows into a gigantic flame-spewing, vengeance-seeking terror.

"The Ring" and "Prick Up Your Ears" showcase how Christianity is treated as dangerous when it legitimates controlling willing participants' sexual behaviors. Commercialism and social-political coercion profane the sacred form of Christian sexual purity, and individual pursuit of sexual pleasure is presented as the socially acceptable ideal. *South Park* and *Family Guy* argue that neither Mickey Mouse nor the Opal Ring Crusade or their real-life counterparts in SRT and the larger purity ring culture should determine the ways that teenagers are taught about sex, its pleasures and dangers, and the consequences of sexual behavior.

This liberated sexuality extends into the programs' treatment of homosexuality and religion, in which *The Simpsons*' ambivalent treatment of same-sex marriage in the episode "There's Something About Marrying" is helpfully paired with *Family Guy*'s episode "You May Now Kiss The . . . Uh . . . Guy Who Receives." Meanwhile, *South Park*'s treatment of how homosexuals are treated in Christian ex-gay movements criticizes conservative Christian approaches to homosexuality in the episode "Cartman Sucks."

Homosexual couples come to Springfield to tie the knot after same-sex marriage is legalized to increase tourism revenue in "There's Something About Marrying." Lovejoy refuses them entrance to the church, saying, "While I have no opinion for or against your sinful lifestyles, I cannot marry two people of the same sex any more than I can put a hamburger on a hot dog bun." When Marge challenges him, saying that love should be the deciding factor, Lovejoy sticks to the text: "The Bible forbids same sex marriage," although it should be noted that he cannot name specific books (e.g., Lev 18:22, Rom 1:26). He rings the church bell to quiet Marge's protests, although we can hear her arguing that scriptural scholars disagree about the significance of something (her voice fades out) and that Jesus' ministry emphasized love. Lovejoy is shown rejecting the liberal sexual attitude *The Simpsons* treats as normative.[36] He becomes another villain in the larger discourse about Christianity in America.[37] Lovejoy's position is conservative, denying marriage rights to homosexuals based on strict biblical interpretation. When taken in light of the larger context of *The Simpsons'* treatment of Christianity and sexuality, "There's Something About Marrying" does not resolve the issue of same-sex marriage, but it reaffirms the program's position that Christians are dangerous.

The dangers of conservative Christian sexual ethics are foregrounded in *Family Guy's* episode "You May Now Kiss The . . . Uh . . . Guy Who Receives." After Chris joins the Young Republicans at his high school because he likes the new girl Alyssa, he asks her what they do at Young Republicans meetings. Alyssa replies, "We help those who already have the means to help themselves. Also, we perpetuate the idea that Jesus chose America to destroy non-believers and brown people." Chris responds, "I don't understand what you're saying, but somehow I feel safer." This sense of safety is illustrated when Chris tells Brian that the Bible says homosexuality is a sin and Brian tells him, "don't give me that Young Republican crap Chris. The Bible also says a senior citizen built an ark and rounded up two of every animal." These jokes establish the Young Republicans as radical fundamentalist Christians who cannot be trusted to intelligently analyze public policy needs. The episode's most damning attack on conservative sexual ethics about homosexuality comes in the form of a propaganda piece that Lois watches when she asks her priest for help thinking through same-sex marriage. Telling her that "these questions are too big to be answered by human beings, which is why God made this film," the priest shows Lois "The Homosexual and You" by "Pat Robertson Industries," which ends with a gay man having deadly corrosive acid in his veins instead of blood. This parodic film production equates irrationality and bigotry with conservative Christianity. The jokes in this episode dismiss conservative concerns by making them into convictions based on stupidity and fear rather than a different religious perspective. *Family Guy* first aired in 1999. Throughout most of the program's run, American family policies that restrict or deny homosexual marriages and adoptions as legitimate have been a persistent feature of the American political landscape. These policies are strongly supported by conservative Christians and are often supported in explicitly Christian terms. This episode positions *Family Guy* against those Christian morals and argues that those Christians should not have the power to shape public policy.

Controlling homosexuality does not always happen in the halls of political power. Sometimes it occurs in selected Christian institutions that are further away from the mainstream, such as ex-gay camps that try to "cure" homosexuals. In *South Park*'s episode "Cartman Sucks," Cartman invites Butters for sleepovers and takes embarrassing pictures of him while he is asleep. Cartman takes a picture of himself with Butters' penis in his mouth and claims that that makes Butters gay. The other boys argue the opposite. Mortified, Cartman tries to get a picture of Butters fellating Cartman so as to "cancel out the gay polarity." After convincing a blindfolded Butters to kneel, Cartman is about to put his penis in Butters' mouth when Butters' father bursts through the door. Deciding that Butters is bi-curious, Mr. Stotch takes Butters to Maxi and the priest suggests a camp to cleanse Butters of this "confusion." "A secluded camp where a bunch of bi-curious boys are all put together?" says Mr. Stotch. "That sounds like a good idea." Butters ends up at "Camp New Grace," which has the tagline "Pray the Gay Away." As he is led to his room, the camp director explains that "even though some people would have you believe you can't control how you feel, the truth is that with the power of Jesus Christ you can be normal." Every camper gets an "accountabilabuddy," but Butters' first acountabilabuddy has hanged himself. The director quickly finds another accountabilabuddy, Bradley, who nervously quotes scripture while the director has someone remove the body.

At the camp the boys sing, "The Lord this love is for/With Jesus I can just say no/And not be confused any more" and listen to a sermon from the flamboyant Pastor Philips, whom the director claims was "cured" after he prayed to Jesus (the obvious implication being that Pastor Philips, who acts like a homosexual male stereotype, has not changed). The director even finishes Pastor Philips' sermon with an analogy, saying that the boys are like paper clips and that "God needs to bend you, and shape you, and make you straight," which causes another boy to shoot himself.

Butters is oblivious to the anti-homosexual innuendo. Whenever people ask if he is confused, he responds affirmatively because he does not understand the situation, not because he has sexual feelings. This becomes especially apparent when Bradley starts falling for Butters and when Butters says he likes the boy, Bradley starts panicking that they are both unfixable and runs away. Bradley is found calling himself an abomination and threatening to jump off a bridge. When Butters tries to help him the director calls Butters back, saying he is just confused. Butters retorts, "I am sick and tired of everyone telling me I'm confused! I wasn't confused until other people started telling me I was! You know what I think? I think maybe you're the ones who are confused. [*Bradley says "Yeah."*] I'm not going to be confused any more just because you say I should be. My name is Butters. I'm eight years old, I'm blood type-O, and I'm bi-curious. And even that's OK. Because if I'm bi-curious and I'm somehow made from God, then I figure God must be a little bi-curious himself!" Bradley comes down and Butters goes home.

Christian moral claims to sexual purity and conduct are attacked in these depictions. Christian scripture and conservative theology are portrayed as illegitimate authorities, the tools of bigots who do not acknowledge that homosexuals are "made from God."[38] Camp New Grace references Christian camps that have employed conversion therapy—a discredited theory that certain therapeutic practices can alter one's sexual orientation from homosexual to heterosexual.[39] This theory was widely disseminated by groups that worked under Exodus International's umbrella until the organization's disbanding in 2013 and had caused substantial negative press for the operation.[40] Exodus' disbanding does not mean that such camps have ceased to exist, however, and some still cling to the promise that Jesus can "fix" sexual orientation.[41] Such claims are *South Park*'s target. All three programs present Christian sexual ethics as destructive and homosexuality as an acceptable practice—a presentation that is part of the larger rearranging of the hierarchy of sacred forms and ties into their larger worldview.

Thus far, our examples of dangerous Christians have focused on Protestant Christians who are portrayed as stupid, manipulative, and politically active. To these characteristics we can add hypocrisy as another quality that marks Christians as dangerous in these shows. The Catholic Church's hypocrisy and the magnitude of damage it has wrought in its sexual scandals are satirized in *South Park*. *South Park* not only views Christianity as culturally dangerous, but the program's creators have directly experienced Christian critics—particularly Catholics—as dangerous. The watchdog group the Catholic League for Religious and Civil Rights (Catholic League) was able to have *South Park* censored in 2005 for its blasphemous humor, and *South Park* fought back aggressively.[42] *South Park* has never been shy about mocking Catholics through blasphemy,[43] and from early episodes featuring Jesus and Satan boxing and equating Christians and Nazis in the persecution of homosexuals, to "Do the Handicapped Go to Hell" and its reduction of the Eucharist to eating crackers and drinking wine or else you are going to hell, *South Park* established early on that it would willfully use humor to undermine the Catholic Church's presentation of an unseen order.[44]

When the Catholic Church's sexual abuse scandal broke, *South Park* was there to satirize its reaction. The episode "Red Hot Catholic Love," which aired on July 3, 2002, satirizes the Catholic Church's sexual abuse scandals and draws its humor from having Maxi travel to the Vatican to stop sexual abuse within the church. After attending a local meeting in which the other priests declare, "We have to stop these boys from going to the public" and "having sex with boys is part of the Catholic priest's way of life," Maxi realizes he has to make serious reforms in the church. He travels to the Vatican, where he encounters a senile Pope and a cadre of church officials, the leader of whom declares, "It is not written anywhere in the holy document of Vatican law that sex with boys is wrong."

Maxi preaches in the Vatican's ruins in *South Park*'s "Red Hot Catholic Love"

When Maxi suggests changing the law, he is attacked and evokes further ire when he suggests allowing priests to have heterosexual sex.

After a series of trials, Maxi retrieves the holy document so that it can be changed, but when the Pope suggests going to the highest source in the Catholic Church—a giant spider—Maxi loses his patience. He then delivers one of *South Park*'s "morals" about the church: "You people have completely lost touch with the outside world. You sit in this big room with your Galgamechs [*an alien race that practices Catholicism*] and your giant spider and none of it applies to what being a Catholic is all about." When another priest restates the holy document's instructions, Maxi interrupts him: "To hell with the holy document of Vatican law." Maxi rips the document in half and the church collapses around him.

Amidst the rubble he reminds the priests what being Catholic is about:

> This book [the Bible]. You see, these are just stories. Stories that are meant to help guide people in the right direction, love your neighbor, be a good

person. That's it. And when you start turning the stories into literal translations of hierarchies and power, well, you end up with this. People are losing faith because they don't see how what you've turned the religion into applies to them. They've lost touch with any idea of any kind of religion and when they don't have any kind of mythology to try and live their lives by they just start spewing a bunch of crap out of their mouths.

Maxi concludes by stating that the church needs to change.

In this episode Parker and Stone follow one of satire's basic rules by taking what is popularly presumed to be morally correct—a group of Catholic priests should be protecting the innocent instead of covering up their sexual misconduct, Vatican law should not be used to hide the misconduct, and the church should embrace reforms that will help its public image—and turn it into a satire by emphasizing the ridiculous and scandalous elements of not following appropriate behavior. On the DVD commentary for "Red Hot Catholic Love," Parker and Stone agree that as the scandals in the American church came to light, the Catholic hierarchy mishandled things. Stone makes this point explicit, saying, "I'm glad we did this episode. This is a bummer man. Just, you know what, don't fuck little boys. And if you're going to, don't cover it up. Just admit you're wrong." For Parker and Stone the issue is straightforward: The Catholic Church needs to be ridiculed and told what to do because it has failed, making it worthy of satire.

South Park uses sacralized moral scripts from the broader American culture to diminish Catholic credibility while employing alternative symbols that are deeply embedded in American religious and secular society. *South Park*'s moral script in "Red Hot Catholic Love" classifies children as unavailable for sexual relationships—especially with adults. It seems obvious to Americans that having sex with minors is wrong and this code legitimates attacking those who have sex with minors. *South Park* frames this moral point within established anti-Catholic prejudices that present priests as sexually deviant and the Church hierarchy as inherently conservative, defensive, and dishonest. The Catholic Church is depicted as a cesspool and, while more cases of priestly misconduct come to light, this pattern of treating Catholic priests as sexually deviant has become more common.[45] This attack on the sexual deviance that the bishops concealed shows the ultimate level of Christian danger.

When Catholic priests can sexually abuse children and not have to face criminal trials, *South Park* demonstrates that the institution has transgressed all civil standards and, as such, must be brought back within the program's boundaries for good and normal religious conduct.

Combating Institutional Dangers: Censorship

This discussion of Christianity's dangers returns us to *South Park*'s episode "Bloody Mary" which aired on December 7, 2005. While the Catholics in this episode were not presented as particularly dangerous, especially compared to the Catholics in "Red Hot Catholic Love," the Catholic League for Religious and Civil Rights' (Catholic League) response to this episode's blasphemy is illustrative of the dangers Catholics pose for the three programs in the wider American culture and explains the politics and jokes that are satirized in other episodes. "Bloody Mary" criticizes Alcoholics Anonymous as a religious group that teaches people that they are helplessly addicted to alcohol and only a higher power can save them. When a news story breaks about a Virgin Mary statue that is "bleeding out her ass" people flock to the statue to bathe in the blood and be healed. Stan's alcoholic father, Randy, has his alcoholism cured after bathing in the Virgin's blood.

Rather than offering an extended satirical attack on Catholic icons and statues that start bleeding and the miraculous cures attributed to them, "Bloody Mary" attacks Alcoholics Anonymous. The scatological humor facilitates the episode's overarching message of moderating one's drinking through self-control rather than saying that you are helpless, sick, and turning to a higher power. Randy's healing is presented as the result of a placebo rather than a miracle. Within this framework, popular Catholicism, with its saints, miracles, healing, and suffering,[46] is treated as little more than a foil for *South Park*'s scatological humor. Yet, the Pope is depicted with the Virgin Mary "shitting blood" on him, and the fact that this episode aired on the night of the Feast of the Immaculate Conception was too much for the Catholic League.

The League responded with a strategic plan to have the episode pulled and convinced Joseph A. Califano, a prominent Catholic public servant who served on Viacom's (Comedy Central's corporate parent) board of directors, to pressure the network and have the episode pulled.[47] The strategy was simple: Convince a prominent Catholic on the board of directors to have the network remove the episode and have him publicly show that there is division and disagreement within the Viacom camp over what the company's products are saying. On December 30, 2005, the Catholic League issued a press release stating that the episode had been pulled. That same release also noted that they were receiving hate mail, but they defended their actions, writing, "We exercised our First Amendment right to request that Comedy Central not offend Catholics again!"[48]

Each program has had different Christian groups write to the Federal Communications Commission to demand that episodes and jokes be censored; the programs' creators typically claim that they have the freedom of speech to say what they want. Christian censorship poses a consistent threat in that it raises the specter of Christian critics possibly dictating the rules for discussing religion in the public square, which would strike an institutionally dissonant note with the different programs' core values. The Catholic League's successful censorship of "Bloody Mary" was accomplished through tactics that go beyond free expression and venture into the realm of using unequal power relationships to accomplish the group's aims. The Catholic League threatened to shame someone not involved with the episode's creation in order to execute power over *South Park*, it mobilized like-minded people to write letters, and it used their platform as a recognized Catholic organization to achieve their goal.[49] These events are not *merely* the free expression of opinion that the Catholic League claims they are. The League's actions are power plays within the marketplace, and this case alerts us to the fact that *South Park* and its humor are commodities that can be censored. Internet file sharing ensured that the episode never completely disappeared, but it was temporarily removed from the normal means of distribution and set a precedent for not insulting Catholics again, or so the Catholic League thought.

Comedy Central eventually put "Blood Mary" back into rotation and released it on DVD. On the episode's DVD commentary, Parker and Stone admit that they allowed the episode's re-run to be pulled because it was set to air in late December and management asked them not to replay it and offend Christians at Christmas time. Parker and Stone agreed, but Comedy Central pulled "Bloody Mary" permanently, setting a precedent that they found themselves fighting the next season when every offended religious group wanted episodes retired. They did not, however, attempt to justify this attack on Catholicism and Parker and Stone admitted that they understood why Catholics would be offended. Instead, they were upset that they were tricked by the network rather than by Catholic League president Bill Donahue and Califano. Removing the episode from regular rotation harmed their image as equal opportunity offenders and gave the Catholic League recognition Parker and Stone do not think it deserves. In the commentary to the later episode "Fantastic Easter Special," they caricature the Catholic League's president Bill Donahue as a talking head that networks use to portray a negative Catholic reaction to media, implying that he is a fringe voice. In "Fantastic Easter Special" Donahue is presented as a fundamentalist who refuses to listen to Jesus when Christ appears in the Vatican and tells the world that he intended for the Popes to all be rabbits. While Pope Benedict XVI is willing to listen to Jesus, Donahue refuses, declares himself Pope, and eventually Jesus kills Donahue with a five-bladed throwing star.

South Park took rhetorical revenge upon Donahue, but "Bloody Mary's" censorship is important because it started a chain reaction of other religions requesting that episodes be pulled from the rotation, which started *South Park's* tenth season fighting Scientologists and Muslim groups who wanted other episodes censored. The Catholic League, as self-proclaimed representatives of the largest Christian denomination in the United States, revealed the dangers competing unseen orders hold for *South Park* (and *The Simpsons* and *Family Guy*). With a substantial history of humorous blasphemy, satirical criticism, and censorship in the dance between all three programs and Christian groups, it behooves us to ask what the incidents in question can teach us about the politics of humor and why certain groups are satirized as dangerous in these programs.

Humor and the Social Construction of Sacredness in the Contemporary United States

As we have seen, *The Simpsons, South Park,* and *Family Guy* have satirized what they have seen as Christianity's dangerous qualities. In order to understand those qualities we need to not only understand how the programs satirize the way Christians live within their unseen orders and try to convince others to adopt their religious worldviews. We also have to draw upon broader civic themes in the United States to understand why these Christian activities are classified as dangerous. These series rely on the "freedom of speech" script's sacredness as justification for publicly criticizing and blaspheming different Christian groups. For the satirists behind these programs, freedom of speech has to be defended as a sacred right. When Christians attempt to censor them, it allows the program's creators the opportunity to position themselves as sacred defenders of the civil religious faith. This position is useful for these programs because it justifies their satire and strengthens their claim that their humor is "equal opportunity," not biased or hateful, and part of a general skewering of religion's role in American public life.

Based in the First Amendment, the "freedom of speech" script transmits significant symbolic information about what it means to be American and is tied to the individual's pursuits at the core of *The Simpsons* and *Family Guy* and permits the unregulated creativity *South Park* values. Within this framework a true American always protects a person's ability to speak freely—no matter their opinion or what is said. *South Park* works hard to maintain its reputation as an "equal opportunity offender," which allows Parker and Stone a substantial amount of leeway in putting forth criticisms that offend different groups. When a group like the Catholic League tries to censor them, they can cast themselves as rebels who offended a powerful religious group that refuses to see the light. In the process, they defend the American way of life, showing us who is good and evil in American civil life. *South Park* becomes more than entertainment through this struggle, it becomes part of the larger debate about who gets to define the public agenda for discussing religion. Satirizing Christians for censorship, promoting sexual ethics that restrict sexual behaviors (especially homosexuality), and for spreading their unseen orders through missionary work communicates to viewers that the people who engage in these behaviors are not to be trusted in civil life.

The power to define how a civil value is interpreted will always be contested. In "Bloody Mary's" case, the Catholic League's counterattack was based on the argument that *South Park* did not actually adhere to the freedom of speech script. According to the Catholic League, instead of speaking courageously and showing freedom of speech's importance, *South Park* used it to regurgitate old prejudices against the Church in America.[50] The League combined this anti-Catholic label with another important cultural script based in the First Amendment, the freedom of religion script. Under this script the Catholic League is free to publicly voice its ideals. When combined with contemporary politics of recognition, the Catholic League takes this to mean not only that it may speak, but that it should expect to be free from insults against its religious identity, as demonstrated by its repeated cries that Catholics not be publicly slandered, insulted, misrepresented, or satirized.[51] While this is wishful thinking on any group's part, freedom of speech provides a political legitimation to the Catholic League's claim that *South Park*'s perspective is bigotry rather than criticism.[52]

When we consider that each example we have considered in this chapter—from ex-gay ministries to missionary work to covering up child sexual abuse—is supported by people who consider these activities an essential part of their adhering to an unseen order, we can see that having the power to interpret the freedoms in the First Amendment is at stake. If freedom of speech and freedom of religion are intertwined into the ability to set the agenda for the public understanding of religion, this bestows the power to exclude voices as dangerous for any reason. This power is an extremely valuable asset for the different groups who are competing to set the public agenda for interpreting religion. For example, if freedom of speech and freedom of religion mean that only the Catholic League gets to set the agenda for how Catholics are understood in the public sphere, then the Catholic League has the power to silence voices that disagree with its agenda. At stake in this discussion of dangerous Christians is the question of whose unseen orders can legitimately set the agenda for publicly discussing religious peoples' actions and their social impacts.

What, then, are we to make of "Bloody Mary"? In light of our discussion about how Christianities are presented as dangerous, we should recognize that profaning Catholic symbols, institutions, and rituals exposes the social construction of their sacredness. As social constructions they are more easily identified as human, rather than divine, creations. Such recognition deprives them of their sacredness. Miracle healing from a saint's statue joins with other examples such as faith healings, missionaries withholding food in exchange for religious conversion, purity culture, and ex-gay ministries. All of these examples come to be seen as historically contingent actions by humans instead of God's will. In *The Simpsons'*, *South Park's*, and *Family Guy's* worlds people can choose to follow these teachings, but that does not mean that they are free from criticism. Nor does it mean that Christians get to set the agenda for how they are interpreted. The power struggles over defining good religious practice, especially when that practice leads to the enforcement of standards of belief and practice on other people, mark the moral boundaries between these programs and Christian groups. The satires we have explored in this chapter speak directly to the importance of discussing religion in American civil life through popular culture, as they present us with pictures of which groups they think their audiences should mistrust and explanations for why we should suspect them.

The politics of religious humor in these three programs exist to facilitate religious criticism and further free speech's sacralization. Humor is not always benevolent; it can be used to criticize religion, and it can both facilitate discrimination and present prejudice in such a way that humorists can argue that their reasons for opposing certain groups and practices are for the greater good. These criticisms of Christian missions, their incorporation into American consumerism and sexual politics, and their threat to freedom of speech set the stage for a final discussion of what makes religion dangerous and how *The Simpsons'*, *South Park's*, and *Family Guy's* humor attacks other religious groups they see as dangerous while protecting their own moral orders.

5

Stigma, Stupidity, and Exclusion

"Cults" and Muslims

Springfield has been overrun by a strange and almost certainly evil sect calling themselves the Movementarians. In
exchange for your home and all your money, the leader of
this way out and wrong religion claims he'll take believers
away on his spaceship to the planet Blisstonia. Excuse my
editorial laugh: Ha, ha, ha.
—Kent Brockman, news anchor in *The Simpsons'* "The Joy
of Sect"

In *The Simpsons* episode "The Joy of Sect," Brockman's statement that
Springfield has been overrun by a strange and evil sect highlights the
way in which certain religions are stigmatized as cults. The "cult" stereotype is often taken for granted as accurately portraying troublesome
religious collectives. It allows for the persistent demonization of different groups, in this case, the caricatured "Movementarians." All three
programs also feature episodes with Muslim terrorists—depicted as men
with brown skin, yelling in Arabic, and threatening to indiscriminately
kill Americans. This is a stereotype North American Muslims have been
combating for decades, but it has gained even more traction since 9/11.
Stigmas do not apply to all groups equally. In each case the shows draw
on their core worldviews to assess and characterize new religious movements (NRMs) and Muslims. How do the different programs use humor
to stigmatize out-groups and, in turn, sacralize their core values? And
under what conditions can members of these stigmatized religions be
redeemed within the programs' moral universes?

NRMs are often pejoratively labeled cults. *The Simpsons, South Park,*
and *Family Guy* have portrayed a variety of specific NRMs and also feature generic "cult" stereotypes. As we meet contemporary Neopagans, Sci-

entologists, and a variety of Christian minority movements in these series, it is useful to ask why they are popularly lumped into the same "cult" category. How does ignorant familiarity with these different groups work to allow them to be consolidated into the same stereotyped category?

The Cult Stereotype

Brockman's editorial echoes a number of "real world" television news broadcasts that negatively portray NRMs, reflecting deeply rooted prejudices against new religious movements in the United States. In 1988, sociologists Barend van Driel and James Richardson identified the most common negative motifs used in "cult" reporting between 1972 and 1984: confining members or depriving them of personal freedoms; charismatic leadership; extreme authoritarianism and discipline; behavioral control using psychological manipulation or brainwashing; a preoccupation with the leaders' wealth and luxury; the group's portrayal of the outside world as evil and something to be feared; and apocalyptic beliefs.[1] This list contains the essential elements of a stereotype. The media often draw upon these ignorant familiarities in explaining NRMs to consumers who have little, if any, contact with these groups.[2] The cult stereotype's motifs are interwoven to disparage marginal religious groups, helping to maintain established moral boundaries for how religious groups should comport themselves.

The cult stereotype did not arise from nothing. There have always been religious groups that have drawn the ire and suspicion of their more prominent neighbors. Indeed, today's established and respected religions were once stigmatized. For example, the label "cult" has been applied to the Methodist and Catholic churches in other times. Throughout American history, marginal religious groups have been effectively attacked and stigmatized as cults, generating considerable fear and inspiring social retaliation. As long as there have been new religions there have been critics.[3] While the United States has a history of fostering new religions, these groups are typically small, and if they attract attention it is often accompanied by vitriol, harassment, false accusations, and attempts to end the groups through theological and state means.[4]

The Simpsons, *South Park*, and *Family Guy* all contain stereotypes that became codified around assaults upon different religions that arose after the 1950s and became especially prominent from the 1970s through the 1990s. Ignorant familiarity about cults in the modern era does not emphasize their theological differences with mainstream religions so much as it stresses dangerous social behaviors such as brainwashing, fraud, holding people against their will, and violence.[5] These ideological narratives dialectically received legitimation from and endorsed the political actions of the secular anti-cult movement (ACM), which provided journalists with expert advice.[6]

The ACM focused on fund-raising, mind control, and charismatic leadership in NRMs, which is believed to eventually lead to violence. These characteristics of NRMs became mass media's framework for reporting on these groups, and there is a direct correlation between anti-cult ideologies and media accounts of NRMs' beliefs and practices. This ideological spectrum legitimates certain religions as "authentic," "real," and/or "valid." How a religion is classified along certain cultural standards that editors, reporters, and audiences take for granted determines how it will be reported to the general populace, and NRMs are disadvantaged from the start as stigma frames the public's initial exposure to them. They are not "newsworthy" unless they draw the attention of civil authorities.[7] News reporters have built a stereotype of cults that feeds into the ACM's agenda, compounds ignorant familiarity among the general populace with regard to the different groups, and legitimates established authority structures by reducing complexity and relying on abnormal behavior to frame their stories. Richardson and van Driel argue that this is dangerous because, although these stories sell newspapers, they also discredit the idea of newsmakers as "fair and balanced" and harm civil liberties.[8] In reducing all NRMs to the status of cult, mass media has helped to marginalize these groups, a pattern that crosses both news and entertainment media.[9] Van Driel and Richardson's components of a cult stereotype: confining members or depriving them of personal freedoms; charismatic leadership; extreme authoritarianism and discipline; behavioral control using psychological manipulation or brainwashing; a preoccupation with the leaders' wealth and luxury; the group's portrayal of the outside world as evil and something to be feared; and apocalyptic beliefs, provide a model that can be effectively implemented to analyze the stereotype's usage in comedy programs as well as news media.[10] Through an analysis of various episodes we can see how the different shows use this stereotype and its accompanying ignorant familiarity to make their cases.

The NRM Spectrum

Accepted NRMs

The Simpsons, South Park, and *Family Guy* rarely treat NRMs positively, though *The Simpsons'* treatment of Wicca represents an exception. *The Simpsons* supports Wicca's feminist politics and creative spirituality, with the most explicit discussion coming in its episode "Rednecks and Broomsticks," in which Lisa is invited to join a coven comprised of three teenage girls. At first Lisa is skeptical because she does not believe in magic. However, when Lisa benefits from her teacher mysteriously falling ill, she decides that there may be more to the religion than she first suspected. After researching the basics on "Wiccapedia," and learning that Wiccans worship nature, Lisa decides to convert. Unfortunately, when she approaches the circle and is about to be initiated, the local police arrest the girls for practicing witchcraft.

Before the trial the girls ask the goddess Lilith to show their persecutors their blindness and, subsequently, citizens start going blind. The girls are tried in court for causing the townspeople's suffering, but the judge finds them innocent. Angered, the people form a mob and take the girls outside, where the mayor says they can persecute the witches under seventeenth-century law. Just before they are to be executed, Lisa reveals the real reason behind the townspeople's suffering: Local hillbillies poured moonshine into the town's water supply, causing temporary blindness. The crowd disperses and Marge tells the Wiccans she thinks they are interesting before ending Lisa's membership in the coven.

This positive portrayal draws on Wicca's reputation as an open and welcoming feminist religion. As we have seen, *The Simpsons* generally favors religious traditions that uphold American individualism and liberal values. Creator Matt Groening has stated that his goal is "to entertain and subvert."[11] Wicca's feminist associations makes it an ideal religion for *The Simpsons* to portray positively because it can be used to support its political position, implicitly attacking other religions that have been criticized for not allowing women's full participation (e.g., Christianity).[12] That "Rednecks and Broomsticks" also includes jokes satirizing witches' treatment throughout American history indicates a greater acceptance of contemporary witchcraft and its practitioners at their critics' expense. While Wiccans have to contend with accusations that they are Satanists, *The Simpsons* defends them as nature loving, pro-woman, and empowering.[13] Their portrayal in "Rednecks and Broom-sticks" introduces such rituals as the esbat (a rite for the new moon) and entering the circle for initiation. These depictions legitimate Wicca, even as the show adds ironic touches such as having music for Lisa's woodland initiation ceremony playing on a stereo-docked "MyPod," and the witches sneaking away in "a manner most Wiccan" by contacting a parent for a drive via cellular phone. These gentle jabs at Wiccan nature worship make Wicca appear both different and familiar, with benign intentions and avoiding the fears sedimented in van Driel and Richard-son's stereotype.

Annoying NRMs

While some NRMs are thus accepted for their political positions, others are presented as obnoxious and strange, but otherwise benign. Jeho-vah's Witnesses are a good example.[14] As a nineteenth-century NRM, they may not immediately come to mind as "new," but they do bear the mantle of being misunderstood and stigmatized for their mission-ary efforts. *The Simpsons* has used Jehovah's Witnesses occasionally for humorous effect. In the episode "Marge Gets a Job," Marge admits, "My life is pretty boring. Last week some Jehovah's Witnesses came to the door and I wouldn't let them leave. They snuck away when I went in the kitchen to get more lemonade." This is an ironic twist on the common perception of Jehovah's Witnesses as annoying and overzealous in their missionizing, a sentiment that is made apparent in an episode entitled "Maximum Homerdrive." While Marge and Lisa wait for somebody to come and ring their new doorbell, they notice two Jehovah's Witnesses walking up their driveway. Just as they are about to ring the doorbell they stop and talk to each other:

NOREEN
Wait Marlin. You know, I just had a thought. Maybe we're bothering people by trying to change their religion. What if we don't have all the answers?

MARLIN
You're right Noreen. Let's go get real jobs.

They then discard their tracts while Marge sighs, "I would have feigned interest." This joke assumes that viewers are familiar with Jehovah's Witnesses and that their efforts are seen as bothersome and unwanted. However, there is no suggestion that the Witnesses are trying to circumvent social norms or deviously force social change. They only exist as time-wasting nuisances. This places them below Wicca, but appreciatively above other groups, without displaying the dangerous elements encoded in the cult stereotype.

Family Guy makes similar jokes about the Jehovah's Witnesses. In the pilot episode "Death Has a Shadow," an African American woman offers the family some pancakes after the Griffins claim that the Bradys from *The Brady Bunch* lived in a bad neighborhood. Peter declines her offer and then says, "See, that's the worst we got is Jemima's Witnesses." Furthermore, in "The Father, the Son, and the Holy Fonz," when Peter is experimenting with different religions he joins the Jehovah's Witnesses, but he cannot remember their teachings about Jesus when going door-to-door. *Family Guy* even gives the Witnesses a bit of credit when the evil monkey who lives in Chris' closet and has been terrorizing him becomes good after converting.[15] These treatments are relatively benign because the Witnesses do not harm anybody and they are not financial or cultural threats, nor are their beliefs explored in any depth. They are simply perceived as annoying and that is sufficient to make jokes about them. That said, another group that is known for its missionary efforts—the Latter Day Saints (the Mormons)—are given a more extensive treatment in *South Park*.

Misguided NRMs

South Park's episode "All About Mormons" tells the story of the LDS' origins after a Mormon family, the Harrisons, moves to South Park and one of the boys, Gary, befriends Stan.[16] Sociologist of religion Douglas Cowan analyzes this episode in greater detail, but the salient point about South Park's presentation is that it tells Joseph Smith's story about discovering the golden plates containing what would later become *The Book of Mormon*, how he translated them with the seer stones in a hat while Martin Harris recorded what Smith read, and how nobody else ever saw the plates.[17] Smith's story is told in such a way that it is presented as fallacious. After hearing how Lucy Harris, Martin Harris' wife, hid the first translations from the plate of Lehi, and that Smith had to translate from the plate of Nephi, Stan is outraged. While the Harrisons insist that the story is all a matter of faith, Stan objects, saying it is a matter of logic: "If you're going to say things that have been proven wrong, like that the first man and woman lived in Missouri, and that Native Americans came from Jerusalem, then you better have something to back it up. All you've got are a bunch of stories about some ass-wipe who read plates nobody ever saw out of a hat, and then couldn't do it again when the translations were hidden."

South Park thus portrays the church's foundational narrative as a lie. Smith made the whole thing up. Choosing to believe in *The Book of Mormon* and the social structures that have been built upon Smith's prophecies is depicted as an exercise in willful ignorance.

While *South Park*'s portrayal presents the Mormons as theologically misguided, they are shown to be otherwise benign. The Harrisons are depicted as ideal neighbors. Stan and his father Randy are attracted to them because they are so close and happy. They enjoy each other's company and never fight, unlike the other families in *South Park*, which are constantly disrupted by domestic tensions. Indeed, the episode's moral message is not Stan's argument for logical critique, but Gary's monologue at the episode's conclusion:

Look, maybe us Mormons do believe in crazy stories that make absolutely no sense, and maybe Joseph Smith did make it all up, but I have a great life and a great family, and I have the Book of Mormon to thank for that. The truth is, I don't care if Joseph Smith made it all up, because what the church teaches now is loving your family, being nice, and helping people. And even though people in this town might think that's stupid, I still choose to believe in it. All I ever did was try to be your friend, Stan, but you're so high and mighty you couldn't look past my religion and just be my friend back. You got a lot of growing up to do, buddy. Suck my balls.

Gary's speech offers the Mormons a moral escape that is consistent with *South Park*'s core values of individual freedom and creativity without impinging on others. While he concedes that perhaps the religion's theological foundations lack logical support, what matters is that his life is good because he is a Mormon. The religion has strong ethical motivations for its practitioners—stronger than anything South Park's residents have. Furthermore, he is not judgmental, accepting Stan's differences in belief while still befriending him. Hence, South Park's treatment of the Mormons presents the LDS as misguided, but while the religion may be a pack of lies, those lies lead to something that is worth having in the world. Parker has reflected that Mormons are so nice that if any religion is going to rule the world, it should be them, saying, "Even if it's all bullshit, that's ok."[18]

Untrustworthy NRMs

While the Mormons' misguided religion is portrayed as nevertheless valuable because it leads to ethical behavior, other NRMs are presented as both misguided and untrustworthy. For South Park the most untrustworthy NRM is Scientology, which it famously lampooned in the episode "Trapped in the Closet." In The Simpsons, the Freemasons receive similar treatment in an episode entitled "Homer the Great."

"Trapped in the Closet" engendered a number of protests from celebrity Scientologists. Tom Cruise threatened to not promote Mission Impossible III for Paramount Pictures, which is owned by Viacom. Furthermore, long-time cast member Isaac Hayes quit, claiming religious prejudice. In this episode, Stan attends a Scientology session where he is given a free personality test and told that he is depressed. He returns the next day to receive audit counseling and registers the highest scores in the Church of Scientology's history. From these results the Scientologists discern that he is the reincarnation of Scientology's founder, L. Ron Hubbard, and they recruit him to write new scriptures for the group.

To facilitate Stan's writing, Scientology's president tells him the group's creation stories from the "Operating Thetan Level III" documents. These are highly guarded Scientology documents that explain how the galactic overlord Xenu solved his overpopulation problem 75 billion years ago by freezing aliens, dropping them into the volcanoes of Hawaii, and detonating them with H-bombs. He then trapped the alien souls and had them brainwashed before being released to wander

Scene from the Xenu myth in *South Park*'s "Trapped in the Closet"

the earth. At the dawn of humanity the alien souls attached themselves to our ancestors, becoming "thetans," which are the cause of everything negative in our lives. When *South Park* reiterates this story, it is captioned with "This is What Scientologists Actually Believe."[19]

Yet, the beliefs are not the most important thing for *South Park*. Instead, when Stan starts writing new doctrines, he develops a controversial one: Scientologists no longer have to pay for services. Scientology's president is furious and he tells Stan that Scientology is a global scam that will make both of them rich if Stan maintains the charade of being Hubbard's reincarnation. Stan cannot; he denounces Scientology, and all the Scientologists threaten to sue him for insulting their religion.[20] This episode reflects Parker and Stone's general disdain for Scientology— Parker later asserted that Scientologists are "all fucked up."[21]

Scientology's untrustworthiness is depicted in its charging people for what *South Park* considers lies. Its *religiousness* is questioned because of the costs involved in progressing through the ranks. This is not an original critique.[22] Intellectuals in the anti-cult movement have accused NRM leaders of defrauding members for years, the assumption being that converts are too ignorant or brainwashed to realize they were being swindled. In this view, Hubbard's greed has led Scientology to become irreversibly corrupted. This popular perception provides *South Park* with fruitful material for its satire.

Similarly, *The Simpsons* attacks Freemasonry in "Homer the Great." In this episode Homer joins "The Stonecutters," an "ancient mystical society" that controls business and government. After undergoing initiation rituals in which he is pushed off a step while blindfolded, paddled by other members, and swears an oath, he is welcomed into the society and everybody spends their time getting drunk and using their connections to manipulate society to their benefit. Ultimately, Homer becomes the group's leader and tries to take them in an ethical direction. Instead of getting drunk and being corrupt, he has the Stonecutters help ordinary citizens by running a day care and painting over graffiti. The Stonecutters revolt and leave to form a new ancient mystical society: No Homers.

Like the Jehovah's Witnesses and Mormons, the Freemasons are not new. Some may even question whether they are a fraternal society or a religious movement, but the religious nature of their rituals and their mythology linking back to Hiram, the architect they claim built Solomon's temple, affords us enough material to analyze them as religious. Indeed, the history of anti-Masonic prejudice and public suspicions of Masonic control over the U.S. government has been couched in religious concerns and ideas about what is normative.[23] Masons have been treated as untrustworthy since the early nineteenth century. *The Simpsons* selects from fragments of popular conspiracies to make its jokes work. This ignorant familiarity reinforces common prejudices and Freemasons remain categorized as untrustworthy.

Dangerous NRMs

Popular fears regarding NRMs relate to concerns about brainwashing and violence. Many believe that NRMs are not only out to defraud people, but they also steal their identities and abilities to think freely through devious psychological methods commonly known as "brainwashing."[24] Moreover, after the tragic mass murders/suicides of Peoples Temple members at Jonestown in 1978, anti-cult activists started to claim that charismatic leaders were not just stealing people's free thoughts and property, but would also lead them to unspeakable acts of violence against themselves or others.[25] This narrative influenced the FBI's decisions confronting the Branch Davidian group in Waco, Texas in 1993, leading to a conflagration that killed seventy-four people.[26] Drawing on these popular fears, brainwashers and violent NRMs have been used for comic effect in animated comedies.

Both *The Simpsons* and *South Park* have employed a generic cult stereotype that plays on concerns about mind control. In *The Simpsons* it is "The Movementarians" from "The Joy of Sect" episode; in *South Park*, it is "The Blainetologists" from the episode "Super Best Friends." There is a great deal to be learned from the parallels in these two episodes. "The Joy of Sect" starts with Homer and Bart walking through the local airport, where different religious groups promote themselves. After passing a member of the International Society for Krishna Consciousness (ISKCON, "Hare Krishna") and a Christian, they meet the Movementarians, whose offer of a free weekend event at their agricultural compound entices Homer. While attending the weekend he is shown a recruitment film, exposed to public ridicule, fed low-protein gruel, resists a "droning, repetitive chant" of "The Leader is good, The Leader is great. We surrender our will as of this date," and is eventually won over by a revised version of the *Batman* theme song. He then gives the Movementarians the deed to the Simpson house and moves his entire family to the agricultural compound, where they pick lima beans in the fields and attend a mass marriage ceremony. Bart is brainwashed at the compound. Everybody wears the same style of robes, demonstrating their loss of individuality. Eventually, Marge escapes and gets Reverend Lovejoy, the school groundskeeper Willie, and Ned to help her kidnap her family and deprogram them. This works on the children, but before Homer can be deconverted, the Movementarians' lawyers break into Flanders' house and extract Homer, returning him to the Movementarian compound. There Homer throws open the doors to the "forbidden barn," revealing a spaceship, which takes off. Everybody thinks they are doomed until the spaceship falls apart, revealing the Movementarians' leader on a helicopter bicycle with bags of money attached to it. He crashes into a nearby farm and the people return home dejected to gather in front of another bastion of brainwashing—FOX television (*The Simpsons'* home network).

"Super Best Friends" starts with magician David Blaine arriving in South Park, where he performs magic tricks on a street corner. Wowing the audience with his abilities, his followers—the Blainetologists—start distributing pamphlets inviting people to the Center for Magic, where they are taught about David Blaine as "a scholar, a visionary, a leader" and refer to his magic tricks as "miracles." Instead of teaching people magic, recruits are told that they are unhappy and that their parents and friends have programmed them to feel isolated. Only by reading from David Blaine's book *Teachings* will they find happiness. This desire for happiness resonates with Stan, Kyle, and Cartman and they join Blainetology by attending "magic camp" for $69.95. The boys have their heads shaved, dress the same, and are sent out to recruit new people to come see Blaine. Stan suspects something is wrong, but is pressured to stay. He sneaks out at night, but Kyle stays behind and their friendship falls apart over the new religion. Stan then goes to see Jesus for help and Christianity's founding figure agrees to assist him. Blaine's miracles, however, are more enticing than Jesus', and people start joining Blainetology. The religion grows so fast that it seems the government will soon have to grant them 501(c)(3) tax-exempt status. Yet, when it turns out that they will be denied tax-exempt status, Blaine sends his followers to Washington to drown themselves in the Reflecting Pool. Only when Jesus bands together with Lao Tzu, the Buddha, Joseph Smith, Krishna, Muhammad, Moses, and Seaman (forming the Super Best Friends) can he fight Blaine's magic. Blaine brings the Lincoln Memorial to life and it starts terrorizing Washington until the Super Best Friends create a giant John Wilkes Booth. Once the terror has been subdued, Blaine escapes and his remaining followers return to their old lives after Stan tells them that any religion requiring people to pay money is wrong (which is the same message he delivered to the Scientologists at the end of the episode "Trapped in the Closet").

Both of these episodes make quick references—both visually and verbally—to famous NRMs and reinforce these associations with negative sentiments embedded in the cult stereotype. The actions the Movementarians and Blainetologists undertake are directly linked to fearsome stories about specific groups that have circulated since the 1970s. The Holy Spirit Association for the Unification of World Christianity (The Unification Church, "The Moonies"), The Children of God (now The Family International), ISKCON, and other groups have been accused of forcefully detaining recruits and using brainwashing. Stories persist about how these groups would trick people into coming to a meeting and, once they were there, would deprive them of sleep and nourishment, using psychological manipulation such as "love-bombing"—a practice whereby Unificationists would inundate a potential convert with positive reinforcement—to bring unsuspecting victims into the fold. Ostensibly, NRMs have a series of tactics that enable them to convert anybody by controlling their behaviors, breaking down old beliefs, and instilling new ones.[27] Yet, sociological studies of actual conversion processes show that converting to a NRM or any other religion is a complex, multi-stage process in which people actively choose to believe and practice their new religion.[28] The oversimplification of the conversion process in these episodes is a reduction for comedic purposes that reinforces the negative assumption that groups have power to deceive a potential convert.

Charismatic leadership, one of the negative characteristics of cults that has been identified by van Driel and Richardson, is often related to another motif, a focus on the leader's wealth and luxury. In *The Simpsons* and *South Park* both the Movementarians and the Blainetologists are led by a charismatic figure. "The Leader" of the Movementarians, a visual caricature of L. Ron Hubbard, is constantly in the background of "The Joy of Sect" and appears at the end of the episode exposed as a fraud. *South Park* also explicitly references popular notions of Hubbard as a fraud in their portrayal of David Blaine as a false miracle worker, scholar, visionary, and prophet. The Blainetologists' language echoes the way Scientologists describe Hubbard, enabling viewers to link Blaine and Hubbard. Even if viewers are unfamiliar with Scientology, they learn that there are frauds whose followers present them as prophets and that one should be suspicious of such figures and their followers.

Bhagwan Shree Rajneesh, an Indian guru who practiced "crazy wisdom" and founded a community at Rajneeshpuram in Oregon, was another controversial leader whom *The Simpsons'* "The Joy of Sect" references. The episode depicts the disparity between the Leader and his followers by having him drive by in a Rolls Royce while the Movementarians harvest lima beans in the fields. This scene parodies Rajneesh, who was notorious for collecting Rolls Royces (he had ninety-three) while Rajneeshpuram's residents did not share this luxury.[29] Even if viewers are unfamiliar with Rajneeshpuram's history, the image of a "cult" leader who has amassed wealth through duplicitous means is constantly reinforced through scenes such as this one. *South Park's* "Super Best Friends," like "Trapped in the Closet," reinforces the dangers of NRMs asking for your money when Stan tells the despondent Blainetologists that the danger in cults lies in the fact that they exchange teaching for money. Because Blainetology and Scientology both end in "-tology," are founded by charismatic individuals who are both portrayed in *South Park's* universe as greedy frauds, and are both subject to speeches about how "real religions" do not take your money, it is easy to see that popular satirizing of Scientology makes for a straightforward contribution to the sedimented stereotype, since treating Blainetology as a parody of Scientology is a logical choice.

As van Driel and Richardson demonstrate, another characteristic attributed to so-called cults is apocalyptic beliefs. Related to fears of brainwashing and control over members is the fear that these members will suddenly become violent. Frequently, this fear of violence is associated with millennialism—"hope for collective earthly or heavenly salvation."[30] Religion scholar Catherine Wessinger identifies two major forms of millennialism: catastrophic millennialism in which the end of the world arrives and sinners are punished while a chosen remnant remains to enjoy the new world which will replace this one, and progressive millennialism in which humans work toward the goals that supernatural beings (i.e., gods, extraterrestrials) put before them, leading the way to a utopian tomorrow.[31] *The Simpsons'* "The Joy of Sect" episode spoofs the progressive millennialism of such UFO groups as the Unarians, whose leader, Uriel (d. 1993), predicted that thirty-three spaceships would come to the earth in 2001 and usher in a new era of human learning; or the Raëlians, who are trying to build a welcome center in Israel for the Elohim (who are seen as benevolent extraterrestrials and not as gods) and usher in a new era of peace.[32] For both groups, extraterrestrials are believed to contact us through channels whose charisma must be constantly maintained. In order for Uriel and Raël to maintain their status as prophets they have/had to continue giving messages and insights from the extraterrestrials. For believers, this appears as spiritual revelation. For outsiders such as *The Simpsons'* creators, this appears to be incredulous and ridiculous.

The Simpsons portrays the Movementarians as working toward an interplanetary migration to Blisstonia (which is "known for its high levels of bliss"), but it inverts the common pattern within UFO religions of a prophet receiving extraterrestrial contact leading to prophecies about how to improve life on Earth. *The Simpsons'* creative team uses general beliefs about UFOs, other planets, and the idea that aliens will provide us with salvation and shifts the focus to the charismatic leader. While the Movementarians apparently have apocalyptic beliefs about a better life on the planet Blisstonia, it is The Leader who will take them there on his spaceship. The humor and criticism in this depiction is directed at The Leader and the fact that gullible people believe him. The spaceship to Blisstonia is just a charade meant to help The Leader to extort Springfielders. This scene reaffirms the "cult" stereotype's assumptions that charismatic leaders' wealth and luxury reflect negatively on their religions as a whole.

Progressive millennialism, however, is not what is commonly associated with apocalyptic beliefs and cults. Catastrophic millennialism is more common in the popular imagination. In *South Park*'s episode "Super Best Friends," the fears of brainwashing and self-inflicted violence coalesce when David Blaine tells his followers to kill themselves so the group can achieve tax-exempt status. Recalling mass suicides by Peoples Temple, Heaven's Gate, and the Solar Temple—events that became symbolic of the dangerous extremes to which cults will go and the reason why they must be stopped—the Blainetologists' deaths in the reflecting pool are for naught.

Even though the reasons why members of groups such as Peoples Temple, Heaven's Gate, and the Solar Temple committed suicide are available, these explanations are not explored in this episode. Cult members are instead presented as delusional. Violent NRMs raise institutional dissonance with *South Park*'s core value of individual creativity, and the program resolves these tensions by reinforcing the idea that the followers are stupid and leaders are evil. Building on the lasting images of the Peoples Temple's members' deaths at Jonestown in 1978, "Super Best Friends" references the Peoples Temple's legacy—the idea that cult members will pointlessly kill themselves and others.[33]

The more explicit use of the violent cult stereotype comes in *Family Guy*'s episode "Chitty, Chitty, Death Bang." Parodying the 1997 Heaven's Gate mass suicides, *Family Guy* introduces us to the "Heaven's Helpers Youth Cult." Meg attends a party hosted by this group consisting of

Mass suicide in *South Park*'s "Super Best Friends"

teenagers who all wear the same blue jumpsuit, share the same blank stare, and live in a mansion with their white-haired leader (modeled on Heaven's Gate leader Marshall Herf Applewhite). The boys are castrated and there is a clock that is counting down the "Time Until Transformation," but otherwise none of the group's beliefs are known. While it is true that some Heaven's Gate members voluntarily castrated themselves, this hardly encompasses the breadth of the group's beliefs.[34] However, rather than trying to unravel or parody the beliefs of this complicated group and explain their mass suicide in a way that reflects their heartfelt belief that they were transcending their bodies to the level beyond human, *Family Guy* uses a generic reason for Meg joining the group (and by extension, anybody who affiliates with an NRM)— they feel like outcasts:

LEADER
Do you have a mind that seeks enlightenment and a heart that seeks purity?

MEG
Well, not really.

LEADER
OK. Are you a confused adolescent desperately seeking acceptance from an undifferentiated ego mass that demands conformity?

MEG
Wow, that sort of sounds more like me.

LEADER
Great! Well then all you need is a dark blue jogging suit.

When the leader leaves to get Meg's jumpsuit, the Heaven's Helpers members prepare a poisonous cocktail and consume it before he returns. When the leader sees them dead, he groans, "Oh for the love of God! Haven't any of you ever been in a cult before?" in frustration because the members killed themselves before they were supposed to. The leader then goes off to find Meg, who has gone home with Peter, because if the leader were to "achieve transcendence" alone he would appear crazy.

In *Family Guy*'s brief use of the dangerous cult stereotype, the teenagers in the group are stupid enough to mix a poisonous cocktail and then drink it, while the leader is aware that he is leading them to their deaths. The Heaven's Gate suicides were also explained by invoking the idea of a dangerous and manipulative cult leader and stupid followers. A closer examination of the group's doctrines, however, uncovers a twenty-year history of trying to master the body and find ways to transcend the flesh. While extreme, ending this life to transcend to the next level was plausible to the group's members. Ridiculing the group after their suicides reinforces the assumption that these people were crazy or brainwashed, and were, therefore, legitimate victims; this does not bring us any closer to understanding the groups.[35] It does, however, reinforce *Family Guy*'s core value that religions are dangerous and should be avoided.

Unlike Scientologists in *South Park* who do not brainwash people (they only lie, cheat, and steal), the Movementarians, Blainetologists, and Heaven's Helpers are seen as dangerous groups because they take away people's wills. The difference lies in the way a person's agency is understood. *South Park* portrays Scientologists and Mormons as willfully stupid. However, they are (ostensibly) free to choose Scientology, LDS, or some other religion. The Movementarians and Blainetologists are portrayed as brainwashing, as taking choice away from people. The anti-cult movement made the same accusations of such groups as The Family International, the Unification Church, and Peoples Temple. American culture prizes self-reliance and individual agency, and as we have seen, all three programs treat the removal of free will as a serious crime against a person's humanity. Such an act marks a group, and especially its leader, as a threat to society.

In *The Simpsons* we see that the core of individual spirituality is preserved, but any sense of submitting to a regimented unseen order is ridiculed in order to protect the program's plausibility structure. The religions that are not as stigmatized—for example, the LDS—are presented more positively, especially by *South Park*, which values individual creativity provided that the religion does not intrude on anybody else's freedoms. *South Park* only considers a group untrustworthy and dangerous when an individual's freedom to think and exercise his or her will is threatened. *Family Guy*'s attack on NRMs is consistent with its worldview, which prizes science and atheism. The moral boundaries the three programs use between dangerous and stupid behaviors span both Christians and NRMs. In each program's unseen order, good Christians hold ideas the programs think are foolish, but they do not impose their unseen orders and dangerous Christians try to force their religious values on others. This pattern of good people not foisting their beliefs on others carries over to NRMs. This consistency in the moral evaluation of different religions demonstrates that the standards upon which the moral boundaries underlying each program's satire are firm and shows us that the core value of individual choice of religion is a defining criterion for evaluating different religions in each program's unseen order.

Islam: Between Threat and Tolerant Religion

Jokes about Islam in *The Simpsons*, *South Park*, and *Family Guy* illuminate its contentious status in the United States. Islam is one of America's most maligned religions. However, *The Simpsons'* and *South Park's* treatments of Islam are instructive for their challenges to Islamic stereotypes.

Scholars studying Islam's portrayal in news media and popular culture have consistently noted the relationship between the United States' foreign interests and the denigration of Muslims, who are often portrayed as Arabs despite the fact that the majority of the world's Muslims live in East Asia (particularly Indonesia) and not all Arabs are Muslims.[36] Unfortunately, Arabs and Muslims are often reduced to a stereotype that media scholar Jack Shaheen summarizes as follows: "Arabs are brute murderers, sleazy rapists, religious fanatics, oil-rich dimwits, and abusers of women" or, even more succinctly, "billionaires, bombers, and belly dancers."[37] Muslims are frequently depicted as oil barons who threaten the American economy and way of life through petroleum embargos; as violent suicide-bombers and terrorists who are willing to die for purely religious reasons; and as belly-dancers, drawing on a highly sexualized vision of Arabic women presumably dominated by oversexed Muslim men. Latent in this concept is the belief that Americans are good, modern, progressive, and truthful compared to Muslims' evil, regressiveness, and untrustworthiness.[38] This stereotype has built steadily over the years and recently has built upon popular perceptions of American international politics in the Middle East through events in which Muslims were viewed as threats to the American way of life that had to be confronted. Major recent confrontations that have shaped American perceptions of Islam include the OPEC oil embargo from October 1973 to March 18, 1974 in which Arabic oil exporting nations withheld oil from the United States and Japan to force geopolitical change;[39] the Iranian hostage crisis which lasted 444 days from November 4, 1979 to January 21, 1981 during which sixty-five Americans were held in the United States' embassy in Tehran during the Iranian Revolution;[40] the Persian Gulf War between the United States and Iraq that lasted from January 17, 1991 until April 6, 1991, when the UN brokered a cease-fire and was broadcast into American homes around the clock by CNN;[41] and the terrorist attacks on New York City and Washington, DC on September 11, 2001 and the subsequent wars in Afghanistan and Iraq. Scholarship on American Islam demonstrates that Muslims in the United States craft their identities by drawing upon American cultural values, the traditions of countries that Muslims and their ancestors have immigrated from, and Islamic doctrine.[42] Mass media, on the other hand, has opted for a narrative emphasizing a dichotomy between oppressed Muslims living under

Islam's tyrannical rule and Americans as their good, freedom-loving liberators.[43]

In all three series the dangerous Muslim stereotypes are repeated. *Family Guy* offers the most uncritical portrayal of Islam in its episode "Turban Cowboy," which aired on March 17, 2013—roughly a month before the Boston Marathon bombings on April 15, 2013. The episode was later removed because of a scene in which Peter drives his car through the Boston Marathon, leaving a trail of destruction in his wake. The episode's plot features Peter converting to Islam after meeting a man named Mahmoud in the hospital. After they watch the end of Muslim Looney Tunes (featuring Porky Pig with stubble and claiming that as a pig he is very dirty), Peter introduces Mahmoud to Quagmire and Joe at the Drunken Clam. When Mahmoud excuses himself to "go bring great shame to myself by using the restroom," Brian takes Quagmire and Joe to task for being uncomfortable with Mahmoud because he is Muslim, claiming that it is their "post-9/11 racism" talking. Peter defends his new friend, arguing that, like all different groups, Muslims have their quirks, before listing other ethnic and racial stereotypes. In the next scene, Peter meets Mahmoud at The Chaste Camel, where people smoke hookahs and listen to Arabic, an atmosphere Peter describes thus: "It's like ear-bloodening sounds had sex with nose-bloodening smells and this is their baby." When Peter tries to excuse himself to pick up his drycleaning, Mahmoud snaps his fingers and has his niqab-wearing wife do his bidding. Peter is astounded, but Mahmoud assures him that in Muslim cultures, "wives are much more obedient." Peter is enthused, but needs clarification, stating, "sweet hat, obedient wife, and I get to yell 'Admiral Akbar' when I do stuff? You, sir, have got yourself a Muslim."

After converting, Peter dresses differently—wearing a taqiyah (prayer hat) and vest—hangs out in small restaurants watching soccer, and shops at "the bazar," where he purchases cobras, silk, and dates. Impressed by Peter's commitment to Islam, Mahmoud introduces him to the rest of his terrorist cell who are planning to blow up the Quahog bridge. Peter gives away the plan at the Clam, but when Joe suggests that he has joined a sleeper cell, Peter calls Mahmoud on a cell phone Mahmoud gave him. We hear an explosion in the background after Peter dials. When Peter realizes what he has done Quagmire proclaims, "Those guys are all bad news," which prompts Joe to say, "Just because these few guys are terror-

Peter befriends Mahmoud at The Chaste Camel in *Family Guy's* "Turban Cowboy"

ists doesn't mean all Muslims are. Every ethnic group has their nut-jobs." Joe convinces Peter to be an informant and eventually they stop Mahmoud from blowing up the Quahog bridge, which leads to thirty terrorists behind bars and Joe proclaiming that "every middle-class Arab in this town is now under suspicion." In *Family Guy's* world, the excluded are those who hold religious beliefs. When those who are excluded become physically violent, then they are ridiculed, shamed, and attacked. The humor of hatred in this episode is less about accurately lampooning Islam than it is about imagining a group of people laughing with you, an act that makes the incongruity appropriate and reinforces the marginalized status of those who deserve exclusion.[44]

Family Guy treats the Muslim terrorist stereotype as a given and paints all Muslims with the same brush. *South Park* tends to treat Muslims in two ways. Either Muslims overreact and should be insulted for that, or terrorists are real, but terrorist threats are exaggerated. *South Park* also draws a line between Muslims as everyday people who just want to live their lives and a violent minority who are subject to the program's satirical gaze.

A good example of *South Park's* balancing act comes in the two-part "Cartoon Wars" saga which parodied the post–*Jyllands Posten* caricatures of Muhammad riots that swept across the Middle East in 2005. This story made international headlines after the Danish newspaper *Jyllands Posten* published twelve editorial cartoons on September 30, 2005 after asking artists to portray the Prophet as they saw him. Five months later these cartoons were circulated throughout the Middle East, leading to public protests and riots demanding that the Prophet not be ridiculed. Meanwhile, Western newspapers were caught between showing the cartoons as a matter of freedom of speech and fears that they would suffer economically, politically, or physically for republishing them.[45] In "Cartoon Wars: Part I," which focuses on fellow animated sitcom *Family Guy*, *Family Guy* airs a cutaway scene with Peter getting tea with Muhammad, but FOX censors the image because nobody is supposed to show the Prophet after the riots rocked the world. People in South Park are hiding in fear, but three of the boys do not think that the depiction is a big deal. Cartman, who hates *Family Guy*, is the exception, arguing that it is wrong to insult millions of people's religion. When Stan and Kyle note that he has never been sensitive about anybody's religion, Cartman responds that he is just a little boy, but *Family Guy* is a cartoon with millions of viewers. He makes his point by asking Kyle how he would like it if there was "a cartoon on television that made fun of Jews all the time" in an example of *South Park*'s self-reflexive humor. *South Park*, however, does not miss an opportunity to include offensive humor in this episode. At school the boys get "Muslim Sensitivity Training" from Ms. Garrison. Her argument is that Muslims are upset about depictions of the prophet because the cartoons are coming from countries where people are having sex, but because the Muslims live in countries filled with sand and they cannot have sex before marriage or masturbate they must be upset (an argument that Cartman immediately points out is racist and wrong). Despite this fear, *Family Guy* announces it will air a second episode with Muhammad uncensored. South Park starts panicking and Cartman heads to Los Angeles to have the episode pulled. When Kyle discovers that Cartman is really going because he wants *Family Guy* pulled off the air, he chases him because he thinks that *Family Guy*'s writers' right to free speech should be defended.

A religion's ability to peacefully argue its position without restricting free speech is a central element of *South Park*'s evaluation of religion. This point is made explicit at a town hall meeting. After it is suggested that everybody literally bury their heads in the sand in order to avoid any complicity with *Family Guy*'s depiction of the prophet, Mr. Stotch stands up and declares:

> No, no, wait a minute, that's ridiculous. What we need to do is just the opposite. Freedom of speech is at stake here, don't you all see? If anything, we should all make cartoons of Muhammad, and show the terrorists and the extremists that we are all united in the belief that every person has a right to say what they want. Look, people, it's been real easy for us to stand up for free speech lately. For the past few decades we haven't had to risk anything to defend it. But those times are going to come, and one of those times is right now. And if we aren't willing to risk what we have, then we just believe in free speech, but we don't defend it.

South Park's residents choose the sand.

In the next episode, "Cartoon Wars: Part II," Cartman continues his quest to use fear to have *Family Guy* pulled from the air, admitting that it is a form of terrorism. Cartman's idea is that if you get one episode of a program pulled it compromises the program's credibility, an argument that is carried across the two episodes. It is important to point this out as this episode aired after "Trapped in the Closet" and "Bloody Mary." When Comedy Central pulled "Bloody Mary," Scientologists tried to have "Trapped in the Closet" pulled as well. The "Cartoon Wars" episodes are as much about Parker and Stone making a statement about *South Park* and its integrity as it is about depicting Muslims, and the rest of "Cartoon Wars: Part II" is a showdown with FOX over airing the *Family Guy* episode. Of course, the underlying script is the way that Comedy Central was censoring *South Park*, which was made explicit when they aired scenes describing what Muhammad was doing, but which also explained that Comedy Central was censoring the images.

Parker and Stone's inspiration for this episode came when they first saw the riots in the Middle East and thought that Muslims there had seen the episode "Super Best Friends." This episode depicted Muhammad and had him shooting fire from his hands (all the religious heroes had super powers—for example, Jesus had carpentry powers, Joseph Smith could breathe ice, and Krishna could change shape). Instead, the issue of Muslims protesting caricatures of the Prophet and Western self-censorship out of the fear of violence helped *South Park's* creators to voice their response to the "Bloody Mary" controversy discussed earlier. Comedy Central did not budge and the network's fears were born out in 2010 when South Park Studios were threatened with violence by the group Revolution Muslim, which posted a picture of Dutch filmmaker Theo van Gogh's death on their website and claimed that Parker and Stone would probably end up like him for their blasphemy. Van Gogh was murdered in 2004 by a Muslim extremist for his film "Submission" about women in Islam. Parker and Stone's Los Angeles studio's address was listed, as was Comedy Central's headquarters'. The website has since been removed, even though its owners claimed in a CNN interview that they were not encouraging violence.[46]

Revolution Muslim was responding to the episode "200" in which *South Park* revisited some of its most controversial moments, including the censorship fight over depicting Muhammad (which carried through to the next episode, "201"). Again, Muhammad was not allowed to be shown, but in these episodes *South Park* drove home their point about free speech and giving in to threats of violence by satirizing other religious figures whose followers do not scare Comedy Central. After Tom Cruise organizes a class action lawsuit, which he will only drop if the boys can bring him Muhammad (Cruise and the celebrities want to steal Muhammad's power to avoid insult), they go to the Super Best Friend's headquarters to try to get the Prophet. Jesus explains to Stan and Kyle that things have changed since they were last there and that it is no longer appropriate to show the Prophet. The boys ask if it is acceptable to dress up Muhammad in a pirate costume, cover his face with a paper bag, or portray him in a suit of armor. None of these options is acceptable to the other religious leaders because they still depict Muhammad in human form. When Kyle gets upset, Joseph Smith sets him straight, saying: "Boys, you need to understand that people get very offended when Muhammad is mocked because he's a religious figure." Then there is a sucking noise in the background and the shot changes, showing the Buddha snorting lines of cocaine with a dollar bill. Jesus chides him: "Buddha! Don't do coke in front of kids!" Eventually they agree that Muhammad can appear in South Park if he appears in the back of a U-Haul without windows (but everybody is unsure if Muhammad can speak). Eventually, they get Muhammad out of the truck covered in a bear mascot uniform, but before the celebrities can take the Prophet, an explosion goes off and a group of "ginger" kids (children with red hair, pale skin, and freckles) claims responsibility—they want the Prophet's power too.

In "201" the Prophet's name is now censored, but Parker and Stone stress their point about being able to insult any other group by having the Buddha snorting cocaine (again), and when Jesus tells him to stop the Buddha responds, "Oh and you're one to talk, with all your Internet porn." Jesus responds, "Watching porn isn't like doing coke, fag." At the episode's conclusion, the speeches that Kyle, Jesus, and Santa Claus give are censored. According to the DVD commentary, this was Comedy Central's decision and in 2014 an anonymously sourced audio clip was leaked on the Internet that ostensibly had the speeches. The argument was that all you need is violence and threats to get what you want, which continues the criticism of radical Muslim groups (and also echoes Catholic League president Bill Donahue's criticisms of Comedy Central).[47]

The "Cartoon Wars" and "200" episodes rely on Islamophobia for their arguments. Censorship is institutionally dissonant with South Park's core values. Creative individuals need to be able to speak their minds without fear of reprisal. Making jokes, for Parker and Stone, requires that they not be afraid to insult anybody, and Muslims who try to censor free speech are treated as some of the most extreme religious people in their examples. That Revolution Muslim actually threatened South Park's creators and their staff is proof enough that what South Park was saying was enough to incite violence in some individuals, but for Parker and Stone the way to fight back is to defy the people who make such threats and live their lives as they see fit. Incorporating Muhammad into the episodes and then explaining why nobody should take offense is a direct attack on the unseen orders that would try to silence South Park. South Park does not portray Muslims as humorless and violent because the Muslims who are problematic in its world are insufficient foils for its moral points. Its commentary in these episodes is particularly important for understanding how ignorant familiarity—in this case the radical Muslim stereotype—is used to frame discourse about civic behavior in the public sphere. South Park uses Muslims who would use violence to silence the program as proof that extreme religious groups are dangerous and that only those who protect freedom of speech should have the right to address others in public. All criticisms of what is said through freedom of speech are secondary to allowing free speech in the first place.

South Park's commentaries on Islamic radicalism are tempered with a critique of Islamophobia in other episodes. For Parker and Stone it is extremism and irrationality which violate other people's personal freedoms that justifies attacking religion, not belief itself. The episode "The Snuke" provides a counterexample to these "terrorist" stereotype and "fear of violent Muslims" episodes. When Baahir Hassan Abdul Hakeem joins the fourth-grade class at South Park Elementary, Cartman is immediately suspicious of the new kid, asking Ms. Garrison if he has been checked for bombs. Ms. Garrison reprimands him, saying that not all Muslims are terrorists. "No," Cartman replies, "but most of them are. And all it takes is most of them." At recess he calls Kyle, who is home sick, to start looking up Baahir's information on the website MySpace. This initiates a parody of FOX's *24 (2001–2010, 2014)*, which featured Kiefer Sutherland as Jack Bauer, a Counter Terrorism Unit agent who used any means necessary to save the United States from terrorists. The series *24* was well known for presenting different religious, ethnic, and national groups (e.g., Muslims, Chinese, Russians) as terrorists whom Bauer eventually thwarted. In *South Park*, the elementary school is evacuated because there is a Hillary Clinton rally in town and Cartman assumes that the rally and Baahir's arrival are connected. He calls the CIA and tips them off to a bomb threat (it turns out that Russians have placed a "snuke," or suitcase nuke, in Clinton's vagina after being hired by the British). Cartman turns the Hakeems over to the CIA, certain that it was them. Baahir, however, is not with them. He is playing checkers with Butters. After Cartman finds Baahir, he chases him outside and gets captured by the Russians. Eventually, the Russians are stopped, the British attempt to take back America is thwarted, and things return to normal. The final scene depicts Kyle and Cartman discussing who helped save the day:

KYLE
You didn't save everyone! I did! You were just out harassing Muslims!

CARTMAN
But if I hadn't called you in the first place to check out the Muslims, you would have just stayed in bed all day, right?

KYLE
Maybe.

CARTMAN
Maybe? If I hadn't called you, you wouldn't have been on your computer checking out the Clinton rally. That means my intolerance of Muslims saved America.

KYLE
That is so missing the point.

CARTMAN
Me being a bigot stopped a nuclear bomb from going off, yes or no?

KYLE
That's not the right way to look at it.

CARTMAN
Yes or no Kyle?

KYLE
NO! Not . . . not like you're saying.

CARTMAN
But that's all I'm saying. Today, bigotry and racism saved the day. Baahir, you get this right?

At this point Baahir's parents arrive and tell him to pack because they are leaving the country. Cartman then starts gloating, asking "Okay, who got rid of the Muslims, huh? That was all me. A simple thank-you will suffice." This conclusion repeats the unsettling problem with Cartman's racism. His bigotry becomes a way of introducing Islamophobia as a potentially good thing into the program. One of Parker and Stone's favorite things to do is sometimes let Cartman and his heinous behavior win, which challenges the moral foundations they normally support. In this case they have let Cartman speak his racist mind, but they have also debunked the "Muslim terrorist" stereotype. Bigotry and racism won the day on dumb luck, rather than accurately assessing people of a specific religion. Unfortunately, they do not make a definitive statement on the problems of racial profiling, which leaves their point on the issue unsettled. Instead of attacking and debunking an ignorant familiarity and incorporating Muslims into *South Park's* unseen order when they play by *South Park's* core values of acting independently and not trying to convert, Islamic stereotypes are allowed to stand as a reason to suspect and exclude Muslims from everyday life in *South Park*.

The Simpsons satirizes the "Muslims as terrorists" stereotype more forcefully in the episode "MyPods and Boomsticks." After causing a scene at the Springfield Mall, Bart meets a Jordanian boy named Bashir who quickly becomes his friend. On the way to school the next day, Bart tells Bashir what he can safely eat in the cafeteria. Only the pork chops are harmless, but Bashir's religion forbids eating pork. Bart does not learn of Bashir's Muslim religion right away, but once he does he warns him not to tell anyone or else he will get beaten up. Overhearing this, the local bullies advance on Bashir. The bald bully, Kearney, looms over Bashir, saying, "You're the reason I can't carry toothpaste on an airplane." Bart defends Bashir and then makes a statement on diversity, identifying Jimbo (the bully in a stocking cap) as Christian, Dolf (the bully with long hair) as Jewish, and Kearney as a member of the "cult Moe started" (it turns out Moe was just acting crazy to get out of jury duty, reinforcing the stereotype of the duplicitous cult leader discussed earlier). Islam is just one religion among many.

Later, Homer meets Bashir and is impressed by the boy's politeness. However, that night Lenny and Carl tease Homer at the bar because of Bashir. Homer initially defends Bashir, but Moe warns him, saying, "This Bashir kid is Muslim, and therefore up to something." Homer contends that he cannot believe it unless he sees "a fictional TV program espousing your [*Moe's*] point of view." Moe turns on a *24* parody and Homer is convinced that Muslims are a threat. Carl suggests that the way to get back at Bashir's family is to discriminate in employment and housing (which, as a suggestion made by an African American, is a darkly satirical point), but Lenny and Moe advocate inviting the family over for dinner and then interrogating them the way Jack Bauer would. Homer chooses the latter, implying that biased, stupid people advocate these methods.

At dinner Homer cannot hide his suspicions. When he learns that Bashir's parents met at Jordan University of Science and Technology he notes that "science is used to make bombs." He then brings out a cake decorated with the American flag and asks if they want to cut it. When they refuse, he bellows, "What's the matter? Don't like the taste of freedom?" Bart defends them, saying, "Dad, these people are my friends. Don't fear them just because they have a different religion, a different culture, and their last name is bin Laden." Bashir's father then models the stark differences between the Muslim family and the Simpsons, saying, "Young man, you do not respect us by disrespecting your father." The bin Ladens leave shortly thereafter and Marge rebukes Homer for his behavior. Homer replies, "I'm sorry, it's just so fun and easy to judge people based on religion." This joke emphasizes the dangers of ignorant familiarity and its ability to facilitate snap decisions made on bad information. *The Simpsons* shows the logical fallacy in Homer's explanation by contrasting the way Muslims are normally judged with a Muslim family that is more mannerly than the Simpsons. Their positive presentation of Muslims opposes other depictions of Muslims on American television, and although the bin Ladens' last name makes for a convenient joke, it works because it inverts the expectations people have for someone named bin Laden. The process of deconstructing the Muslim stereotype and combating the ignorant familiarity that *Family Guy* and *South Park* used for laughs is under way.

Marge then sends Homer over to the bin Ladens' to apologize. However, when he arrives he sees Bashir's father handling dynamite in the garage and goes home proclaiming that he was right about them. Homer's dream that night parodies Disney's *Aladdin*. The genie claims he will "destroy your decadent Western society," and proceeds to turn the First Church of Springfield into a mosque, makes the bullies dress like Arab gangsters, and changes every CD in the local music store into a Cat Stevens album (Stevens converted to Islam in 1977 and is now known as Yusuf Islam). Homer awakens reassured that Muslims are a threat.

The next morning he goes to the bin Ladens' to confirm his suspicions. Homer overhears Bashir's father proclaiming his love for blowing up buildings, but does not hear the part where he states that it must be done safely and legally. Homer's eavesdropping reveals that Mr. bin Laden is "killing myself, but it is all for the profit" (a clever homonym) and that he will be in a better place. What Homer does not hear is that the better place is a corner office. After snooping around the house, Homer learns that Mr. bin Laden will demolish the Springfield Mall. The condemned building is the old Springfield Mall which is scheduled for demolition, but Homer ruins the explosion, taking the dynamite and throwing it into the Springfield River where it destroys a bridge to the Duff brewery. After this escapade, the Simpsons have the bin Ladens over for an apology dinner under Homer's "Please Forgive My Intolerance" banner.

On Exclusion

"MyPods and Boomsticks" shows that not all groups that start out hated have to remain that way. The NRMs that get compressed into the Movementarians and Blainetologists are complicated, complex religions. Their strengths and weaknesses are built on a whole host of ideological, sociological, and political complications. The same goes for Muslims, who are members of the second largest religion on Earth—an internally diverse and complex body of different religious traditions.

The exclusion of these religions across the three programs by reducing them to basic ignorant familiarities connects the major themes of this book. To understand these jokes one does not need to know anything about Islam's diversity or the various NRMs that The Simpsons, South Park, and Family Guy parody with generic "cults." Two widespread stereotypes are sufficient. When we rely on ignorant familiarity to present information, it is difficult to show how these simple presentations lead to superficial and incorrect portrayals of different religions' participants and histories. These incomplete depictions can lead to superficial dismissal of different religions and their adherents. As we have seen, every religious tradition has its easily mocked elements. The question is not whether or not there are beliefs and stories in the world's different religious traditions that seem incongruous. The question is why we can easily dismiss some groups' (such as Muslims and NRMs) ideas and practices without ever engaging the social and ideological structures that sustain people's lives. The easiest answer is that these groups are not considered relevant enough for their members to be engaged as full citizens. For this reason, they can be interpreted through stereotypes and generalities in a handful of episodes.

These superficial representations are what facilitate easy discussions of excluding religions in civil life through popular culture. Each program presents its core values by showing how NRMs or Muslims measure up to their standards for public acceptance. In *The Simpsons* NRMs are only welcomed when they allow individual spiritual experimentation such as Lisa's conversion to Wicca. When they brainwash people and take their money, like the Movementarians, then they are portrayed as fraudulent and dangerous organizations that need to be exposed and shut down. *South Park* is interested in regulating certain kinds of religion—those religions that try to impose their interpretation of reality upon others through force or falsehood—but that does not mean that they are always fighting back. *South Park's* treatment of Muslims reflects its larger systematic view of religious people as good citizens if they hold beliefs that do not lead to violence or coerce people to join a religion against their will. Using violent and coercive behavior as their standards for inclusion and exclusion allows *South Park* to evaluate religions without evaluating their theologies. The Mormons and Scientology illustrate this rule. While the episodes "All About the Mormons" and "Trapped in the Closet" discuss Scientology's and the LDS' unseen orders, the deciding factor between which religions are good and bad are the way that members of those religions behave in public. Mormons are welcomed in *South Park*, but Scientologists are not.[48] For *Family Guy*, NRMs and Muslims are more of the same. We have established that *Family Guy* is the most exclusive of all the programs and sees no reason to allow any religious discourse to shape the way public life should be conducted. They ridicule and stereotype Muslims and NRMs as dangerous and violent because in *Family Guy's* world they are not worthy of respect or inclusion.

Deploying ignorant familiarity for humorous purposes is made possible through a comparative discussion of "religion" related to each program's core values. It would be incorrect to say that all the groups discussed in this chapter are hated. They exist as replications of stigmatized stereotypes about generic "religions" that are filtered through each program's core values because they are only momentarily engaged and are not given enough time to be sufficiently fleshed out as regular contributors to the fictional American towns in which each program is set. The characters or groups that the main characters encounter are not recurring; they exist as examples of how to evaluate idealized others in the world. In each case, the programs use these groups as means to sacralize their core values, while also reaffirming the idea that the groups can be dealt with simply. None of the NRM or Muslim characters recur, we do not have to seriously deal with their beliefs, and easy stereotypes rule the day in a discussion that centers on the sacred politics at each program's core. Their humor reduces complexity, dismisses theology, and reinforces their own ideology. That is an easy way of dealing with danger when you are in control of the script. It is also how you teach people to interpret religions without seriously engaging a different unseen order. The process of presenting ignorant familiarity as sufficient knowledge for evaluating other religions is a contribution to civil life. Portrayals that deal with religious groups at the margins of American society remain a part of popular culture as constantly repeated sediments for viewers to reference when thinking about religion, its place in civic life, and why some groups should be included and excluded. These satires are not objective and the audience will not always accept each program's portrayals of the different religions, but through constant repetition of ignorant familiarity the agenda is set for future discussions of these religions and what they have to contribute to our collective good. The question now becomes, what do we do with that knowledge?

Conclusion

What can we learn about religion from satire in *The Simpsons*, *South Park*, and *Family Guy*? Let us return to our three major questions: (1) *What do you have to believe about different groups classified as "religions" and the role of "religion" in society to find jokes in the three sitcoms humorous?* (2) *What do the patterns in these programs tell us about the popular construction of "religion's" significance in America?* and (3) *What can a critical assessment of religion in the public sphere through popular culture tell us about American civil life?* Revisiting these inquiries will help us to understand why religious satire in these three programs is useful for those who want to understand religion in the United States.

As we have seen, religious satire occurs when a satirist uses humor to attack an opposing plausibility structure's unseen order. When humorists desecrate an opposing unseen order they reinforce their own sacred center and reaffirm the bodies of knowledge that underlie their worldview. Satire is based in a common stock of knowledge and affirms the moral boundaries that make the satirist's plausibility structures seem valid. It attacks opponents' unseen orders by making them look ridiculous, stupid, and dangerous. In so doing, satirists emphasize these "others'" outsider status. Humorous exclusion is often facilitated through ignorant familiarity, because this kind of knowledge is widespread, superficial, often erroneous, directed at outsiders, and deployed with a degree of certainty as to the validity of the knowledge. Neither the satirist nor the audience of the programs in this book need to have specialized knowledge of any of the religions discussed. The general stock of knowledge deployed through ignorant familiarity makes it easier for satirists to rank and order those who are deemed different and excluded. It also makes it easy to use different moral boundaries to exclude people for varying reasons, adding variety and nuance to humorous criticisms. Through the process of humorously criticizing others, satirists reinforce their own plausibility structures and the unseen orders they support.

Satire's moral force helps to make its own cultural center into a sacred center.

Satire and Religious Literacy

Our first question is: What do you have to believe about different groups classified as "religions" and the role of religion in society to find jokes in the three sitcoms humorous? When we consider what one has to know to find the depictions of religious groups in these programs funny, we should think about how ignorant familiarity about religion is based on religious illiteracy. This book has argued that the stereotypes and events that inform the depictions of different religions in these programs are distilled into easily interpreted caricatures that can be mass mediated to a broad audience. Those caricatures are framed so that audiences understand the messages about religion through the way the characters are portrayed relative to a set of core values in each program. No one should take these programs as the last word on any of the religions covered. We do not learn much about Islam except for a few superficial stereotypes in *Family Guy*'s episode "Turban Cowboy." *The Simpsons*' Ned Flanders is a caricature of evangelicals; if this were all anybody knew about evangelicals, we would not know what motivates members of this Christian subculture. The contentious politics of representing Native American religions are completely lost on *The Simpsons* in the episode "El Viaje Misterioso de Nuestro Jomer" and on *Family Guy* in the episode "The Son Also Draws." The humor in these episodes is based on religion, but not on a deep knowledge of how these religions shape their adherents' lives. The smaller, more marginalized, and more stigmatized the religion, the harder it is to overcome this ignorance.

Stereotypes based on limited knowledge enable ignorant familiarity to fester in dangerous ways. When we think about the popular construction of religion's significance in America, we need to consider the ways in which ignorant familiarity reinforces already existing moral boundaries. This book has demonstrated that *The Simpsons*, *South Park*, and *Family Guy* are engaged in bolstering their own unseen orders when they tell jokes. By presenting a religion as incapable of engaging in the modern world, as each program does through its jokes about Christianity, for example, they reinforce the idea that the programs know that a different unseen order can meet our modern needs. In *The Simpsons*, that honor falls to individual spiritual seeking. In *Family Guy* it is atheism based in scientific understanding of the world. For *South Park*, individual creativity and living according to the golden rule is sufficient. Regardless of one's personal approach to religion, critically engaging different traditions and seeking to understand why people adhere to them and how they shape people's lives is vital for understanding our fellow humans. By contrast, ignorant familiarity enables the creators of these programs to construct superficial criticisms of different traditions that teach audiences to accept or reject the religions out of hand. This superficiality has consequences for American civil life.

In *Cultural Literacy*, English literature professor E. D. Hirsch argued that even if people's "schoolchild knowledge had become vague with the passage of time, it was still functional, because the information essential to literacy is rarely detailed or precise. This haziness is a key characteristic of literacy and cultural literacy."[1] In other words, Hirsh argues that there is an ignorant familiarity with key ideas in our culture that makes us literate—but here this "literacy" rests on a tenuous foundation. This ignorant familiarity is not just a conceptual or definitional knowledge. It is also wrapped in moral and political sentiment. The combination of ignorant familiarity and emotional, institutional resonance enables people to make quick decisions on bad information. When it comes to religious knowledge, this haziness is dangerous. It is an ignorance that can reinforce one unseen order in a pluralistic world through factual errors and can lead to individual and collective decisions that damage other humans. Prothero's point about the civic duty to become religiously literate becomes increasingly relevant in light of the dangers of these ignorant familiarities.[2] Knowing more about the world's religious traditions will help citizens to analyze problematic depictions of religion such as those discussed in this book. Increased knowledge will also enable them to criticize arguments presented by civic, media, and religious leaders who rely on ignorant familiarity to bolster their agendas. Finally, it will empower people to make informed decisions when they do everything from interact with their neighbors to publicly criticize foreign policy. Overcoming religious illiteracy requires not just learning facts, but also combating the haziness that characterizes Hirsch's cultural literacy. While knowledge will never be perfect, being informed and capable of working with people across religious boundaries requires an intersection of cultural, political, religious, and media literacies and the critical facilities to sort through the ways in which ignorant familiarity is being manipulated to serve competing interests.

With religious literacy concerns in mind, let us return to the question at hand: What do you have to believe about different groups classified as "religions" and the role of "religion" in society to find jokes in the three sitcoms humorous? You need to "know" each program's unseen order in the hazy sense to which Hirsch refers. You must understand how each program bases its humor on certain central values—individual spirituality and scientific rationality in *The Simpsons*, individual creativity in *South Park*, and scientific atheism in *Family Guy*—and generates laughter by showing how other religions fall short of the program's moral standards. A viewer's understanding does not have to be a logically organized and defended position. One does not need a deep knowledge of the different religions to understand the humorous material covered in this book. That is the point. When general ignorance characterizes the broader social stock of knowledge, it can be played down to by emphasizing the basic moral sentiments that make groups appear good or bad, stupid or dangerous. Popular culture creations are important locations for disseminating and acquiring religious literacy because of their ability to reach broad audiences with easily accessible information that connects with other social institutions and events that may also be poorly understood. A lot of knowledge is distilled into ignorant familiarity, which enables these programs to craft successful jokes for diverse audiences. *The Simpsons*, *South Park*, and *Family Guy* are discussion partners with other media, religious institutions, political actors, and academics when it comes to shaping public understandings of religion and its place in contemporary society. If our knowledge is based on ignorance or error, however, it can lead to decisions that unjustly damage other people and demean the morals we claim to uphold.

Humor, Boundaries, and Religious Satire

There is another level of understanding that one needs to analyze when studying satire. We need to comprehend the signs, symbols, and sentiments that create the sense of certainty at the core of the unseen order upon which jokes are based. This analytical step takes us to our second question: What do the patterns in these programs tell us about the popular construction of "religion's" significance in America? Our knowledge of each program's unseen order allows us to understand how the programs project their creators' values and moral boundaries by finding appropriate incongruities between the satirists' worldview and their opponents'. We find evidence for these boundaries in the way an opponent's failures are constructed. How a religious group is presented will tell us not only about their failures, but about the program's standards for goodness. Whenever one of the three programs targets a religious tradition it reinforces the program's unseen order. For example, when *South Park* makes fun of Jesus for using drugs to perform his miracles in the episode "A Scause for Applause," it presents him as very human and diminishes the perspective taken by Christians that Jesus is both fully human and fully divine. Those who would take offense at *South Park's* portrayal of Jesus as just a man and not somebody who was divine are excluded from the moral foundations underlying *South Park's* unseen order. Returning to the previous point about religious literacy, how "religion" is presented in popular culture tells us that religion remains a significant way of morally and socially positioning oneself as a moral person in the United States. In a pluralistic society, each program's unseen order becomes a tool for viewers to use when navigating relationships with idealized others.

Some readers may have found certain examples in this book to be shocking, disgusting, or personally offensive. Maybe you found yourself agreeing with the Catholic League that mocking Catholicism is indecent and should not be aired, or perhaps the Scientologists were right to pressure Viacom to have *South Park* censored because the episode "Trapped in the Closet" was a cruel mockery of their tradition. The Federal Communications Commission (FCC) receives hundreds of complaints about the content of these three programs, some of which have been made available by the website Governmentattic.org through Freedom of Information Act requests. Sexual references, blasphemy, religious characters performing sexual or violent acts, and using the names of God or Jesus as swearing in the different programs are all reasons why people write to the FCC arguing that this content is obscene and should be censored. Meanwhile, others are offended by the censorship of Muhammad's name in the *South Park* episode "201." Just as religion and media scholar Diane Alters had found that there were a variety of reactions to *The Simpsons* in 2001, these shows continue to elicit numerous responses in viewers.[3] FCC complaints are but one way of discovering what people think about the programs. Other ways of publicly engaging with their content include works like Mark Pinsky's and Jamey Heit's books, which argue that *The Simpsons* has moral and redeeming qualities, or the books about each program in the "and Philosophy" series which contain essays arguing that these programs contain opportunities for philosophical reflection.[4] Blogs, message boards, and other reproductions of jokes and commentary on social media are additional examples of viewer feedback. These voices circle the programs and they are important data sets for those interested in audience reception theories about the programs. As was previously noted, such resources were not pivotal in shaping the analysis in this book because their impact on the content of the three programs is questionable. They are echoes that start from individual human beings viewing the products that this book discusses and bringing their personal interpretive frameworks to the program.

Our personal reactions and others' interpretations of the programs offer an invitation to reflect upon, clarify, challenge, and change our common stock of knowledge by using popular culture to understand the depth of our own unseen order. Perhaps these programs inspire a response to show how their representations fall short of reality. This would put offended readers in a position of countering the satire and reasserting the moral boundaries of their own world. People calling for the FCC to censor the programs share this position. Offenses to our sensibilities and agreements with the points each program makes engage all three questions at the heart of this book. They show us what we believe about religion when we laugh or are offended by a joke. Religion's popular constructions in the programs show us how we evaluate our own and others' unseen orders and how the way we engage—either by letting the moment pass or by using the episodes for further reflection—can move us toward a deeper understanding of religion in American civil life or can reaffirm our ignorance.

Critically Assessing Religious Satire

Our third question is: What can a critical assessment of religion in the public sphere through popular culture tell us about American civil life? Critically examining satire in the three programs shows us how popular representations of religion can help us to understand how religious diversity and politics in the United States are made into something comprehensible for millions of people who want to be entertained. Religious satire in these three programs is further proof that societies are rarely unified collectives. Instead, they are competitive arenas in which people jockey for status, power, and survival. This dynamic conflict illuminates a great deal of the derisive humor that humor theorists have categorized under superiority theory. Modern societies are comprised of competing groups, which is why institutional resonance in its consonant and dissonant dimensions is vital for understanding how satire transmits knowledge. Knowledge itself reflects the competitive and conflicting social environments in which it was made and continues to dwell. The sociological approach to humor and satire has outlined this conflictual element.[5] This book has argued that the groups widely identified as religions are social competitors. They jockey with competing groups to define the unseen order that shapes society as a whole. For example, Muslims are depicted either as threats to the social order or as potentially good citizens with the rest of American society. Christian denominations and subcultures have been shown as competitors for the power to define such things as appropriate sexual conduct and who has a right to avoid insult. Scientific advancements are presented as insights into reality to be embraced and positioned against opposing religious understandings of reality. Every group presented in this book has its arguments reflected through the filters that the programs' creators put in place, and there is an ongoing dialogue that is meant to both entertain and inform viewers about the ideas with which they are being presented. The programs' creators are not neutral, impassive observers of social phenomena. They are actively engaged in interpretation and they attempt to convince their audience through humor that their perceptions of other groups are correct. This maneuvering for power over the ability to define the unseen order is the religious element of their satire, which gives satirical humor its powerful moral resonance and goes beyond what the sociology of humor has thus far explored. It also invites people to participate in the larger religious enterprise of positioning themselves among competing ideologies that shape the world.

This book has argued between two intertwined uses of the phrase "religious satire." First, religious satire is satire directed at groups deemed religious. When the three programs told jokes about different religious groups, they reinforced the core values that sustained their plausibility structure. Without an assumption that the audience found deviations from these core values as incongruous and in need of correction, these jokes could not have been told the way they were.

Satirizing religious groups is also "religious" work. Our working definition of religion has been a modified version of William James': A religion consists of the social structures and institutions that facilitate, support, and protect the belief that there is an unseen order and that our ultimate good relies on harmoniously adjusting to it. Each criticism of religion is built on the unseen order at each program's core, and these criticisms reaffirm the sacredness of the unseen order that the program's creators build upon to make their jokes comprehensible. Each program's creators are both setting their opponents apart as less than themselves and setting themselves apart as people in a position to judge others' moral failures. In the Durkheimian language of sacralization that has permeated the book, religious satire is engaged in making one's core sacred. It is a tool for simultaneously attacking opponents and reifying one's unseen order. This is why satire is based in a common stock of knowledge and how it marks the moral boundaries that order that knowledge as valid and comprehensible.

Religious satire confounds the normal division between things deemed religious and irreligious. Yet, as religion scholars David Chidester and Gary Laderman have demonstrated in their studies of popular culture and religion, humans are sacralizing animals.[6] As a species, we sacralize our social worlds, making everything comprehensible through the interrelations between social actors and their environments. On the surface, religious satire looks like a criticism of existing religious traditions. Yet, this book has examined portrayals of religions not only as attacks against a tradition, but also as ways of supporting each program's unseen orders. That is satire's dual nature. It desecrates opponents' unseen orders while sacralizing the satirist's. Competition between unseen orders is constant, ongoing, and part of our everyday socialization. That socialization is partially facilitated through popular culture and satire. This is why religious literacy and media literacy are essential bodies of knowledge for today's consumers of popular culture. Popular culture teaches us how to interpret the seen order in light of the unseen. Popular culture producers engage different groups' stocks of knowledge and arrange that knowledge to serve the producers' interpretive goals. Avoiding critical engagement leads to passive socialization and encourages ignorant familiarity to develop. Laughter at satire, whether one's own or someone else's, is an invitation to reflect on what was presented as funny. It is an appeal to own the arguments presented through jokes. Knowing that human beings will sacralize their worlds, whether through religious language favored by the groups studied in this book or through the language of secularism and morality without reference to any divine beings, we should use religious satire in both senses of the term to consciously own the legitimations that comprise the plausibility structures undergirding our unseen orders. In this way, we hope to be able to overcome divisive difference by recognizing the basic humanity that has gone into the creation of other unseen orders, learn the legitimations that justify those ways of life, and engage in intelligent criticism based on comprehending others and accepting the fact that there may be fundamental reasons for differences between varying human groups. Critical engagement with popular culture and entertainment can foster a more nuanced understanding of the sacred dimensions of human life and intergroup interaction. Whether or not you agree with the examples presented in this book, if the tools presented herein help to facilitate this kind of understanding and dialogue, then it has served its purpose.

APPENDIX

Episodes Referenced

Family Guy. FOX Television Network. Created by Seth McFarlane. 1999–2002; 2004–Present.

Episode Name	Original Airdate	Production Code	Writer(s)	Director(s)
Death Has a Shadow	January 31, 1999	1ACX01	Seth MacFarlane	Peter Shin
Chitty, Chitty, Death Bang	April 18, 1999	1ACX04	Danny Smith	Dominic Polcino
The Son Also Draws	May 9, 1999	1ACX06	Ricky Blitt	Neil Affleck
Holy Crap	September 30, 1999	1ACX11	Danny Smith	Neil Affleck
Fifteen Minutes of Shame	April 25, 2000	2ACX08	Steve Callaghan	Scott Wood
One if By Clam, Two if by Sea	August 1, 2001	2ACX19	Jim Bernstein & Michael Shipley	Dan Povenmire
The Kiss Seen Around the World	August 29, 2001	3ACX02	Mark Henteman	Pete Michels
Brian Wallows and Peter's Swallows	January 17, 2002	3ACX03	Allison Adler	Dan Povenmire
When You Wish Upon a Weinstein	November 9, 2003*	2ACX05	Ricky Blitt	Dan Povenmire
Blind Ambition	May 15, 2005	4ACX04	Steve Callaghan	Chuck Klein
The Court-ship of Stewie's Father	November 20, 2005	4ACX19	Kirker Butler	Kurt Dumas
The Father, the Son, and the Holy Fonz	December 18, 2005	4ACX22	Danny Smith	James Purdum

Episode Name	Original Airdate	Production Code	Writer(s)	Director(s)
You May Now Kiss the . . . Uh . . . Guy Who Receives	April 30, 2006	4ACX28	David A. Goodman	Dominic Polcino
Untitled Griffin Family History	May 14, 2006	4ACX30	John Viener	Zac Moncrief
Stu & Stewie's Excellent Adventure	May 21, 2006	4ACX07	Steve Callaghan	Pete Michels
Prick Up Your Ears	November 19, 2006	5ACX01	Chevy Chevap-ravatdumrong	James Purdum
Airport '07	March 4, 2007	5ACX08	Tom Devanney	John Holmquist
It Takes a Village Idiot, and I Married One	May 13, 2007	5ACX12	Alex Borstein	Zac Moncrief
Padre de Familia	November 18, 2007	5ACX20	Kirker Butler	Pete Michels
I Dream of Jesus	October 5, 2008	6ACX05	Brian Scully	Mike Kim
Not All Dogs Go to Heaven	March 29, 2009	6ACX17	Danny Smith	Greg Colton
Family Goy	October 4, 2009	7ACX01	Mark Hentemann	James Purdum
April in Quahog	April 11, 2010	7ACX18	John Viener	Joseph Lee
Partial Terms of Endearment^	June 20, 2010	7ACX10	Danny Smith	Joseph Lee
Excellence in Broadcasting	October 3, 2010	8ACX03	Patrick Meighan	John Holmquist
Brian Writes a Bestseller	November 21, 2010	8ACX07	Gary Janetti	Joseph Lee
And I'm Joyce Kinney	January 16, 2011	8ACX12	Alec Sulkin	Dominic Bianchi
Friends of Peter G.	February 13, 2011	8ACX13	Brian Scully	John Holmquist
Meg and Quagmire	January 8, 2012	9ACX03	Tom Devanney	Joseph Lee
Burning Down the Bayit	March 4, 2012	9ACX13	Chris Sheridan	Jerry Langford
Internal Affairs	May 20, 2012	9ACX20	Wellesley Wild	Julius Wu
Yug Milaf	November 11, 2012	AACX04	Mike Desilets & Anthony Blasucci	Brian Iles

Episode Name	Original Airdate	Production Code	Writer(s)	Director(s)
Jesus, Mary, and Joseph!	December 23, 2012	AACX07	Tom Devanney	Julius Wu
The Giggity Wife	January 27, 2013	AACX09	Andrew Goldberg	Brian Iles
Turban Cowboy	March 17, 2013	AACX13	Artie Johann & Shawn Ries	Joe Vaux
3 Acts of God	March 16, 2014	AACX17	Alec Sulkin	Bob Bowen

* "When You Wish Upon a Weinstein" originally aired November 9, 2003 during Cartoon Network's Adult Swim lineup. It first aired on FOX on December 10, 2004.
^ "Partial Terms of Endearment" originally aired June 20, 2010 on BBC Three in the United Kingdom, and as of June 1, 2014, had not aired on FOX due to its sensitive content. It is available in the United States on DVD and digital download.

The Simpsons. FOX Television Network. Created by James L. Brooks, Matt Groening, and Sam Simon. 1989–Present.

Episode Name	Original Airdate	Production Code	Writer(s)	Director(s)
The Telltale Head	February 25, 1990	#7G07	Al Jean, Mike Reiss, Sam Simon, & Matt Groening	Rich Moore
Krusty Gets Busted	April 29, 1990	#7G12	Jay Kogen & Wallace Wolodarsky	Brad Bird
Homer vs. Lisa and the 8th Commandment	February 7, 1991	#7F13	Steve Pepoon	Rich Moore
Brush with Greatness	April 11, 1991	#7F18	Brian K. Roberts	Jim Reardon
Like Father, Like Clown	October 24, 1991	#8F05	Jay Kogen & Wallace Wolodarsky	Jeffrey Lynch with Brad Bird
I Married Marge	December 26, 1991	#8510	Jeff Martin	Jeffrey Lynch
Lisa the Greek	January 23, 1992	#8F12	Jay Kogen & Wallace Wolodarsky	Rich Moore
The Otto Show	April 23, 1992	#8F22	Jeff Martin	Wes Archer

Episode Name	Original Airdate	Production Code	Writer(s)	Director(s)
Brother, Can You Spare Two Dimes?	August 27, 1992	#8F23	John Swartzwelder	Rich Moore
Homer the Heretic	October 8, 1992	#9F01	George Meyer	Jim Reardon
Marge Gets a Job	November 5, 1992	#95F05	Bill Oakley & Josh Weinstein	Jeff Lynch
Mr. Plow	November 19, 1992	#9F07	Jon Vitti	Jim Reardon
Lisa's First Word	December 3, 1992	#9F08	Jeff Martin	Mark Kirkland
Homer's Triple Bypass	December 17, 1992	#9F09	Gary Apple & Michael Carrington	David Silverman
Homer's Barbershop Quartet	September 30, 1993	#9F22	Jeff Martin	Mark Kirkland
Cape Feare	October 7, 1993	#9F22	Jon Vitti	Rich Moore
Homer and Apu	February 10, 1994	#1F10	Greg Daniels	Mark Kirkland
Homer Loves Flanders	March 17, 1994	#1F14	David Richardson	Wes Archer
Bart's Girlfriend	November 6, 1994	#2F04	Jonathan Collier	Susie Dietter
Lisa on Ice	November 13, 1994	#2F05	Mike Scully	Bob Anderson
Homer the Great	January 8, 1995	#2F09	John Swartzwelder	Jim Reardon
A Star is Burns	March 5, 1995	#2F31	Ken Keeler	Susie Dietter
Home Sweet Homediddly-Dum-Doodily	October 1, 1995	#3F01	Jon Vitti	Susie Dietter
Bart Sells His Soul	October 8, 1995	#3F02	Greg Daniels	Wesley Archer
Team Homer	January 7, 1996	#3F10	Mike Scully	Mark Kirkland
Much Apu About Nothing	May 5, 1996	#3F20	David S. Cohen	Susie Dietter
Homerpalooza	May 19, 1996	#3F21	Brent Forrester	Wesley Archer
Bart After Dark	November 24, 1996	#4F06	Richard Appel	Dominic Polcino

Episode Name	Original Airdate	Production Code	Writer(s)	Director(s)
Hurricane Neddy	December 29, 1996	#4F07	Steve Young	Bob Anderson
El Viaje Misterioso de Nuestro Jomer (The Mysterious Voyage of Homer)	January 5, 1997	#3F24	Ken Keeler	Jim Reardon
The Springfield Files	January 12, 1997	#3G01	Reid Harrison	Steven Dean Moore
The Two Mrs. Nahasapeemapetilons	November 16, 1997	#5F04	Richard Appel	Steven Dean Moore
Lisa the Skeptic	November 23, 1997	#5F05	David S. Cohen	Neil Affleck
In Marge We Trust	April 27, 1997	#4F18	Donick Cary	Steven Dean Moore
The Joy of Sect	February 8, 1998	#5F23	Steve O'Donnell	Steven Dean Moore
Das Bus	February 15, 1998	#5F11	David S. Cohen	Pete Michels
Bart the Mother	September 27, 1998	#5F22	David S. Cohen	Steven Dean Moore
Take My Wife, Sleaze	November 28, 1999	#BABF05	John Swartzwelder	Neil Affleck
Viva Ned Flanders	January 10, 1999	#AABF06	David M. Stern	Neil Affleck
Make Room for Lisa	February 28, 1999	#AABF12	Brian Scully	Matthew Nastuk
Maximum Homerdrive	March 28, 1999	#AABF13	John Swartzwelder	Swinton Scott
Simpsons Bible Stories	April 4, 1999	#AABF14	Tim Long, Larry Doyle, and Matt Selman	Nancy Kruse
Mom and Pop Art	April 11, 1999	#AABF15	Al Jean	Steven Dean Moore
Little Big Mom	January 9, 2000	#BABF04	Carolyn Omine	Mark Kirkland
Faith Off	January 16, 2000	#BABF06	Frank Mula	Nancy Kruse
Alone Again, Natura-Diddly	February 13, 2000	#BABF11	Ian Maxtone-Graham	Jim Reardon

Episode Name	Original Airdate	Production Code	Writer(s)	Director(s)
Missionary: Impossible	February 20, 2000	#BABF10	Ron Hauge	Steven Dean Moore
HOMЯ	January 7, 2001	#BABF22	Al Jean	Mike B. Anderson
Trilogy of Error	April 29, 2001	#CABF14	Matt Selman	Mike B. Anderson
I'm Going to Praiseland	May 6, 2001	#CABF15	Julie Thacker	Chuck Sheetz
She of Little Faith	December 16, 2001	#DABF02	Bill Freiberger	Steven Dean Moore
The Old Man and the Key	March 10, 2002	#DABF09	Jon Vitti	Lance Kramer
The Sweetest Apu	May 5, 2002	#DABF14	John Swartzwelder	Matthew Nastuk
Pray Anything	February 9, 2003	#EABF06	Sam O'Neil & Neil Boushell	Michael Polcino
The Bart of War	May 18, 2003	#EABF16	Marc Wilmore	Michael Polcino
Treehouse of Horror XIV	November 2, 2003	#EABF21	John Swartzwelder	Steven Dean Moore
Today, I Am a Clown	December 7, 2003	#FABF01	Joel H. Cohen	Nancy Kruse
'Tis the Fifteenth Season	December 14, 2003	#FABF02	Michael Price	Steven Dean Moore
Milhouse Doesn't Live Here Anymore	February 15, 2004	#FABF07	Julie Chambers & David Chambers	Matthew Nastuk
Co-Dependents Day	March 21, 2004	#FABF10	Matt Warburton	Bob Anderson
Treehouse of Horror XV	November 7, 2004	#FABF23	Bill Odenkirk	David Silverman
Homer and Ned's Hail Mary Pass	February 6, 2005	#GABF02	Tim Long	Steven Dean Moore
There's Something About Marrying	February 20, 2005	#GABF04	J. Stewart Burns	Nancy Kruse
Home Away From Homer	May 15, 2005	#GABF15	Joel H. Cohen	Bob Anderson
The Father, the Son, and the Holy Guest Star	May 15, 2005	#GABF09	Matt Warburton	Michael Polcino

Episode Name	Original Airdate	Production Code	Writer(s)	Director(s)
Treehouse of Horror XVI	November 6, 2005	#GABF17	Marc Wilmore	David Silverman
Simpsons Christmas Stories	December 18, 2005	#HABF01	Don Payne	Steven Dean Moore
Bart Has Two Mommies	March 19, 2006	#HABF07	Dana Gould	Mike Marcantel
Kiss Kiss, Bang Bangalore	April 9, 2006	#HABF10	Deb Lacusta & Dan Castellaneta	Mark Kirkland
The Monkey Suit	May 14, 2006	#HABF14	J. Stewart Burns	Raymond S. Persi
Little Big Girl	February 11, 2007	#JABF04	Don Payne	Raymond S. Persi
You Kent Always Say What You Want	May 20, 2007	#JABF15	Tim Long	Matthew Nastuk
Midnight Towboy	October 7, 2007	#JABF21	Stephanie Gillis	Matthew Nastuk
Treehouse of Horror XVIII	November 4, 2007	#JABF16	Marc Wilmore	Chuck "Bloody" Sheetz
Smoke on the Daughter	March 30, 2008	#KABF08	Billy Kimball	Lance Kramer
Mona Leaves-a	May 11, 2008	#KABF12	Joel H. Cohen	Mike B. Anderson & Ralph Sosa
Sex, Pies, and Idiotscrapes	September 28, 2008	#KABF17	Kevin Curran	Lance Kramer
MyPods and Broomsticks	November 30, 2008	#KABF20	Marc Wilmore	Steven Dean Moore
No Loan Again, Naturally	March 8, 2009	#LABF03	Jeff Westbrook	Mark Kirkland
Bart Gets a 'Z'	October 4, 2009	#LABF15	Matt Selman	Mark Kirkland
Rednecks and Broomsticks	November 29, 2009	#LABF19	Kevin Curran	Bob Anderson and Rob Oliver
The Food Wife	November 13, 2011	#NABF20	Matt Selman	Timothy Bailey
Pulpit Friction	April 28, 2013	#RABF11	Bill Odenkirk	Chris Clements

South Park. Comedy Central. Created by Trey Parker and Matt Stone. 1997–Present.

Episode Name	Original Airdate	Production Code	Writer(s)	Director(s)
Big Gay Al's Big Gay Boat Ride	September 3, 1997	104	Trey Parker & Matt Stone	Trey Parker
Death	September 17, 1997	106	Trey Parker & Matt Stone	Trey Parker
Starvin' Marvin	November 19, 1997	109	Trey Parker	Trey Parker
Mr. Hankey, the Christmas Poo	December 17, 1997	110	Trey Parker & Matt Stone	Trey Parker
Damien	February 4, 1998	112	Trey Parker, Philip Stark, Matt Stone	Trey Parker
Ike's Wee Wee	May 27, 1998	204	Trey Parker, Matt Stone, and David Goodman	Trey Parker
The Mexican Staring Frog of Southern Sri Lanka	June 10, 1998	206	Trey Parker & Matt Stone	Trey Parker
Rainforest Shmainforest	April 7, 1999	301	Trey Parker and Matt Stone	Trey Parker & Eric Stough
Jewbilee	July 28, 1999	309	Trey Parker	Trey Parker
Starvin' Marvin in Space	November 17, 1999	311	Trey Parker, Matt Stone, and Kyle McCulloch	Trey Parker
Are You There God? It's Me, Jesus	December 29, 1999	316	Trey Parker	Eric Stough
Cherokee Hair Tampons	June 28, 2000	407	Trey Parker	Trey Parker
Something You Can Do With Your Finger	July 12, 2000	409	Trey Parker	Trey Parker
Do the Handi-capped go to Hell?	July 19, 2000	410	Trey Parker	Trey Parker
. . . Probably	July 26, 2000	411	Trey Parker	Trey Parker
Super Best Friends	July 4, 2001	503	Trey Parker	Trey Parker

Episode Name	Original Airdate	Production Code	Writer(s)	Director(s)
The Entity	November 21, 2001	511	Trey Parker	Trey Parker
Kenny Dies	December 5, 2001	513	Trey Parker	Trey Parker
Simpsons Already Did It	June 26, 2002	607	Trey Parker	Trey Parker
Red Hot Catholic Love	July 3, 2002	608	Trey Parker	Trey Parker
Christian Rock Hard	October 29, 2003	709	Trey Parker	Trey Parker
All About Mormons	November 19, 2003	712	Trey Parker	Trey Parker
It's Christmas in Canada	December 17, 2003	714	Trey Parker	Trey Parker
The Passion of the Jew	March 31, 2004	804	Trey Parker	Trey Parker
Mr. Garrison's Fancy New Vagina	March 9, 2005	901	Trey Parker	Trey Parker
Two Days Before the Day After Tomorrow	October 19, 2005	908	Trey Parker & Kenny Hotz	Trey Parker
Trapped in the Closet	November 16, 2005	912	Trey Parker (as John Smith)	Trey Parker (as John Smith)
Bloody Mary	December 7, 2005	914	Trey Parker	Trey Parker
Cartoon Wars: Part I	April 5, 2006	1004	Trey Parker	Trey Parker
Cartoon Wars: Part II	April 12, 2006	1005	Trey Parker	Trey Parker
Go God Go	November 1, 2006	1012	Trey Parker	Trey Parker
Go God Go XII	November 8, 2006	1013	Trey Parker	Trey Parker
Cartman Sucks	March 14, 2007	1102	Trey Parker	Trey Parker
Lice Capades	March 21, 2007	1103	Trey Parker	Trey Parker
The Snuke	March 28, 2007	1104	Trey Parker	Trey Parker
Fantastic Easter Special	April 4, 2007	1105	Trey Parker	Trey Parker

Episode Name	Original Airdate	Production Code	Writer(s)	Director(s)
Le Petit Tourette	October 3, 2007	1108	Trey Parker	Trey Parker
Imagination-land I: Kyle Sucks Cartman's Balls	October 17, 2007	1110	Trey Parker	Trey Parker
Imagination-land II: The Drying of the Balls	October 24, 2007	1111	Trey Parker	Trey Parker
Imagination-land III: The Moistening of the Scrotum	October 31, 2007	1112	Trey Parker	Trey Parker
The Ring	March 11, 2009	1301	Trey Parker	Trey Parker
200	April 14, 2010	1405	Trey Parker	Trey Parker
201	April 21, 2010	1406	Trey Parker	Trey Parker
Humancentipad	April 27, 2011	1501	Trey Parker	Trey Parker
Jewpacabra	April 4, 2012	1604	Trey Parker	Trey Parker
Insecurity	October 10, 2012	1610	Trey Parker	Trey Parker
A Scause for Applause	October 31, 2012	1613	Trey Parker	Trey Parker

NOTES

INTRODUCTION

1 Episodes are hereafter referenced by their name in quotation marks and are listed chronologically in the appendix. In this sentence specific episodes referenced are, in order, *Family Guy* "The Son Also Draws," "I Dream of Jesus," *South Park* "Bloody Mary."

2 I use "America" and "United States of America" interchangeably in this book to avoid repetition. That said, I acknowledge that "America" is bigger than the United States.

3 Giroux (2001).

4 See, e.g., Alberti (2004), Alters (2002), Gournelos (2009), Johnson-Woods (2007).

5 Nielsen Company (2014b).

6 Nielsen Company (2014a).

7 See, e.g., Gray (2008), Mittell (2004, 2010), Mittell and Thompson (2013).

8 See, e.g., Lotz (2007), Spigel and Olsson (2004). See also Murphy (2011) on how television continues to inspire "new media."

9 See, e.g., Dalton and Linder (2005), Jones (1993), Marc (1997), Mills (2009), Morreale (2003).

10 The Pew Forum on Religion and Public Life (2010), Prothero (2007).

11 Prothero (2007).

12 I am thankful to Douglas E. Cowan for coining this term in private communication (ca. 2009). The theoretical development of ignorant familiarity as a concept is my own.

13 Box Office Mojo (2012), Grala (2007).

14 Booker (2006), Turner (2004).

15 Crawford (2009), Henry (2003), Knox (2006), Mittell (2004), Wood and Todd (2005).

16 Alberti (2004), Delaney (2008). Cf. Cantor (2001).

17 *New York Times*, January 28, 1992, sec. 1, p. 17.

18 E.g., Bowler (1996/1997), Pinsky (2007).

19 E.g., Dark (2002), Heit (2008).

20 E.g., Dalton, Mazur, and Siems (2010), Todd Lewis (2002).

21 Pinsky (2007, 226).

22 Heit (2008, 150).

23 Ibid., 143–151. Note that Heit's arguments are influenced by the fact that he was writing during President George W. Bush's second term when neoconservative evangelical politics and economics were particularly strong in the United States.
24 This is known in *South Park* fan circles as *The Spirit of Christmas: Jesus vs. Santa* (Parker and Stone 1995). *The Spirit of Christmas: Jesus vs. Frosty* (Parker and Stone 1992) was released three years earlier and was what originally caught the executive's attention.
25 See also Johnson-Woods (2007).
26 "Red Hot Catholic Love," "Super Best Friends," "Damien."
27 This controversy is covered in "Cartoon Wars: Part I" and "Cartoon Wars: Part II" and is discussed in chapter 5.
28 Dawkins (2006).
29 E.g., Terry Clark (2012), DeLashmutt and Hancock (2008), Dueck (2007), Johnson-Woods (2007, 227–242), Jacoby (2007), Jacquette (2007), Koepsell (2007), Lipoma (2009), Murtagh (2007), David Scott (2011).
30 Cowan (2005), Gournelos (2009). Cf. David Scott (2011).
31 Johnson-Woods (2007, 241).
32 MacFarlane (1995, 1997).
33 See Carlin (2012), David Johnson (2007), VanArragon (2007) for short discussions on religion in *Family Guy*.
34 Jonathan Smith (1998).
35 James (2002 [1902], 61).
36 Ibid., 61–89.
37 See also Cowan (2008, 2010).
38 Taves (2009).
39 See Chidester (2005), Laderman (2009).
40 Berger (1967, 29).
41 Berger and Luckmann (1966).
42 Berger (1967, 3–18).
43 Berger and Luckmann (1966, 155).
44 Ibid., 41.
45 Berger (1967, 31–32).
46 Berger and Luckmann (1966, 67).
47 Ibid., 54.
48 Durkheim (1995 [1912], 207–241, 418–448).
49 Ibid., 44.
50 Ibid., 216–241.
51 Ibid., 224.
52 Bellah (1967).
53 Gorski (2010).
54 See, e.g., Alexander (2006), Chidester (2005), Gorski (2010), Laderman (2009).
55 Kercher (2006).
56 Wuthnow (2005, 78; emphasis in original).

57 See also Bender and Klassen (2010), Eck (2001), Herberg (1960 [1955]), Hutchison (2003), Prothero (2006), Wuthnow (2005).

58 Hunter (1991).

59 Lamont (1992, 4). See also Bourdieu (1977, 1984, 1993).

60 Douglas (2002 [1966]).

61 See also Christian Smith (2003).

62 Swidler (1986).

63 Schudson (1989).

64 See also Swidler and Arditi (1994).

65 Lynch (2012, 65).

66 Illouz (2008, 9).

67 S. Hall (1975, 18).

68 See, e.g., Attardo and Raskin (1991), Christie Davies (1990, 1998, 2002, 2011), M. Davis (1993), Fine (1983, 1984), Fine and de Soucey (2005), Griffin (1994), Kuipers (2006), Morreall (1983, 1987, 1999, 2004, 2009), Oring (2003), Raskin (1985), Zijderveld (1983). Cf., Bergson (1956 [1911]), Douglas (1975, 90–114), Freud (1990).

69 Davis (1993, 7).

70 Morreall (1983), Oring (2003).

71 "In Marge We Trust."

72 Zijderveld (1983, 9). See also Paolucci and Richardson (2006a, 2006b).

73 Zijderveld (1983, 4).

74 Ibid., 6–27, 41–54.

75 Zijderveld (1983). For additional studies on humor as a means of solidifying group solidarity and reinforcing symbolic universes, see Fine (1983, 1984), Fine and de Soucey (2005), Francis (1994), Kuipers (2006), Lowney and Best (1996), Sanford and Eder (1984), and Zillman and Cantor (1996 [1976]). For critiques of sociological approaches to the study of humor, see M. Davis (1995) and Fine (1983). Fox (1990) provides a good example of how humor can disrupt a social group to the point that its taken-for-granted reality is brought into question.

76 See, e.g., Ferguson and Ford (2008), Ford (2000), Ford, Wentzel, and Lorion (2001), Ford and Ferguson (2004), Zillmann (1983).

77 Cf. Randall Collins (1975, 108; 2004), McCarthy (1996, 2). See also Kuipers (2006).

78 See, e.g., Cowan (1999, 2003a, 2003b, 2004).

79 See Fine (1983, 169).

80 Kuipers (2006, 13–18).

81 Christie Davies (1990, 1998, 2002, 2011).

82 Ibid. (1990, 15).

83 Ibid.

84 Ibid. (1998, 164–165).

85 Ibid. (2002, 201–227). This does not mean that jokes are not threatening to political orders. On contemporary satire and politics, see Baumgartner and Morris (2008), Gournelos (2009), Gray, Jones, and Thompson (2009), and Lamb (2004). Conversely, Oring and Raskin argue against any political significance of humor

in their contributions to *Humor*'s forum on the caricatures of Muhammad (Paul Lewis 2008, 21–30, 37–42).

86 Christie Davies (1990, 9).

87 "Hurricane Neddy."

88 Oring (2003, 41–57).

89 Freud (1990).

90 Oring (2003, 48).

91 Ibid., 46–47.

92 Ibid., 56–57. See also Paul Lewis (2006).

93 On how microsociological interactions build a social structure defined by inter-group conflict, see Randall Collins (1975, 103–111). See also Mannheim (1936).

94 Cowan (2003a).

95 "Homerpalooza."

96 Berger (1997, 157).

97 One of the more confusing distinctions in the study of religion arises when scholars use "profane" to indicate something that is "evil" or "impure." I use the terms positive and negative sacred because what is evil can still be set apart. Satan, for example, is an evil figure in the Christian and Islamic traditions, but he is still "set apart and forbidden," marking him as a sacred figure. That which is considered monstrously evil is sacred because it is of great, cosmic importance and is part of the unseen order (Beal 2002).

98 Berger (1997). See also Arbuckle (2008), Hyers (1969, 1981, 1987, 1989, 1996). For a more extended criticism of this approach, see Feltmate (2013a, 2013b, 2013c).

99 Berger (1970).

100 Berger and Luckmann (1966, 25). See also Proudfoot (1985), Taves (2009).

101 Berger (1961, 1970, 1997). See also Feltmate (2013c).

102 Douglas (1975, 98).

103 Stuart Hall (1975, 15).

104 "The Old Man and the Key."

105 Goffman (1959). See also Paolucci and Richardson (2006a, 2006b).

106 Stuart Hall (1975, 15; emphasis in original).

107 Cowan (2003a, 2003b, 2008, 2010), Hendershot (2004), Lofton (2011), Lynch (2012), McAlister (2005). For a broader application that just religion and television, see the essays in Mittell and Thompson (2013).

108 E.g., Lynn Clark (2003), Hoover (2006).

109 E.g., Henry Jenkins (2006a, 2006b).

110 E.g., Campbell (2010), Wagner (2012).

111 See also Booker (2006), Gray (2006), Kercher (2006), Mittell (2004, 2010).

CHAPTER 1. SACRED CENTERS

1 Pinsky (2007, 20, 23).

2 Pinsky and Parvin (2002, 57–62).

3 Keslowitz (2006, 207–211).

4 Lynch (2005, 154–160).

5 Romanowski (2007, 174–175), Heit (2008, 14–15, 104–106).

6 Turner (2004, 267; emphasis in original).

7 Henry (2012, 177–179).

8 Dalton et al. (2010, 245).

9 Roof (1999, 75).

10 Bellah et al. (2008, 221, 235).

11 Albanese (2007), Aupers and Houtman (2006), Bellah et al. (2008), Bender (2010), Chandler (2008, 2011), Fuller (2001), Hanegraaff (1996), Heelas (1996, 2008), Heelas and Woodhead (2005), Roof (1999), Stuart Rose (1998, 2001), Sutcliffe (2003), Wuthnow (1998), Zinnbauer et al. (1997).

12 Roof (1999).

13 For a discussion of this episode in light of whether or not the Church of the Holy Fonz is a "real" religion, see David Johnson (2007).

14 Ammerman (2013, 275).

15 Moore (1994).

16 Einstein (2008, 210). See also Vincent Miller (2003).

17 Moore (1994, 269). See also McDannell (1995), Morgan (2007), Schmidt (1995).

18 According to Carrette and King, neoliberal ideology "puts profits before people, promotes privatisation of public utilities, services and resources, and is in the process of eroding many individual liberties that were established under its forerunner—political liberalism" (2005, 7).

19 Carrette and King (2005, 5).

20 Heelas (2008, 14; emphasis in original).

21 Ibid., 8. See also Chandler (2011).

22 For more on Lisa, see Gray (2006, 58), Henry (2007), and Skoble (2001).

23 Turner (2004, 274).

24 Iwamura (2005, 34–38).

25 See, e.g., Prebish and Baumann (2002), Queen (2000, 2002), Seager (1999), Tanaka (1998).

26 Cox (1977). See also Wuthnow (1998).

27 Pinsky (2001, 39–46).

28 See also Wilson (2012).

29 Tweed (2002).

30 Iwamura (2005, 32).

31 Iwamura (2005, 32–38).

32 McLeod (1999).

33 The Numbers (2010).

34 Yoffe (2007).

35 Bashir and Apton (2007).

36 Armstrong (2009).

37 Ibid., 82.

38 Ibid., 83.

39 The Stonecutters are a parody of the Freemasons. Homer joins the group in the season 6 episode "Homer the Great." "Make Room for Lisa" aired in season 10, which assumes a consistent audience that will make the connection.

40 See Possamai (2003), York (2001).

41 Zaidman (2007, 364).

42 Heelas (2008). See also Heelas and Woodhead (2005, 82–110).

43 Heelas (2008), Chandler (2011).

44 Jessie Smith (2011). Zuckerman's (2008) comparison between the religious United States and the secular Denmark and Sweden provides a helpful contrast in how disbelief can be a normal, everyday occurrence.

45 Cragun et al (2012), Edgell, Gerteis, and Hartmann (2006).

46 Pew Forum on Religion and Public Life (2015, 3).

47 Ibid., 4.

48 Pew Forum on Religion and Public Life (2013a).

49 Woods (2009).

50 The video of this speech is available on YouTube. The quote is transcribed from part three, available at http://www.youtube.com.

51 See American Civil Liberties Union of Pennsylvania (2009), Humes (2007), Moran (2002), Slack (2007).

52 Harris (2004). See also, e.g., Dawkins (2006), Dennett (2006), Hitchens (2007).

53 Dawkins (2006).

54 "Go God Go."

55 The Flying Spaghetti Monster was introduced when Bobby Henderson, a computer programmer with satirical talent, wrote to the Kansas School Board in 2005 demanding that all viewpoints be taught in science class, including the theory that everything was created by an invisible Flying Spaghetti Monster. It has since been adopted by proponents of the separation of Church and State, and Dawkins has referenced it in his lectures. For more information, see The Church of the Flying Spaghetti Monster's website (http://www.venganza.org/). See also Laycock (2013a).

56 Forrest and Gross (2004, 5).

57 "Intelligent Design" developed from "creation science" after the U.S. Supreme Court case *Edwards v. Aguillard* declared teaching the latter unconstitutional (see, e.g., Numbers [2007], Eugene Scott [2007]). However, it differs because, while it posits an intelligent designer as the reason for life, it also accepts a broad range of scientific theories, for example, accepting that the Earth is billions of years old as opposed to the thousands of years that some creationists posit. For discussions against ID, see Forrest and Gross (2004), Petto and Godfrey (2007), and Shermer (2006). Pennock (1999) helpfully locates ID within neo-creationism while also defending Darwinian evolutionary theory. For a theistic position that also endorses evolution, see Francis Collins (2006).

58 ID's foundational figure and driving force, Berkeley law professor emeritus Phillip Johnson, has proposed an agenda for infiltrating the scientific community's Darwinian orthodoxy. Dubbing this plan "the wedge," its goal is to undermine

Darwinian materialism by creating a volume of books and articles that generate enough publicity to draw people's attention. This will "wedge" ID into scientific debate and eventually break Darwinian thinking, leaving ID as the dominant paradigm (Philip Johnson [1999]; see also Center for the Renewal of Science & Culture [1998], Dembski [2006], Philip Johnson [2000]). The problem is that in this light the arguments appear less than scientific, especially once scientists start challenging them (see, e.g., Behe [1996; 2000]; Shanks and Joplin [1999]). Rather, they start appearing as systematic attempts to influence public policy without adhering to accepted scientific standards.

59 Behe (1996, 39). See also Behe (2000, 2001, 2007), and Shanks and Joplin (1999).
60 See, e.g., Francis Collins (2006, 181–195), Forrest and Gross (2004), Petto and Godfrey (2007), Shermer (2006).

CHAPTER 2. THE DIFFERENCE RACE MAKES

1 See, e.g., Brodkin (1998), Conley (1999), Cornell and Hartmann (1997), McIntosh (1998 [2004]), Omi and Winart (1986), Pager (2007).
2 Cornell and Hartmann (1997, 72–101).
3 Ibid., 24.
4 Bramadat (2005, 8).
5 Cornell and Hartmann (1997).
6 de Mille (1976, 1980), Hardman (2007), Wendy Rose (1992).
7 See Heit (2008, 100–104) for a different perspective on Homer's spiritual seeking.
8 Castaneda (1968, 120–123; 1971, 231; 1972, 83–89).
9 A similar pattern occurs in *The Simpsons Movie* (Silverman 2007) when Homer experiences an epiphany while throat singing with an Inuit elder.
10 See, e.g., Aldred (2000), Philip Deloria (1998), Vine Deloria (1992a, 1992b, 1999a), Grim (2000), Hernández-Ávila (2000), Jocks (2000), Owen (2008), Wendy Rose (1992).
11 Philip Jenkins (2004, 254–255).
12 Parkhill (1997, 82–87). See also Gill (1987).
13 Quoted in Parkhill (1997, 85). See also V. Deloria (1999b).
14 P. Deloria (1998, 154–180).
15 Visually, the clod is Alfred E. Neuman—*MAD Magazine*'s infamous mascot—while Lorne Michaels is famous as the creator of *Saturday Night Live* where some *Simpsons* writers worked before coming to FOX.
16 Eck (1998).
17 Reichenbach (1988), Sharma (1973).
18 This episode is an explicit parody of the anti-immigrant Proposition 187 that appeared on California's 1994 ballot that denied illegal aliens social services including health care and education. Although it passed on the original ballot, it was found unconstitutional in 1998 and overturned by the Supreme Court (American Civil Liberties Union 1999).
19 Kurien (2007, 53).

20 See, e.g., Gupta (2003); Jacob and Thaku (2000); Kurien (2007); Mazumdar and Mazumdar (2003); Min (2003); Waghorne (1999).

21 See *Hinduism Today* (1999).

22 Sri Venkateswara Temple (1999).

23 Crosland (1927).

24 In Judaism the Torah refers to the whole of the law (including the oral Torah, also known as the Mishnah and Talmud), as well as the first five books (the Pentateuch) of the Tanak. However, some American nontraditionalist groups (e.g., Reform Jews) will call into question some laws in the Torah and may not even acknowledge the oral Torah as legally binding (Raphael [2003, 18]). Any of these meanings works here, so even if non-Jews in the audience are only familiar with the Torah referring to the Pentateuch, the exchange still makes sense.

25 Diner (1999), Raphael (2003).

26 See, e.g., Diner (1999), Kaplan (2009), Raphael (2003), Sarna (2004).

27 Cf. Gans' characterization of American Jews's "symbolic ethnicity" (1999, 178) with Cohen and Eisen (2000, 27–42), Kaufman (2005), and Winter (1992, 1996).

28 Herberg (1960 [1955]), cf. Brodkin (1998).

29 Ritterband (1995).

30 Devlin (2007), Morefield (2009).

31 "Rainforest Shmainforest," "Mr. Garrison's Fancy New Vagina."

32 "Mr. Hankey, the Christmas Poo."

33 Devlin (2007).

34 Brodkin (1998).

35 Fishman (2000, 10).

36 Ibid., 1.

37 See also Auerbach (1995), Feingold (1995), Glazer (1995), Ritterband (1995).

38 Cohen and Eisen (2000, 5).

39 Wuthnow (1998, 4).

40 Cohen and Eisen (2000, 27–42).

41 A counterpoint to this comes from the Pew Forum on Religion & Public Life's report on American Jews, which found that 22% of American Jews are "Jews of no religion," suggesting that there has been a change over the last decade in how many Jews see religion as a substantive component of Jewish identity (2013b, 32).

42 Sarna (2004, 371).

43 Pew Forum (2013b).

44 Neusner (1990). See also Glazer (2005), Sklare (1990), Woocher (1990). None of the programs deal intimately with Israel and its politics and for spatial reasons I have not discussed the few times Israel is noted.

45 Pew Forum on Religion & Public Life (2013b, 55).

46 Glazer (2005), Waxman (2005, 104–112).

47 Steven Cohen (1995).

48 Morefield (2009).

49 In "The Entity," Kyle B is known as Kyle and Kyle becomes "Kyle 2." On the DVD commentary, however, Parker and Stone refer to Kyle B as Kyle 2 and this switching of names between episode and commentary, not to mention the general confusion of reading about Kyle and Kyle 2, is why I have switched his name to Kyle B.

50 Victor Marsden (1986). See also Landes and Katz (2011).

51 On the self-hating Jew, see Gilman (1986) and Lerman (2008).

52 "Blind Ambition."

53 Christie Davies (1990, 1998, 2002, 2011).

54 "Padre de Familia."

55 In the original version of "When You Wish Upon a Weinstein" the lyric is "Even though they killed my Lord." The "I don't think they killed my Lord" line was a later edit to reduce the episode's offensiveness for audiences (Keys 2004). For more on the problem of the Christ-killer motif in anti-Semitism, see Jeremy Cohen (2007).

56 Keys (2004).

57 "Something You Can Do With Your Finger."

58 "Simpsons Already Did It."

59 "Two Days Before the Day After Tomorrow."

60 "Jewpacabra."

61 Gibson (2004).

62 This reflects the concerns among American Jewish leaders that *The Passion* would spark anti-Semitic sentiments and violence (Ariel [2004]).

63 See Cohen (2007).

CHAPTER 3. AMERICAN CHRISTIANITY, PART 1

1 A portion of this chapter was previously published as Feltmate (2013b).

2 "Homerpalooza."

3 Christie Davies (1990, 15).

4 Butler (1990), Finke and Stark (2005), Hatch (1989).

5 Herberg (1960).

6 Pew Forum on Religion & Public Life (2015).

7 Hunter (1991), Putnam and Campbell (2010), Wuthnow (1988).

8 Pinsky (2007, 16).

9 Heit (2008, 36).

10 Delaney (2008, 203–207).

11 "The Courtship of Stewie's Father."

12 "The Kiss Seen Around the World."

13 "The Giggity Wife."

14 Edwards (1741).

15 Whitfield (1738).

16 Finney (1835, 274).

17 Tom Smith (2012). According to the survey, 16.6% of respondents said that "While I have doubts, I feel that I do believe in God" accurately describes them, and 58.4% chose "I know God really exists and have no doubts about it."

18 Froese and Bader (2007), Hunter (1991), Jensen (1998, 2009), Kunkel et al. (1999), Noffke and McFadden (2001), Wuthnow (1989). Cf. Stark (2008, 75–78).

19 Gorsuch and Smith (1983), Hunter (1991), Maynard, Gorsuch, and Bjorck (2001), Stark (2008), Wuthnow (1989).

20 Pew Forum on Religion & Public Life (2015).

21 "Das Bus"; "Mom and Pop Art"; "Homer and Ned's Hail Mary Pass."

22 Ratliff (2001); see also Bivins (2008, 129–168).

23 Hutchison (1976).

24 Channing (1967, 197).

25 The other entity in the Christian Trinity is the Holy Spirit. This confusing mystery of how Christians can be monotheists, but their God be three people, is satirically questioned in "Treehouse of Horror XV," in which Ned acquires the power to see people's deaths. Begging Homer not to go to work, where he will cause Springfield's destruction, Ned says, "Homer, please, don't tempt the gods. I mean God. There's one God. Only one. Well, sometimes there's three."

26 Finney (1835, 334–352).

27 Rauschenbusch (1967).

28 Jim Wallis (2005, 209–293).

29 Ibid., 218–219.

30 Heit (2008, 31).

31 Henry (2012, 175).

32 Ibid., 175–176. See also, e.g., Bade and Cook (2008), Baesler (2002), Baker (2008), Harris et al. (2005), and Ladd and Spilka (2002, 2006).

33 Blum and Harvey (2012), Prothero (2003).

34 Blum and Harvey (2012, 268).

35 "Death."

36 See, e.g., Karimi (2013), White (2012).

37 "A Scause for Applause." Pussy Riot is the name of a Russian feminist protest rock group that came to international attention after three of its members were arrested for staging a guerilla performance on February 21, 2012 in Moscow's Cathedral of Christ the Savior, in which they protested the Russian Orthodox Church's support of Vladimir Putin, whom they saw as a dictator. Pussy Riot's arrest became a major story in the West over their freedom of speech and the group became a symbol of the Russian government's attempts to control dissidents (see BBC 2013).

38 "The Mexican Staring Frog of Southern Sri Lanka," "Mr. Hankey the Christmas Poo."

39 For a theological analysis of this episode, see David Scott (2011).

40 Blum and Harvey (2012), Prothero (2003).

41 Prothero (2003).

42 "Milhouse Doesn't Live Here Anymore."

43 Blum and Harvey (2012, 265).

44 Prothero (2003, 301).

45 Tom Smith (2012).

46 American Bible Society (2014, 6, 9–10).
47 For extended analyses of "Simpsons Bible Stories," see Heit (2008, 58–63), Myles (2015), and Pinsky (2007, 122–126).
48 See, e.g., Whitmire (2014).
49 American Bible Society (2014, 11).
50 Ibid., 23.
51 Pew Forum on Religion & Public Life (2010).
52 "Lisa on Ice."
53 "Lisa the Greek."
54 "The Otto Show."
55 "Marge Gets a Job."
56 Heit (2008, 52).
57 Ibid., 55.
58 "The Father, the Son, and the Holy Guest Star."
59 Haskin (1953).
60 Cowan (2007, ¶20). On the difficulty of identifying what constitutes a "mainline" denomination, see Lantzer (2012), Roof and McKinney (1987), Tom Smith (1990). I continue using the "mainline" label because it is still used in popular literature and it is known as a differentiating marker from the more castigated fundamentalist and evangelical labels.
61 See, e.g., Ahlstrom (2004, 731–824), Hutchison (1968, 1976), Lofton (2006), Ogden (1976), Thuesen (2002).
62 Pinsky (2007, 75); see also Heit (2008, 72), Turner (2004, 263–264).
63 Silverman (2007).
64 "Bart's Girlfriend"; "In Marge We Trust."
65 E.g., "Homer the Heretic"; "In Marge We Trust"; "Simpsons Bible Stories."
66 "The Telltale Head."
67 "Take My Wife, Sleaze."
68 "Bart Sells His Soul."
69 "Bart's Girlfriend."
70 Silverman (2007).
71 "The Telltale Head."
72 "Homer vs. Lisa and the 8th Commandment."
73 "Homer's Triple Bypass."
74 "Bart's Girlfriend."
75 See, e.g., Demerath (1995), Finke and Stark (2005, 235–283), Hout, Greely, and Wilde (2001), Hutchison et al. (1991), McKinney (1998), Roof and McKinney (1987); cf. Percy and Markham (2006), Wuthnow and Evans (2002).
76 Finke and Stark (2005). See also Stark and Finke (2000).
77 See also McGaw (1979), cf. Wellman (2002).
78 "Co-Dependents Day."
79 "Mona Leaves-a."
80 "Simpsons Bible Stories."

81 Tae-Bo is a mass marketed aerobics program that combines martial arts, boxing, and dance.
82 Hutchison (1976).
83 "Bart After Dark."
84 "Lisa the Skeptic"; "The Monkey Suit."
85 "Krusty Gets Busted."
86 "Bart the Mother."
87 Heit (2008, 76–78).
88 Ibid., 82.
89 See Heit (2008, 83–95), Pinsky (2007, 46–69).
90 "Home Away From Homer."
91 George Marsden (2005).
92 Hankins (2008), George Marsden (1991, 62–82), Christian Smith et al. (1998, 2–19; Christian Smith 2000), Stone (1997).
93 Christian Smith (2000).
94 See, e.g., Ammerman (1987), Noll (2001), Reimer (2003), Shires (2007), Christian Smith (1998), Stone (1997).
95 Balmer (2006).
96 Becker (1963, 149).
97 Cf. Comments from upset viewers of *The Simpsons* to the Federal Communications Commission in the Freedom of Information Act documents posted by governmentattic.org (2008c, 2013b).
98 "Smoke on the Daughter."
99 "The Bart of War."
100 "Cape Feare."
101 "Trilogy of Error."
102 "НОМЯ."
103 See, e.g., Evans (2002), Hadley (1994), Hoffman and Johnson (2005), Hughes (2006), Jelen and Wilcox (2003), Maxwell and Jelen (1995).
104 See, e.g., Chancey (2007), Ebel (2009), Elifson and Hadaway (1985); Green and Guth (1989).
105 "Bart Has Two Mommies," "Lisa's First Word," "Alone Again Natura-Diddly."
106 See also Cantor (2001).
107 "Brother, Can You Spare Two Dimes?"
108 "Little Big Mom."
109 "Homer Loves Flanders," "The Bart of War," "'Tis the Fifteenth Season."
110 Turner (2004, 267).

CHAPTER 4. AMERICAN CHRISTIANITY, PART 2
1 Portions of this chapter were previously published in Feltmate (2013a).
2 On blasphemy as a label groups apply to something that threatens the perceived sacredness legitimating their socially constructed worlds rather than a quality that is inherent in an image, sound, or action, see Levy (1993) and Plate (2006).

3 See, e.g., Butler (1990), Dorsett (1991), Evensen (2003), Hatch (1989), Luhr (2009), McClymond (2004, 2007), McGirr (2001), McLoughlin (1978), Stout (1991).

4 See Cuneo (1997).

5 For another perspective on Francis' dogmatism and its problems, see David Johnson (2007, 45).

6 Psalm 68:21–23.

7 Sanneh (2009), Walls (1996).

8 Wuthnow (2009, 154).

9 Wuthnow notes that the Southern Baptist Convention reports sending 150,000 members abroad annually and the United Methodist Church sends 100,000 (2009, 167).

10 McClymond (2004, 10).

11 Ibid., 10–14.

12 There is another main plot device in these two episodes about Satan's sexual relationship with Saddam Hussein that starts in *South Park: Bigger, Longer, and Uncut* (Parker 1999) and that provides numerous jokes about different religious beliefs regarding who gets into Heaven (it turns out that only the Mormons do ["Probably"]), but that is not explored here for reasons of space.

13 Steinberg and Kincheloe (2009).

14 Praiseland is inspired by Heritage USA, a South Carolina theme park that was run by Jim and Tammy Faye Bakker's PTL (Praise the Lord) Ministries from 1978 to 1989 before it shut down in the wake of Hurricane Hugo and IRS investigations.

15 "Homer's Barbershop Quartet."

16 "Bart Has Two Mommies."

17 "Sex, Pies, and Idiotscrapes." The AC/DC reference is to their song "Dirty Deeds Done Dirt Cheap."

18 "The Food Wife."

19 To the best of my knowledge, this song was written for this episode and does not exist in an alternate format. Bruce Howell is the guitarist in Parker and Stone's band DVDA.

20 For an introduction to some more prominent CCM songs, see CCM Magazine (2006). See Brenneman (2014) on sentimentality in evangelicalism.

21 Howard and Streck (1999, 213). See also Rowmanowski (2005).

22 See Howard and Streck (1999, especially 49–72), Stowe (2011), Wilder and Rehwaldt (2012).

23 On evangelicals, popular culture, moral regulation, and sexuality see, e.g., Bivins (2008), Hendershot (2004, 87–142), Luhr (2009), Moslener (2011), Regnerus (2007).

24 DeLashmutt and Hancock (2008, 179).

25 On evangelicals and monogamous sex, see DeRogatis (2015).

26 See, e.g., Barton (2012), Jordan (2011).

27 See, e.g., Delaney (2008), Gournelos (2009), Henry (2012), Johnson-Woods (2007), Turner (2004). Cf. Feltmate and Brackett (2014).

28 Lynch (2012, 65).

29 American Civil Liberties Union of Massachusetts (2005, 2006).

30 Silver Ring Thing (2014b).
31 Silver Ring Thing (2014a).
32 Moslener (2011). See also Einstein (2008, 188–189).
33 Regnerus (2007, 98–103).
34 Ibid., 99.
35 Ibid., 158.
36 Olson and Cadge (2002) argue that debates about homosexuality raise questions that are pivotal to a church's identity, stating, "Homosexuality is about scripture: How is the Bible to be read, interpreted, and understood? It is about creation: How ought the people that God creates behave sexually? Homosexuality is about families and reproduction: Who can be married? Bear children? Adopt children? Raise children? What lessons should those children be taught about sexual behavior?" (155). See also Cadge (2002), Cadge, Day, and Wildeman (2007), and Thumma (2006).
37 See, e.g., Moon (2004).
38 See Barton (2012) for an excellent overview of how "Bible Belt" Christianity has influenced homosexuals and their relationships with their conservative families.
39 Glassgold et al. (2009).
40 Exodus International announced it was ceasing operations on June 19, 2013, and issued an apology from former President Alan Chambers. For the full text of Chambers' apology, see Steffan (2013). For exposés of Exodus events, see, e.g., Barton (2012, 116–150), Besen (2003).
41 For an ethnographic analysis inside one group for homosexual men (not teenagers), see Erzen (2006).
42 For a more detailed analysis of the exchange between the Catholic League and *South Park*, see Feltmate (2013a).
43 I use the term blasphemy as a label groups apply to something that threatens the perceived sacredness legitimating their socially constructed worlds rather than a quality that is inherent in an image, sound, or action. Levy (1993), Plate (2006).
44 "Damien," "Big Gay Al's Big Gay Boatride."
45 Bishopaccountability.org, a website dedicated to cataloguing the sexual abuse scandals in the Catholic Church, puts the number of known abusers at 5.6% of all priests serving from 1950 to 2002 (2014).
46 See, e.g., Orsi (2005).
47 Catholic League for Religious and Civil Rights (2005a).
48 Ibid. (2005b).
49 Compare this to their ability to get *The Simpsons* episode "Sunday Cruddy Sunday" censored. This episode features a parody of Superbowl ads in which a man's car breaks down outside a gas station in the desert and three scantily clad women come out and "service" his car. One of the women leans over the car's windshield and a cross pops out of her cleavage. The original (and DVD) version of this scene had a voiceover saying "The Catholic Church, we've made a few changes." In the edited version "Catholic" is removed, a fight that *Simpsons* producers are annoyed at losing (Catholic League for Religious and Civil Rights 1999a, 1999b, 1999c).

50 Ibid. (2002).
51 Ibid. (2005b).
52 See Binder (1993).

CHAPTER 5. STIGMA, STUPIDITY, AND EXCLUSION

1   van Driel and Richardson (1988).
2   See also Beckford (1994), Bromley (1994), Cowan and Hadden (2004), McCloud (2004), Neal (2011), Robbins and Anthony (1994), and Wright (1997).
3   Cowan (2003a), Philip Jenkins (2000).
4   Philip Jenkins (2000). Cf. R. Laurence Moore (1986).
5   Cowan and Hadden (2004), McCloud (2004), Wessinger (2000).
6   For voices from the anti-cult movement (ACM), see Conway and Siegelman (1978), Rudin and Rudin (1980), Singer and Lalich (1995). For analysis of the ACM, see Shupe and Bromley (1980, 1985), Shupe and Darnell (2006).
7   Cowan and Hadden (2004, 69–77), Possamai and Lee (2004), Shupe and Hadden (1995).
8   Richardson and van Driel (1997).
9   Laycock (2013b), Neal (2011).
10 van Driel and Richardson (1988, 177).
11 Griffiths (2000).
12 Adler (2006, 178–239), Salomonsen (2002), Starhawk (1999). Cf. Bado-Fralick (2005).
13 Barner-Barry (2005), Pike (2001, 87–122).
14 For a general introduction to the Jehovah's Witnesses, see Beckford (1975), Howden (2002), and Penton (1997).
15 "It Takes a Village Idiot, and I Married One."
16 For a general introduction to the LDS, see Ostling and Ostling (1999) and Douglas Davies (2003).
17 Cowan (2005).
18 Gillespie and Walker (2006, 3).
19 See also Rothstein (2009).
20 For more on Scientology see James Lewis (2009), Melton (2000), Urban (2012), Roy Wallis (1977).
21 Gillespie and Walker (2006, 4).
22 See, e.g., Behar (1991), Russell Miller (1987).
23 Barkun (2003), Dumenil (1984).
24 Singer and Lalich (1995). cf. Barker (1984).
25 Barker (1986).
26 John Hall (1995).
27 See Singer and Lalich (1995, 63).
28 For a counter-analysis to claims of brainwashing and love-bombing in the Unification Church, see Barker (1984, 173–188). For a summary of brainwashing literature and why brainwashing is insufficient to explain conversion to a NRM, see Dawson (2006, 95–124).

29 Carter (1990), Urban (2005).
30 Wessinger (2000, 12).
31 Ibid., 16–17.
32 Palmer (2004), Tumminia (2003), Tumminia and Kirkpatrick (1995). See also Wojcik (2003).
33 Peoples Temple has a more complicated history than *South Park*'s parody. For more, see Chidester (1988), John Hall (2004 [1987]), Hall, Schuyler, and Trinh (2000), Wessinger (2000).
34 Balch (1995), Balch and Taylor (1977, 2002), Zeller (2014).
35 Wessinger (2000).
36 See, e.g., Gottschalk and Greenberg (2008), Karim (2003), McAlister (2005), Said (1981), Semmerling (2006), Shaheen (2003).
37 Shaheen (2003, 2, 7).
38 Gottschalk and Greenberg (2008, 76).
39 OAPEC refers to the Organization of Arab Petroleum Exporting Countries, as opposed to the Organization of Petroleum Exporting Countries (OPEC) which also included countries such as Venezuela and Nigeria, which did not join the embargo (Licklider 1988). See also, e.g., Gottschalk and Greenberg (2008), Knorr (1975), McAlister (2005), Rustow (1982), Said (1979).
40 See Esposito (1990a; 1990b), Esposito and Voll (1996), Gottschalk and Greenberg (2008), McAlister (2005), Said (1981).
41 See also, e.g., Gottschalk and Greenberg (2008), Jeffords and Rabinovitz (1994), Karim (2003), McAlister (2005), Saliba (1994).
42 GhaneaBassiri (2010), Haddad (1990), Haddad and Smith (1994), Jane Smith (1999).
43 See, e.g., Abrahamian (2003), Gottschalk and Greenberg (2008), Lincoln (2006), Martin and Phelan (2002), McAlister (2005), Tweed (2008), Wicks (2006).
44 Oring (2003, 56–57).
45 Klausen (2009).
46 CNN (2010a, 2010b).
47 O'Neil (2014).
48 For more on how *South Park* strikes back against corporate, religious, and extremist attempts to silence them through satire, see Gournelos (2009, 123–145).

CONCLUSION
1 Hirsch (1987, 14).
2 Prothero (2007).
3 Alters (2002).
4 Arp (2007); Heit (2008); Irwin, Conard, and Skoble (2001); Pinsky (2007); Wisnewski (2007).
5 As outlined in the introduction, for sociological studies of humor, superiority, and conflict see Davies (1990; 2002), Kuipers (2006), and Oring (2003).
6 Chidester (2005), Laderman (2009).

BIBLIOGRAPHY

Abrahamian, Ervand. 2003. The US Media, Huntington and September 11. *Third World Quarterly* 24 (3): 529–544.

Adler, Margot. 2006. *Drawing Down the Moon: Witches, Druids, Goddess-Worshippers and other Pagans in America.* Completely revised and updated edition. New York: Penguin.

Ahlstrom, Sydney E. 2004. *A Religious History of the American People.* 2nd ed. With a new Foreword and concluding chapter by David D. Hall. New Haven and London: Yale University Press.

Albanese, Catherine. 2007. *A Republic of Mind and Spirit: A Cultural History of American Metaphysical Religion.* New Haven: Yale University Press.

Alberti, John, ed. 2004. *Leaving Springfield: The Simpsons and the Possibility of Oppositional Culture.* Detroit, MI: Wayne State University Press.

Aldred, Lisa. 2000. Plastic Shamans and Astroturf Sundances: New Age Commercialization of Native American Spirituality. *American Indian Quarterly* 24 (3): 329–352.

Alexander, Jeffrey C. 2006. *The Civil Sphere.* New York: Oxford University Press.

Alters, Diane. 2002. The Family Audience: Class, Taste and Production in Late Modernity. PhD diss., University of Colorado.

American Bible Society. 2014. The State of the Bible: 2014. Research conducted by the Barna Group. Retrieved from http://www.americanbible.org.

American Civil Liberties Union. 1999. CA's anti-immigrant Proposition 187 is voided, ending state's five-year battle with ACLU, rights groups. *American Civil Liberties Union,* July 29. Retrieved from http://www.aclu.org.

American Civil Liberties Union of Massachusetts. 2005. American Civil Liberties Union of Massachusetts v. Leavitt, Horn, and Wilson. *American Civil Liberties Union.* May 16. Retrieved from https://www.aclu.org.

American Civil Liberties Union of Massachusetts. 2006. American Civil Liberties Union of Massachusetts v. Leavitt, Horn, and Wilson Settlement Agreement. *American Civil Liberties Union.* February 21. Retrieved from https://www.aclu.org

American Civil Liberties Union of Pennsylvania. 2009. Dover Trial Transcripts. *American Civil Liberties Union of Pennsylvania.* Retrieved from http://www.aclupa.org/legal.

Ammerman, Nancy Tatom. 1987. *Bible Believers: Fundamentalists in the Modern World.* New Brunswick, NJ: Rutgers University Press.

———. 2013. Spiritual but Not Religious? Beyond Binary Choices in the Study of Religion. *Journal for the Social Scientific Study of Religion* 52 (2): 258–278.

Arbuckle, Gerald A. 2008. *Laughing with God: Humor, Culture, and Transformation.* With a foreword by Jean Vanier. Collegeville, MN: Liturgical Press.

Ariel, Yaakov. 2004. *The Passion of the Christ* and the Passion of the Jews: Mel Gibson's Film in Light of Jewish-Christian Relations. In *Re-Viewing the Passion: Mel Gibson's Film and Its Critics,* ed. S. Brent Plate, 21–41. New York: Palgrave Macmillan.

Armstrong, Jolene. 2009. Miss Information: Consumer Excess, Health Care and Historical Guilt in "Cherokee Hair Tampons." In *The Deep End of* South Park: *Critical Essays on Television's Shocking Cartoon Series,* ed. Leslie Stratyner and James R. Keller, 78–90. Jefferson, NC: McFarland & Company.

Arp, Robert. 2007. South Park *and Philosophy: You Know, I Learned Something Today.* Malden, MA: Blackwell.

Attardo, Salvatore and Victor Raskin. 1991. Script Theory Revis(it)ed: Joke Similarity and Joke Presentation Model. *Humor: International Journal of Humor Research* 4 (3/4): 293–347.

Auerbach, Jerold S. 1995. Liberalism, Judaism, and American Jews: A Response. In *The Americanization of the Jews,* ed. Robert M. Seltzer and Norman J. Cohen, 144–148. New York: New York University Press.

Aupers, Stef and Dick Houtman. 2006. Beyond the Spiritual Supermarket: The Social and Public Significance of New Age Spirituality. *Journal of Contemporary Religion* 21 (2): 201–222.

Bado-Fralick, Nikki. 2005. *Coming to the Edge of the Circle: A Wiccan Initiation Ritual.* New York: Oxford University Press.

Bade, Mark K. and Stephen W. Cook. 2008. Functions of Christian Prayer in the Coping Process. *Journal for the Scientific Study of Religion* 47 (1): 123–133.

Baesler, E. James. 2002. Prayer and Relationship with God II: Replication and Extension of the Relational Prayer Model. *Review of Religious Research* 44 (1): 58–67.

Baker, Joseph O. 2008. An Investigation of the Sociological Patterns of Prayer Frequency and Content. *Sociology of Religion* 69 (2): 169–185.

Balch, Robert W. 1995. Waiting for the Ships: Disillusionment and the Revitalization of Faith in Bo and Peep's UFO Cult. In *The Gods Have Landed: New Religions from Other Worlds,* ed. James R. Lewis, 137–166. Albany: State University of New York Press.

Balch, Robert W. and David Taylor. 1977. Seekers and Saucers: The Role of the Cultic Milieu in Joining a UFO Cult. *American Behavioral Scientist* 20 (6): 839–860.

———. 2002. Making Sense of the Heaven's Gate Suicides. In *Cults, Religion, & Violence,* ed. David G. Bromley and J. Gordon Melton, 209–228. Cambridge: Cambridge University Press.

Balmer, Randall. 2006. *Mine Eyes Have Seen the Glory: A Journey into the Evangelical Subculture in America.* 4th ed. New York: Oxford University Press.

Barker, Eileen. 1984. *The Making of a Moonie: Choice or Brainwashing?* Oxford: Basil Blackwell.

———. 1986. Religious Movements: Cult and Anti-cult Since Jonestown. *Annual Review of Sociology* 12: 329–46.

Barkun, Michael. 2003. *A Culture of Conspiracy: Apocalyptic Visions in Contemporary America*. Berkeley: University of California Press.

Barner-Barry, Carol. 2005. *Contemporary Paganism: Minority Religions in a Majoritarian America*. New York: Palgrave and MacMillan.

Barton, Bernadette. 2012. *Pray the Gay Away: The Extraordinary Lives of Bible Belt Gays*. New York: New York University Press.

Bashir, Martin and Deborah Apton. 2007. Rick Warren and Purpose-Driven Strife. *ABCNews.com*. June 22. Retrieved from http://abcnews.go.com .

Baumgartner, Jody C. and Jonathan S. Morris, eds. 2008. *Laughing Matters: Humor and American Politics in the Media Age*. London and New York: Routledge.

BBC. 2013. Pussy Riot: The Story So Far. *BBC News Europe*. December 23. Retrieved from http://www.bbc.com.

Beal, Timothy K. 2002. *Religion and Its Monsters*. London and New York: Routledge.

Becker, Howard S. 1963. *Outsiders: Studies in the Sociology of Deviance*. New York: Free Press.

Beckford, James A. 1975. *The Trumpet of Prophecy: A Sociological Study of Jehovah's Witnesses*. Oxford: Basil Blackwell.

———. 1994. The Media and New Religious Movements. In *From the Ashes: Making Sense of Waco*, ed. James R. Lewis, 143–148. Lanham: Rowman & Littlefield.

Behar, Richard. 1991. The Thriving Cult of Greed and Power. *Time*, May 6, 50–57.

Behe, Michael J. 1996. *Darwin's Black Box: The Biochemical Challenge to Evolution*. New York: Touchstone.

———. 2000. Self-organization and Irreducibly Complex Systems: A Reply to Shanks and Joplin. *Philosophy of Science* 67 (1): 155–162.

———. 2001. Reply to My Critics: A Response to Reviews of *Darwin's Black Box: The Biochemical Challenge to Evolution*. *Biology and Philosophy* 16 (5): 685–709.

———. 2007. *The Edge of Evolution: The Search for the Limits of Darwinism*. New York: Free Press.

Bellah, Robert N. 1967. Civil Religion in America. *Daedalus* 96 (1): 1–21.

Bellah, Robert N. with Richard Madsen, William M. Sullivan, Ann Swidler, and Steven M. Tipton. 2008. With a new preface. *Habits of the Heart: Individualism and Commitment in American Life*. Berkeley: University of California Press.

Bender, Courtney. 2010. *The New Metaphysicals: Spirituality and the American Religious Imagination*. Chicago: University of Chicago Press.

Bender, Courtney and Pamela E. Klassen, eds. 2010. *After Pluralism: Reimagining Religious Engagement*. New York: Columbia University Press.

Berger, Peter L. 1961. *The Precarious Vision: A Sociologist Looks at Social Fictions and Christian Faith*. Garden City, NY: Doubleday.

———. 1967. *The Sacred Canopy: Elements of a Sociological Theory of Religion*. Boston: Anchor Books.

———. 1970. *A Rumor of Angels: Modern Society and the Rediscovery of the Supernatural*. Boston: Anchor Books.

————. 1997. *Redeeming Laughter: The Comic Dimension of Human Experience*. Berlin: Walter de Gruyter.

Berger, Peter L. and Thomas Luckmann. 1966. *The Social Construction of Reality: A Treatise in the Sociology of Knowledge*. Boston: Anchor Books.

Bergson, Henri. 1956. *Laughter*. In *Comedy*, ed. Wylie Sypher. Garden City, NY: Doubleday. (Orig. pub. 1911.)

Besen, Wayne R. 2003. *Anything but Straight: Unmasking the Scandals and Lies Behind the Ex-Gay Myth*. New York: Harrington Park Press.

Binder, Amy. 1993. Constructing Racial Rhetoric: Media Depictions of Harm in Heavy Metal and Rap Music. *American Sociological Review* 58 (6): 753–767.

Bishopaccountability.org. 2014. "Data on the Crisis: The Human Toll." Retrieved from http://www.bishop-accountability.org.

Bivins, Jason C. 2008. *Religion of Fear: The Politics of Horror in Conservative Evangelicalism*. New York: Oxford University Press.

Blum, Edward J. and Paul Harvey. 2012. *The Color of Christ: The Son of God & the Saga of Race in America*. Chapel Hill: University of North Carolina Press.

Booker, Keith M. 2006. *Drawn to Television: Prime-Time Animation from* The Flintstones *to* Family Guy. Westport, CT: Praeger.

Bourdieu, Pierre. 1977. *Outline of a Theory of Practice*. Trans. Richard Nice. Cambridge: Cambridge University Press. (Orig. pub. 1972.)

————. 1984. *Distinction: A Social Critique of the Judgement of Taste*. Trans. Richard Nice. Cambridge, MA: Harvard University Press. (Orig. pub. 1979.)

————. 1993. *The Field of Cultural Production: Essays on Art and Literature*. Edited and Introduced by Randall Johnson. New York: Columbia University Press.

Bowler, Gerry. 1996/1997. God and the Simpsons: The Religious Life of an Animated Sitcom. *North American Religion* 5: 1–20.

Box Office Mojo. 2012. *The Simpsons Movie*. Retrieved from http://www.boxofficemojo.com.

Bramadat, Paul A. 2005. Beyond Christian Canada: Religion and Ethnicity in a Multicultural Society. In *Religion and Ethnicity in Canada*, ed. Paul A. Bramadat and David Seljak, 2–25. Toronto: Pearson Longman.

Brenneman, Todd M. 2014. *Homespun Gospel: The Triumph of Sentimentality in Contemporary Evangelicalism*. New York: Oxford University Press.

Brodkin, Karen. 1998. *How Jews Became White Folk & What That Says About Race in America*. New Brunswick, NJ: Rutgers University Press.

Bromley, David G. 1994. The Mythology of Cults. In *From the Ashes: Making Sense of Waco*, ed. James R. Lewis, 121–124. Lanham, MD: Rowman & Littlefield.

Butler, Jon. 1990. *Awash in a Sea of Faith: Christianizing the American People*. Cambridge, MA: Harvard University Press.

Cadge, Wendy. 2002. Vital Conflicts: The Mainline Denominations Debate Homosexuality. In *The Quiet Hand of God: Faith-Based Activism and the Public Role of Mainline Protestantism*, ed. Robert Wuthnow and John H. Evans, 265–286. Princeton: Princeton University Press.

Cadge, Wendy, Heather Day, and Christopher Wildeman. 2007. Bridging the Denomination-Congregation Divide: Evangelical Lutheran Church in America Congregations Respond to Homosexuality. *Review of Religious Research* 48 (3): 245–259.

Campbell, Heidi. 2010. *When Religion Meets New Media*. New York: Routledge.

Cantor, Paul A. 2001. *The Simpsons*: Atomistic Politics and the Nuclear Family. In *The Simpsons and Philosophy: The D'oh of Homer*, ed. William Irwin, Mark T. Conard, and Aeon J. Skoble, 160–178. Chicago and La Salle: Open Court.

Carlin, Nathan. 2012. "The Sayings of Jesus in *Family Guy*: A Pastoral Reading of 'I Dream of Jesus.'" *Pastoral Psychology* 61: 531–553.

Carrette, Jeremy and Richard King. 2005. *Selling Spirituality: The Silent Takeover of Religion*. London and New York: Routledge.

Carter, Lewis F. 1990. *Charisma and Control in Rajneeshpuram: The Role of Shared Values in the Creation of a Community*. Cambridge: Cambridge University Press.

Castaneda, Carlos. 1968. *The Teachings of don Juan: A Yaqui Way of Knowledge*. Berkeley: University of California Press.

———. 1971. *A Separate Reality: Further Conversations with Don Juan*. Pocket Book Edition. Richmond Hill: Simon & Schuster Canada.

———. 1972. *Journey to Ixtlan*. New York: Simon & Schuster.

Catholic League for Religious and Civil Rights. 1999a. 'The Simpsons' Gets Too Cute. *Catalyst* January–February. Retrieved from http://www.catholicleague.org.

———. 1999b. 'The Simpsons' Offends Again. *Catalyst* March. Retrieved from http://www.catholicleague.org.

———. 1999c. FOX gets message on 'Simpsons.' *Catalyst* July–August. Retrieved from http://www.catholicleague.org.

———. 2002. "'South Park' Shows Cowardice" in *Catalyst Online*, September 23. Retrieved from http://www.catholicleague.org.

———. 2005a. "Virgin Mary Defiled on 'South Park'" in *Catalyst Online*, December 8. Retrieved from http://www.catholicleague.org.

———. 2005b. "Vile 'South Park' Episode Pulled" in *Catalyst Online*, December 30. Retrieved from http://www.catholicleague.org.

CCM Magazine. 2006. *CCM Magazine Presents: 100 Greatest Songs in Christian Music: The Stories Behind the Music that Changed our Lives Forever*. Nashville: Integrity Publishing.

Center for the Renewal of Science & Culture. 1998. The Wedge. Retrieved from http://www.antievolution.org.

Chancey, Mark A. 2007. A Textbook Example of the Christian Right: The National Council on Bible Curriculum in Public Schools. *Journal of the American Academy of Religion* 75 (3): 554–581.

Chandler, Siobhan. 2008. The Social Ethic of Religiously Unaffiliated Spirituality. *Religion Compass* 2 (2): 240–256.

———. 2011. The Social Ethic of Religiously Unaffiliated Spirituality. PhD diss., Wilfrid Laurier University, Waterloo, ON.

Channing, William Ellery. 1967. The Essence of the Christian Religion. In *Theology in America: The Major Protestant Voices From Puritanism to Neo-orthodoxy*, ed.

Sydney E. Ahlstrom, 196–210. The American Heritage Series. Indianapolis: Hackett. (Orig. pub. 1831.)

Chidester, David. 1988. *Salvation and Suicide: An Interpretation of Jim Jones, the Peoples Temple, and Jonestown*. Bloomington and Indianapolis: Indiana University Press.

———. 2005. *Authentic Fakes: Religion in American Popular Culture*. Berkeley: University of California Press.

Clark, Lynn Schofield. 2003. *From Angels to Aliens: Teenagers, the Media, and the Supernatural*. New York: Oxford University Press.

Clark, Terry Ray. 2012. Saved by Satire? Learning to Value Popular Culture's Critique of Sacred Traditions. In *Understanding Religion and Popular Culture*, ed. Terry Ray Clark and Dan W. Clanton, 13–27. New York: Routledge.

CNN. 2010a. Security Brief: Radical Islamic Website Takes on 'South Park.' April 19. Retrieved from http://news.blogs.cnn.com.

———. 2010b. Islamic Group: 'South Park' Post a Call to Protest, Not Violence. April 21. Retrieved from http://www.cnn.com.

Cohen, Jeremy. 2007. *Christ Killers: The Jews and the Passion from the Bible to the Big Screen*. New York: Oxford University Press.

Cohen, Steven M. 1995. Jewish Continuity Over Judaic Content: The Moderately Affiliated American Jew. In *The Americanization of the Jews*, ed. Robert M. Seltzer and Norman J. Cohen, 395–416. New York: New York University Press.

Cohen, Steven M. and Arnold M. Eisen. 2000. *The Jew Within: Self, Family, and Community in America*. Bloomington and Indianapolis: Indiana University Press.

Collins, Francis S. 2006. *The Language of God: A Scientist Presents Evidence for Belief*. New York: Free Press.

Collins, Randall. 1975. *Conflict Sociology: Toward an Explanatory Science*. With a contribution by Joan Annett. New York: Academic Press.

———. 2004. *Interaction Ritual Chains*. Princeton: Princeton University Press.

Conley, Dalton. 1999. *Being Black, Living in the Red: Race, Wealth, and Social Policy in America*. Berkeley: University of California Press.

Conway, Flo and Jim Siegelman. 1978. *Snapping: America's Epidemic of Sudden Personality Change*. Philadelphia and New York: J. B. Lippincott Company.

Cornell, Stephen and Douglas Hartmann. 1997. *Ethnicity and Race: Making Identities in a Changing World*. Thousand Oaks, CA: Pine Forge Press.

Cowan, Douglas E. 1999. 'Bearing False Witness?': Propaganda, Reality-Maintenance, and Christian Anticult Apologetics. PhD diss., University of Calgary.

———. 2003a. *Bearing False Witness?: An Introduction to the Christian Countercult*. Foreword by Jeffrey K. Hadden. Westport, CT: Praeger.

———. 2003b. *The Remnant Spirit: Conservative Reform in Mainline Protestantism*. Foreword by Irving R. Hexam. Westport, CT: Praeger.

———. 2004. Contested Spaces: Movement, Countermovement, and E-space Propaganda. In *Religion Online: Finding Faith on the Internet*, ed. Lorne L. Dawson and Douglas E. Cowan, 255–271. New York and London: Routledge.

———. 2005. Episode 712: *South Park*, Ridicule, and the Cultural Construction of Religious Rivalry. *Journal of Religion and Popular Culture* 10: 54 paragraphs. Retrieved from http://utpjournals.metapress.com.

———. 2007. Intellects Vast and Cool and Unsympathetic: Science, Religion, and *The War Of The Worlds*, Part 1. *Journal of Religion and Film* 11 (1). Retrieved from http://www.unomaha.edu.

———. 2008. *Sacred Terror: Religion and Horror on the Silver Screen.* Waco, TX: Baylor University Press.

———. 2010. *Sacred Space: The Quest for Transcendence in Science Fiction Film and Television.* Waco, TX: Baylor University Press.

Cowan, Douglas E. and Jeffrey K. Hadden. 2004. God, Guns, and Grist for the Media's Mill: Constructing the Narratives of New Religious Movements and Violence. *Nova Religio* 8 (2): 64–82.

Cox, Harvey. 1977. *Turning East: The Promise and Peril of the New Orientalism.* New York: Simon & Schuster.

Cragun, Ryan T., Barry Kosmin, Ariela Keysar, Joseph H. Hammer, and Michael Nielsen. 2012. On the Receiving End: Discrimination Toward the Non-Religious in the United States. *Journal of Contemporary Religion* 27 (1): 105–127.

Crawford, Alison. 2009. 'Oh Yeah!': *Family Guy* as Magical Realism? *Journal of Film and Video* 61 (2): 52–69.

Crosland, Alan, dir. 1927. *The Jazz Singer.* MGM.

Cuneo, Michael W. 1997. *The Smoke of Satan: Conservative and Traditionalist Dissent in Contemporary American Catholicism.* New York: Oxford University Press.

Dalton, Lisle, Eric Michael Mazur, and Monica Siems. 2010. Homer the Heretic and Charlie Church: Parody, Piety, and Pluralism in *The Simpsons.* In *God in the Details: American Religion in Popular Culture,* ed. Eric Michael Mazur and Kate McCarthy, 2nd ed., 237–254. New York and London: Routledge.

Dalton, Mary M. and Laura R. Linder, eds. 2005. *The Sitcom Reader: America Viewed and Skewed.* Albany: State University of New York Press.

Dark, David. 2002. *Everyday Apocalypse: The Sacred Revealed in Radiohead, The Simpsons, and Other Pop Culture Icons.* Grand Rapids, MI: Brazos Press.

Davies, Christie. 1990. *Ethnic Humor Around the World: A Comparative Analysis.* Bloomington and Indianapolis: Indiana University Press.

———. 1998. *Jokes and Their Relation to Society.* Humor Research, ed. Victor Raskin and Willibald Ruch, 4. Berlin and New York: Mouton de Gruyter.

———. 2002. *The Mirth of Nations.* New Brunswick, NJ: Transaction.

———. 2011. *Jokes and Targets.* Bloomington and Indianapolis: Indiana University Press.

Davies, Douglas. 2003. *An Introduction to Mormonism.* Cambridge: Cambridge University Press.

Davis, Murray S. 1993. *What's So Funny? The Comic Conception of Culture and Society.* Chicago: University of Chicago Press.

————. 1995. Review: The Sociology of Humor: A Stillborn Field? *Sociological Forum* 10 (2): 327–339.

Dawkins, Richard. 2006. *The God Delusion*. Boston: Houghton Mifflin.

Dawson, Lorne L. 2006. *Comprehending Cults: The Sociology of New Religious Movements*. 2nd ed. Toronto: Oxford University Press.

Delaney, Tim. 2008. *Simpsonology*. Amherst, MA: Prometheus Books.

DeLashmutt, Michael W. and Brannon Hancock. 2008. Prophetic Profanity: *South Park* on Religion or Thinking Theologically with Eric Cartman. In *Taking South Park Seriously*, ed. Jeffrey Andrew Weinstock, 173–191. Albany: State University of New York Press.

Deloria, Philip J. 1998. *Playing Indian*. New Haven, CT: Yale University Press.

Deloria Jr., Vine. 1992a. *God Is Red: A Native View of Religion*. 2nd ed. Golden, CO: North American Press.

————. 1992b. Is Religion Possible? An Evaluation of Present Efforts to Revive Traditional Tribal Religions. *Wicazo Sa Review* 8 (1): 35–39.

————. 1999a. Native American Spirituality. In *For This Land: Writings on Religion in America*. Edited with an Introduction by James Treat, 130–134. New York and London: Routledge.

————. 1999b. Religion and the Modern American Indian. In *For This Land: Writings on Religion in America*. Edited with an Introduction by James Treat, 122–129. New York and London: Routledge.

Dembski, William A., ed. 2006. *Darwin's Nemesis: Phillip Johnson and the Intelligent Design Movement*. Foreword by Senator Rick Santorum. Downers Grove, IL: IVP Academic.

Demerath, N. J. 1995. Cultural Victory and Organizational Defeat in the Paradoxical Decline of Liberal Protestantism. *Journal for the Scientific Study of Religion* 34 (4): 458–469.

de Mille, Richard. 1976. *Castaneda's Journey: The Power and the Allegory*. Santa Barbara: Capra Press.

————, ed. 1980. *The don Juan Papers: Further Castaneda Controversies*. Santa Barbara: Ross-Erikson Publishers.

Dennett, Daniel C. 2006. *Breaking the Spell: Religion as a Natural Phenomenon*. London: Penguin Books.

DeRogatis, Amy. 2015. *Saving Sex: Sexuality and Salvation in American Evangelicalism*. New York: Oxford University Press.

Devlin, William J. 2007. The Philosophical Passion of the Jew: Kyle the Philosopher. In *South Park and Philosophy*, ed. Robert Arp, 87–94. Malden, MA: Blackwell.

Diner, Hasia R. 1999. *Jews in America*. New York: Oxford University Press.

Douglas, Mary. 2002 [1966]. *Purity and Danger*. London: Routledge.

————. 1975. *Implicit Meanings: Essays in Anthropology*. London: Routledge and Kegan Paul.

Dorsett, Lyle W. 1991. *Billy Sunday and the Redemption of Urban America*. Grand Rapids, MI: W.B. Eerdmans.

Dueck, Jeffrey. 2007. Religious Pluralism and the Super Best Friends. In South Park and Philosophy: You Know, I Learned Something Today, ed. Robert Arp, 224–235. Malden, MA: Blackwell.

Dumenil, Lynn. 1984. Freemasonry and American Culture 1880–1930. Princeton: Princeton University Press.

Durkheim, Emile. 1995 [1912]. The Elementary Forms of Religious Life. Translated by Karen E. Fields. New York: Free Press.

Ebel, Jonathan H. 2009. Jesus Freak and the Junkyard Prophet: The School Assembly as Evangelical Revival. Journal of the American Academy of Religion 77 (1): 1–54.

Eck, Diana L. 1998. Darśan: Seeing the Divine Image in India. 3rd ed. New York: Columbia University Press.

———. 2001. A New Religious America: How a "Christian Country" Has Become the World's Most Religiously Diverse Nation. San Francisco: HarperSanFrancisco.

Edgell, Penny, Joseph Gerteis, and Douglas Hartmann. 2006. Atheists as "Other": Moral Boundaries and Cultural Membership in American Society. American Sociological Review 71: 211–234.

Edwards, Jonathan. 1741. Select Sermons: Sinners in the Hands of an Angry God. Christian Classics Ethereal Library. Retrieved from http://www.ccel.org.

Einstein, Mara. 2008. Brands of Faith: Marketing Religion in a Commercial Age. London and New York: Routledge.

Elifson, Kirk W. and C. Kirk Hadaway. 1985. Prayer in Public Schools: When Church and State Collide. Public Opinion Quarterly 49 (3): 317–329.

Erzen, Tanya. 2006. Straight to Jesus: Sexual and Christian Conversions in the Ex-Gay Movement. Berkeley: University of California Press.

Esposito, John L. 1990a. The Iranian Revolution: A Ten-Year Perspective. In The Iranian Revolution: Its Global Impact, ed. John L. Esposito, 17–39. Miami: Florida International University Press.

———, ed. 1990b. The Iranian Revolution: Its Global Impact. Miami: Florida International University Press.

Esposito, John L. and John O. Voll. 1996. Islam and Democracy. New York: Oxford University Press.

Evans, John H. 2002. Polarization in Abortion Attitudes in U.S. Religious Traditions. Sociological Forum 17 (3): 397–422.

Evensen, Bruce J. 2003. God's Man for the Gilded Age: D. L. Moody and the Rise of Modern Mass Evangelism. New York: Oxford University Press.

Feingold, Henry L. 1995. From Equality to Liberty: The Changing Political Culture of American Jews. In The Americanization of the Jews, ed. Robert M. Seltzer and Norman J. Cohen, 97–118. New York: New York University Press.

Feltmate, David. 2013a. Cowards, Critics, and Catholics: The Catholic League for Religious and Civil Rights, South Park and the Politics of Religious Humor in the United States. Bulletin of Religious Studies 42 (3): 2–11.

——. 2013b. It's Funny Because It's True?: *The Simpsons*, Satire, and the Significance of Religious Humor in Popular Culture. *Journal of the American Academy of Religion* 81 (1): 222–248.

——. 2013c. The Sacred Comedy: The Problems and Possibilities of Peter Berger's Theory of Humor. *Humor: International Journal of Humor Research* 26 (4): 531–549.

Feltmate, David and Kimberly P. Brackett. 2014. A Mother's Value Lies in Her Sexuality: *The Simpsons*, *Family Guy*, and *South Park* and the Preservation of Traditional Sex Roles. *Symbolic Interaction* 37 (4): 541–557.

Ferguson, Mark A. and Thomas E. Ford. 2008. Disparagement Humor: A Theoretical and Empirical Review of Psychoanalytic, Superiority, and Social Identity Theories. *Humor: International Journal of Humor Research* 21 (3): 283–312.

Fincher, David, dir. *Fight Club*. Twentieth Century FOX.

Fine, Gary Alan. 1983. Sociological Approaches to the Study of Humor. In *Handbook of Humor Research: Volume I Basic Issues*, ed. Paul E. McGhee and Jeffrey H. Goldstein, 159–181. New York: Springer-Verlag.

——. 1984. Humorous Interaction and the Social Construction of Meaning: Making Sense in a Jocular Vein. *Studies in Symbolic Interaction* 5: 83–101.

Fine, Gary Alan and Michaela de Soucey. 2005. Joking Cultures: Humor Regulation in Group Life. *Humor: International Journal of Humor Research* 18 (1): 1–22.

Finke, Roger and Rodney Stark. 2005. *The Churching of America 1776–2005: Winners and Losers in Our Religious Economy*. New Brunswick, NJ: Rutgers University Press.

Finney, Charles G. 1835. *Lectures on Revivals of Religion*. From notes by the editor of the *N.Y. Evangelist*, revised by the author. 2nd ed. New York: Leavitt, Lord & Co.

Fishman, Sylvia Barack. 2000. *Jewish Life and American Culture*. Albany: State University of New York Press.

Ford, Thomas E. 2000. Effects of Sexist Humor on Tolerance of Sexist Events. *Personality and Social Psychology Bulletin* 26 (9): 1094–1107.

Ford, Thomas E. and Mark A. Ferguson. 2004. Social Consequences of Disparagement Humor: A Prejudiced Norm Theory. *Personality and Social Psychology Review* 8 (1): 79–94.

Ford, Thomas E., Erin R. Wentzel, and Joli Lorion. 2001. Effects of Exposure to Sexist Humor on Perceptions of Normative Tolerance of Sexism. *European Journal of Social Psychology* 31: 677–691.

Forrest, Barbara and Paul R. Gross. 2004. *Creationism's Trojan Horse: The Wedge of Intelligent Design*. New York: Oxford University Press.

Fox, Stephen. 1990. The Ethnography of Humour and the Problem of Social Reality. *Sociology* 24 (3): 431–446.

Francis, Linda E. 1994. Laughter, the Best Mediation: Humour as Emotion Management in Interaction. *Symbolic Interaction* 17 (2): 147–163.

Freud, Sigmund. 1990. *Jokes and Their Relation to the Unconscious*. Translated and edited by James Strachey with a biographical introduction by Peter Gay. New York: W. W. Norton.

Froese, Paul and Christopher D. Bader. 2007. God in America: Why Theology IS Not Simply the Concern of Philosophers. *Journal for the Scientific Study of Religion* 46 (4): 465–481.

Fuller, Robert C. 2001. *Spiritual, but not Religious: Understanding Unchurched America*. Oxford: Oxford University Press.

Gans, Herbert J. 1999. Symbolic Ethnicity: The Future of Ethnic Groups and Cultures in America. In *Making Sense of America: Sociological Analyses and Essays*, 167–201. Lanham, MD: Rowman & Littlefield. (Orig. pub. 1979 and 1996.)

GhaneaBassiri, Kambiz. 2010. *A History of Islam in America: From the New World to New World Order*. Cambridge: Cambridge University Press.

Gibson, Mel, dir. 2004. *The Passion of the Christ*. Icon Productions.

Gill, Sam D. 1987. *Mother Earth*. Chicago: University of Chicago Press.

Gillespie, Nick and Jessie Walker. 2006. South Park Libertarians: Trey Parker and Matt Stone on Liberals, Conservatives, Censorship, and Religion. Retrieved from http://reason.com.

Gilman, Sander L. 1986. *Jewish Self-Hatred: Anti-Semitism and the Hidden Language of the Jews*. Baltimore and London: Johns Hopkins University Press.

Giroux, Henry A. 2001. Breaking into the Movies: Pedagogy and the Politics of Film. *JAC: A Journal of Composition Theory* 21 (3): 583–598.

Glassgold, Judith M., Lee Beckstead, Jack Drescher, Beverly Greene, Robin Lin Miller, and Roger L. Worthington. 2009. Report of the American Psychological Association Task Force on Appropriate Therapeutic Responses to Sexual Orientation. *American Psychological Association*. Retrieved from http://www.apa.org.

Glazer, Nathan. 1995. The Anomalous Liberalism of American Jews. In *The Americanization of the Jews*, ed. Robert M. Seltzer and Norman J. Cohen, 133–143. New York: New York University Press.

———. 2005. "Sacred Survival" Revisited: American Jewish Civil Religion in the New Millennium. In *The Cambridge Companion to American Judaism*, ed. Dana Evan Kaplan, 283–297. Cambridge: Cambridge University Press.

Goffman, Erving. 1959. *The Presentation of Self in Everyday Life*. Boston: Anchor Books.

Gorski, Philip S. 2010. Civil Religion Today (ARDA Guiding Paper Series). State College, PA: The Association of Religion Data Archives at The Pennsylvania State University, retrieved from http://www.thearda.com.

Gorsuch, Richard L. and Craig S. Smith. 1983. Attributions of Responsibility to God: An Interaction of Religious Beliefs and Outcomes. *Journal for the Scientific Study of Religion* 22 (4): 340–352.

Gottschalk, Peter and Gabriel Greenberg. 2008. *Islamophobia: Making Muslims the Enemy*. Lanham, MD: Rowman & Littlefield.

Gournelos, Ted. 2009. *Popular Culture and the Future of Politics: Cultural Studies and the Tao of South Park*. Lanham, MD: Lexington Books.

Governmentattic.org. 2008a. Informal Complaints About *Family Guy* Television Show Made to the Federal Communications Commission (FCC), Washington, DC, 2005–2007. Retrieved from http://www.governmentattic.org.

———. 2008b. Informal Complaints About *South Park* Television Show Made to the Federal Communications Commission (FCC), Washington, DC, 2004–2007. Retrieved from http://www.governmentattic.org.

———. 2008c. Informal Complaints About *The Simpsons* Television Show Made to the Federal Communications Commission (FCC), Washington, DC, 2003–2007. Retrieved from http://www.governmentattic.org.

———. 2013a. Informal Complaints Received by the Federal Communications Commission (FCC) Regarding the Television Show 'South Park,' 2010–2013. Retrieved from http://www.governmentattic.org.

———. 2013b. Informal Complaints Received by the Federal Communications Commission (FCC) Regarding the Television Show 'The Simpsons,' 2010–2013. Retrieved from http://www.governmentattic.org.

Grala, Alyson. 2007. A Salute to *The Simpsons*. *Licensemag.com*. Retrieved from http://www.licensemag.com.

Gray, Jonathan. 2006. *Watching with The Simpsons: Television, Parody, and Intertextuality*. London and New York: Routledge.

———. 2008. *Television Entertainment*. New York: Routledge.

Gray, Jonathan, Jeffrey P. Jones, and Ethan Thompson, eds. 2009. *Satire TV: Politics and Comedy in the Post-Network Era*. New York: New York University Press.

Green, John C. and James L. Guth. 1989. The Missing Link: Political Activists and Support for School Prayer. *Public Opinion Quarterly* 53 (1): 41–57.

Griffin, Dustin H. 1994. *Satire: A Critical Reintroduction*. Lexington: University Press of Kentucky.

Griffiths, Nick. 2000. America's First Family. *Times Magazine* 5 (16): 25, 27–28. Retrieved from http://www.snpp.com.

Grim, John A. 2000. Cultural Identity, Authenticity, and Community Survival: The Politics of Recognition in the Study of Native American Religions. In *Native American Spirituality: A Critical Reader*, ed. Lee Irwin, 37–60. Lincoln: University of Nebraska Press.

Gupta, Himanee. 2003. Staking a Claim on American-ness: Hindu Temples in the United States. In *Revealing the Sacred in Asian and Pacific America*, ed. Jane Naomi Iwamura and Paul Spickard, 193–208. London and New York: Routledge.

Haddad, Yvonne Yazbeck, ed. 1990. *The Muslims of America*. New York: Oxford University Press.

Haddad, Yvonne Yazbeck and Jane Idleman Smith. 1994. *Muslim Communities in North America*. Albany: State University of New York Press.

Hadley, Janet. 1994. God's Bullies: Attacks on Abortion. *Feminist Review* 48: 94–113.

Hall, John R. 1995. Public Narratives and the Apocalyptic Sect: From Jonestown to Mt. Carmel. In *Armageddon in Waco: Critical Perspectives on the Branch Davidian Conflict*, ed. Stuart A. Wright, 205–235. Chicago: University of Chicago Press.

———. 2004 [1987]. *Gone from the Promised Land: Jonestown in American Cultural History*. Second paperback edition with a new introduction by the author. New Brunswick, NJ: Transaction.

Hall, John R. with Philip D. Schuyler and Sylvaine Trinh. 2000. *Apocalypse Observed: Religious Movements and Violence in North America, Europe, and Japan.* New York: Routledge.

Hall, Stuart R. 1975. Introduction. In *Paper Voices: The Popular Press and Social Change 1935–1965,* Anthony Charles H. Smith with Elizabeth Immirzi and Trevor Blackwell, 11–24. Totowa, NJ: Rowman & Littlefield.

Hanegraaff, Wouter. 1996. *New Age Religion and Western Culture: Esotericism in the Mirror of Secular Thought.* Leiden: E.J. Brill.

Hankins, Barry. 2008. *American Evangelicals: A Contemporary History of a Mainstream Religious Movement.* Lanham, MD: Rowman & Littlefield.

Hardman, Charlotte E. 2007. 'He May be Lying but What He Says Is True': The Sacred Tradition of don Juan as Reported by Carlos Castaneda, Anthropologist, Trickster, Guru, Allegorist. In *The Invention of Sacred Tradition,* ed. James R. Lewis and Olav Hammer, 38–55. Cambridge: Cambridge University Press.

Harris, J. Irene, Sean W. Schoneman, and Stephanie R. Carrera. 2005. Preferred Prayer Styles and Anxiety Control. *Journal of Religion and Health* 44 (4): 403–412.

Harris, Sam. 2004. *The End of Faith: Religion, Terror and the Future of Reason.* With a New Afterword. New York: W. W. Norton.

Haskin, Byron, dir. 1953. *The War of the Worlds.* Paramount Pictures.

Hatch, Nathan O. 1989. *The Democratization of American Christianity.* New Haven, CT: Yale University Press.

Heelas, Paul. 1996. *The New Age Movement: The Celebration of the Self and the Sacralization of Modernity.* Oxford: Blackwell.

———. 2008. *Spiritualities of Life: New Age Romanticism and Consumptive Capitalism.* Oxford: Blackwell.

Heelas, Paul and Linda Woodhead with Benjamin Seel, Bronislaw Szerszynski, Karin Tusting. 2005. *The Spiritual Revolution: Why Religion Is Giving Way to Spirituality.* Oxford: Blackwell.

Heit, Jamey. 2008. *The Springfield Reformation: The Simpsons, Christianity, and American Culture.* New York: Continuum.

Hendershot, Heather. 2004. *Shaking the World for Jesus: Media and Conservative Evangelical Culture.* Chicago: University of Chicago Press.

Henry, Matthew. 2003. The Triumph of Popular Culture: Situation Comedy, Postmodernism, and *The Simpsons.* In *Critiquing the Sitcom: A Reader,* ed. Joanne Morreale, 262–273. Syracuse, NY: Syracuse University Press.

———. 2007. "Don't Ask Me, I'm Just a Girl": Feminism, Female Identity, and *The Simpsons. Journal of Popular Culture* 40 (2): 272–303.

———. 2012. The Simpsons, *Satire, and American Culture.* New York: Palgrave MacMillan.

Herberg, Will. 1960 [1955]. *Protestant, Catholic, Jew: An Essay in American Religious Sociology.* New edition, completely revised. Garden City: Anchor Books.

Hernández-Ávila, Inés. 2000. Mediations of the Spirit: Native American Religious Traditions and the Ethics of Representation. In *Native American Spirituality: A Critical Reader,* ed. Lee Irwin, 11–36. Lincoln: University of Nebraska Press.

Hinduism Today. 1999. *Hinduism Today* and *Christianity Today* Craft a Point-Counterpoint. In *Asian Religions in America: A Documentary History*, ed. Thomas A. Tweed and Stephen Prothero, 304–306. New York: Oxford University Press. (Orig. pub. 1996.)

Hirsch Jr., E. D. 1987. *Cultural Literacy: What Every American Needs to Know*. With an updated appendix. New York: Vintage.

Hitchens, Christopher. 2007. *God Is Not Great: How Religion Poisons Everything*. Toronto: McClelland & Stewart.

Hoffman, John P. and Sherrie Mills Johnson. 2005. Attitudes Toward Abortion Among Religious Traditions in the United States: Change or Continuity? *Sociology of Religion* 66 (2): 161–182.

Hoover, Stewart M. 2006. *Religion in the Media Age*. London and New York: Routledge.

Hout, Michael, Andrew Greely, and Melissa J. Wilde. 2001. The Demographic Imperative in Religious Change in the United States. *American Journal of Sociology* 107 (2): 468–500.

Howard, Jay R. and John M. Streck. 1999. *Apostles of Rock: The Splintered World of Contemporary Christian Music*. Lexington: University Press of Kentucky.

Howden, Andrew. 2002. *Jehovah's Witnesses: Portrait of a Contemporary Religious Movement*. London and New York: Routledge.

Hughes, Richard L. 2006. 'The Civil Rights Movement of the 1990s?': The Antiabortion Movement and the Struggle for Racial Justice. *Oral History Review* 33 (2): 1–24.

Humes, Edward. 2007. *Monkey Girl: Evolution, Education, Religion, and the Battle for America's Soul*. New York: Harper Perennial.

Hunter, James Davidson. 1991. *Culture Wars: The Struggle to Define America*. New York: Basic Books.

Hutchison, William R. 1976. *The Modernist Impulse in American Protestantism*. Cambridge, MA: Harvard University Press.

———. 2003. *Religious Pluralism in America: The Contentious History of a Founding Ideal*. New Haven, CT: Yale University Press.

Hutchison, William R., ed. 1968. *American Protestant Thought in the Liberal Era*. Lanham, MD: University Press of America.

Hutchison, William R., Catherine L. Albanese, Max L. Stackhouse, and William McKinney. 1991. The Decline of Mainline Religion in American Culture. *Religion and American Culture* 1 (2): 131–153.

Hyers, M. Conrad, ed. 1969. *Holy Laughter: Essays on Religion in the Comic Perspective*. New York: Seabury Press.

———. 1981. *The Comic Vision and the Christian Faith: A Celebration of Life and Laughter*. New York: Pilgrim Press.

———. 1987. *And God Created Laughter: The Bible as Divine Comedy*. Atlanta: John Knox Press.

———. 1989. *The Laughing Buddha: Zen and the Comic Spirit*. Rev. ed. of *Zen and the Comic Spirit*, 1974. Wolfeboro, NH: Longwood Publishing Group.

———. 1996. *The Spirituality of Comedy: Comic Heroism in a Tragic World*. New Brunswick, NJ: Transaction.

Illouz, Eva. 2008. *Saving the Modern Soul: Therapy, Emotions, and the Culture of Self-Help*. Berkeley: University of California Press.

Irwin, William, Mark T. Conard, and Aeon J. Skoble. 2001. *The Simpsons*: Atomistic Politics and the Nuclear Family. In *The Simpsons and Philosophy: The D'oh of Homer*. Chicago and La Salle: Open Court.

Iwamura, Jane Naomi. 2005. The Oriental Monk in American Popular Culture. In *Religion and Popular Culture in America*, revised edition, ed. Bruce David Forbes and Jeffrey H. Mahan, 25–43. Berkeley: University of California Press.

Jacob, Simon and Pallavi Thaku. 2000. Jyothi Hindu Temple: One Religion, Many Practices. In *Religion and the New Immigrants: Continuities and Adaptations in Immigrant Congregations*, ed. Helen Rose Ebaugh and Janet Saltzman Chafetz, 229–242. Walnut Creek, CA: Altamira Press.

Jacoby, Henry. 2007. You Know, I Learned Something Today: Stan Marsh and the Ethics of Belief. In *South Park and Philosophy: You Know, I Learned Something Today*, ed. Robert Arp, 57–65. Malden, MA: Blackwell.

Jacquette, Dale. 2007. Satan Lord of Darkness in *South Park* Cosmology. *South Park and Philosophy: You Know, I Learned Something Today*, ed. Robert Arp, 250–262. Malden, MA: Blackwell.

James, William. 2002 [1902]. *The Varieties of Religious Experience*. New York: Modern Library.

Jeffords, Susan and Lauren Rabinovitz, eds. 1994. *Seeing Through the Media: The Persian Gulf War*. New Brunswick, NJ: Rutgers University Press.

Jelen, Ted G. and Clyde Wilcox. 2003. Causes and Consequences of Political Attitudes Toward Abortion: A Review and Research Agenda. *Political Research Quarterly* 56 (4): 489–500.

Jenkins, Henry. 2006a. *Convergence Culture: Where Old and New Media Collide*. Updated and with a new Afterword. New York and London: New York University Press.

———. 2006b. *Fans, Bloggers, and Gamers: Exploring Participatory Culture*. New York and London: New York University Press.

Jenkins, Philip. 2000. *Mystics and Messiahs: Cults and New Religions in American History*. New York: Oxford University Press.

———. 2004. *Dream Catchers: How Mainstream America Discovered Native Spirituality*. New York: Oxford University Press.

Jensen, Lene Arnett. 1998. Different Habits, Different Hearts: The Moral Languages of the Culture War. *American Sociologist* 29 (1): 83–101.

———. 2009. Conceptions of God and the Devil Across the Lifespan: A Cultural-Development Study of Religious Liberals and Conservatives. *Journal for the Scientific Study of Religion* 48 (1): 121–145.

Jocks, Christopher Ronwanièn:te. 2000. Spirituality for Sale: Sacred Knowledge in the Consumer Age. In *Native American Spirituality: A Critical Reader*, ed. Lee Irwin, 61–77. Lincoln: University of Nebraska Press.

Johnson, David Kyle. 2007. Francis Griffin and the Church of the Holy Fonz: Religious Exclusivism and "Real" Religion. In Family Guy *and Philosophy: A Cure for the Petarded,* ed. Jeremy Wisnewski, 36–48. Malden, MA: Blackwell.

Johnson, Phillip E. 1999. The Wedge. *Touchstone: A Journal of Mere Christianity* July/August. Retrieved from http://www.touchstonemag.com.

———. 2000. *The Wedge of Truth: Splitting the Foundations of Naturalism.* Downers Grove, IL: InterVarsity Press.

Johnson-Woods, Toni. 2007. *Blame Canada!* South Park *and Contemporary Culture.* New York: Continuum.

Jones, Gerald. 1993. *Honey, I'm Home! Sitcoms: Selling the American Dream.* New York: St. Martin's Press.

Jordan, Mark D. 2011. *Recruiting Young Love: How Christians Talk About Homosexuality.* Chicago and London: University of Chicago Press.

Kaplan, Dana Evan. 2009. *Contemporary American Judaism: Transformation and Renewal.* New York: Columbia University Press.

Karim, Karim H. 2003. *Islamic Peril: Media and Global Violence.* Montréal, New York, and London: Black Rose Books.

Karimi, Faith. 2013. Lance Armstrong Says His Doping Still 'Polarizing Topic' For Many. *CNN.com.* Retrieved from http://www.cnn.com.

Kaufman, Debra Renee. 2005. The Place of Judaism in American Jewish Identity. *The Cambridge Companion to American Judaism,* ed. Dana Evan Kaplan, 169–183. Cambridge: Cambridge University Press.

Kercher, Stephen. 2006. *Revel with a Cause: Liberal Satire in Postwar America.* Chicago: University of Chicago Press.

Keslowitz, Steven. 2006. *The World According to* The Simpsons: *What Our Favorite TV Family Says About Life, Love and the Pursuit of the Perfect Donut.* Foreword by Rick Miller. Naperville, IL: Sourcebooks.

Keys, Lisa. 2004. Bar Mitzvah-gate, Courtesy of Fox. *The Jewish Daily Forward.* Retrieved from http://forward.com.

Klausen, Jytte. 2009. *The Cartoons That Shook the World.* New Haven, CT: Yale University Press.

Knorr, Klaus. 1975. The Limits of Economic and Military Power. *Daedalus* 104 (4): 229–243.

Knox, Simone. 2006. Reading the Ungraspable Double-Codedness of *The Simpsons. Journal of Popular Film and Television* 34 (2): 72–81.

Koepsell, David R. 2007. They Satirized My Prophet . . . Those Bastards! South Park and Blasphemy. South Park *and Philosophy: You Know, I Learned Something Today,* ed. Robert Arp, 131–140. Malden, MA: Blackwell.

Kuipers, Giselinde. 2006. *Good Humor, Bad Taste: A Sociology of the Joke.* Trans. Kate Simms. Humor Research, ed. Victor Raskin and Willibald Ruch, 7. Berlin: Walter de Gruyter.

Kunkel, Mark A., Stephen Cook, David S. Meshel, Donald Daughtry, and Anita Hauenstein. 1999. God Images: A Concept Map. *Journal for the Scientific Study of Religion* 38 (2): 193–202.

Kurien, Prema. 2007. *A Place at the Multicultural Table: The Development of an American Hinduism*. New Brunswick, NJ: Rutgers University Press.

Ladd, Kevin L. and Bernard Spilka. 2002. Inward, Outward, and Upward: Cognitive Aspects of Prayer. *Journal for the Scientific Study of Religion* 41 (3): 475–484.

———. 2006. Inward, Outward, Upward Prayer Scale: Scale Reliability and Validation. *Journal for the Scientific Study of Religion* 45 (2): 233–251.

Laderman, Gary. 2009. *Sacred Matters: Celebrity Worship, Sexual Ecstasies, the Living Dead, and Other Signs of Religious Life in the United States*. New York: New Press.

Lamb, Chris. 2004. *Drawn to Extremes: The Use and Abuse of Editorial Cartoons in the United States*. New York: Columbia University Press.

Lamont, Michèle. 1992. *Money, Morals, & Manners: The Culture of the French and American Upper-Middle Class*. Chicago: University of Chicago Press.

Landes, Richard and Steven T. Katz, eds. 2011. *A Hundred-Year Retrospective on The Protocols of the Elders of Zion*. New York: New York University Press.

Lantzer, Jason S. 2012. *Mainline Christianity: The Past and Future of America's Majority Faith*. New York: New York University Press.

Laycock, Joseph. 2013a. Laughing Matters: "Parody Religions" and the Command to Compare. *Bulletin for the Study of Religion* 42 (3): 19–27.

———.2013b. Where Do They Get These Ideas? Changing Ideas of Cults and the Mirror of Popular Culture. *Journal of the American Academy of Religion* 18 (1): 80–106.

Lerman, Antony. 2008. Jewish Self-Hatred: Myth or Reality? *Jewish Quarterly: A Magazine of Contemporary Writing, Politics & Culture*, Summer. Retrieved from http://www.jewishquarterly.org.

Levy, Leonard W. 1993. *Blasphemy: Verbal Offense Against the Sacred, from Moses to Salman Rushdie*. New York: Alfred A. Knopf.

Lewis, James R., ed. 2009. *Scientology*. Oxford: Oxford University Press.

Lewis, Paul. 2006. *Cracking Up: American Humor in a Time of Conflict*. Chicago and London: University of Chicago Press.

———, ed. 2008. The Muhammad Cartoons and Humor Research: A Collection of Essays. *Humor* 21 (1): 1–46.

Lewis, Todd V. 2002. Religious Rhetoric and the Comic Frame in *The Simpsons*. *Journal of Media and Religion* 1 (3): 153–165.

Licklider, Roy. 1988. The Power of Oil: The Arab Oil Weapon and the Netherlands, the United Kingdom, Canada, Japan, and the United States. *International Studies Quarterly* 32 (2): 205–226.

Lincoln, Bruce. 2006. *Holy Terrors: Thinking About Religion After September 11*. 2nd ed. Chicago: University of Chicago Press.

Lipoma, Lori. 2009. Kierkegaard, Contradiction, and *South Park*: The Jester's View of Religion. In *The Deep End of South Park: Critical Essays on Television's Shocking Cartoon Series*, ed. Leslie Stratyner and James R. Keller, 15–27. Jefferson, NC: McFarland & Company.

Lofton, Kathryn. 2006. The Methodology of the Modernists: Process in American Protestantism. *Church History* 75 (2): 374–402.

———. 2011. *Oprah: The Gospel of an Icon*. Berkeley: University of California Press.

Lotz, Amanda D. 2007. *The Television Will Be Revolutionized*. New York: New York University Press.

Lowney, Kathleen S. and Joel Best. 1996. What Waco Stood For: Jokes as Popular Constructions of Social Problems. *Perspectives on Social Problems* 8: 77–97.

Luhr, Eileen. 2009. *Witnessing Suburbia: Conservatives and Christian Youth Culture*. Berkeley: University of California Press.

Lynch, Gordon. 2005. *Understanding Theology and Popular Culture*. Oxford: Blackwell.

———. 2012. *The Sacred in the Modern World: A Cultural Sociological Approach*. New York: Oxford University Press.

MacFarlane, Seth, dir. 1995. *The Life of Larry*. Rhode Island School of Design. Retrieved from http://www.youtube.com.

———, dir. 1997. *Larry & Steve*. Hanna-Barbera Productions. Retrieved from http://www.youtube.com.

Mannheim, Karl. 1936. *Ideology and Utopia: An Introduction to the Sociology of Knowledge*. Trans. Louis Wirth and Edward Shils. San Diego: Harcourt.

Marc, David. 1997. *Comic Visions: Television Comedy and American Culture*. 2nd ed. Malden, MA: Blackwell.

Marsden, George M. 1991. *Understanding Fundamentalism and Evangelicalism*. Grand Rapids, MI: Eerdmans.

———. 2005. *Fundamentalism and American Culture*. New edition. New York: Oxford University Press.

Marsden, Victor, trans. 1986. *The Protocols of the Meetings of the Learned Elders of Zion: With Preface and Explanatory Notes*. Costa Mesa, CA: Noontide Press.

Martin, Patrick and Sean Phelan. 2002. Representing Islam in the Wake of September 11: A Comparison of US Television and CNN Online Messageboard Discourses. *Prometheus* 20 (3): 263–269.

Maxwell, Carol J. C. and Ted G. Jelen. 1995. Commandos for Christ: Narratives of Male Pro-life Activists. *Review of Religious Research* 37 (2): 117–131.

Maynard, Elizabeth A., Richard L. Gorsuch, and Jeffrey P. Bjorck. 2001. Religious Coping Style, Concept of God, and Personal Religious Variables in Threat, Loss, and Challenge Situations. *Journal for the Scientific Study of Religion* 40 (1): 65–74.

Mazumdar, Shampa and Sanjoy Mazumdar. 2003. Creating the Sacred: Altars in the Hindu American Home. In *Revealing the Sacred in Asian and Pacific America*, ed. Jane Naomi Iwamura and Paul Spickard, 143–157. London and New York: Routledge.

McAlister, Melani. 2005. *Epic Encounters: Culture, Media & U.S. Interests in the Middle East Since 1945*. Updated edition, with a post-9/11 chapter. Berkeley: University of California Press.

McCarthy, E. Doyle. 1996. *Knowledge as Culture: The New Sociology of Knowledge*. London and New York: Routledge.

McCloud, Sean. 2004. *Making the American Religious Fringe: Exotics, Subversives and Journalists, 1955–1993*. Chapel Hill: University of North Carolina Press.

McClymond, Michael J. 2004. Issues and Explanations in the Study of North American Revivalism. In *Embodying the Spirit: New Perspective on North American Revivalism*, ed. Michael J. McClymond, 1–46. Baltimore: Johns Hopkins University Press.

———. 2007. Revivals. In *The Blackwell Companion to Religion in America*, ed. Philip Goff, 306–320. Malden, MA: Blackwell.

McDannell, Colleen. 1995. *Material Christianity: Religion and Popular Culture in America*. New Haven, CT: Yale University Press.

McGaw, Douglas B. 1979. Commitment and Religious Community: A Comparison of a Charismatic and a Mainline Congregation. *Journal for the Scientific Study of Religion* 18 (2): 146–163.

McGirr, Lisa. 2001. *Suburban Warriors: The Origins of the New American Right*. Princeton: Princeton University Press.

McIntosh, Peggy. 1988 [2004]. White Privilege: Unpacking the Invisible Knapsack. In *Race, Class, and Gender in the United States*, ed. Paula S. Rothberg, 188–192, 6th ed. New York: Worth.

McKinney, William. 1998. Mainline Protestantism 2000. *Annals of the American Academy of Political and Social Science* 558: 57–66.

McLeod, Melvin. 1999. Richard Gere: My Journey as a Buddhist. *Shambahala Sun*, May. Retrieved from http://www.shambhalasun.com.

McLoughlin, William G. 1978. *Revivals, Awakenings, and Reform*. Chicago: University of Chicago Press.

Melton, J. Gordon. 2000. *The Church of Scientology*. Studies in Contemporary Religions. Salt Lake City: Signature Books in cooperation with CENSUR.

Miller, Russell. 1987. *Bare-faced Messiah: The True Story of L. Ron Hubbard*. New York: Henry Holt and Company.

Miller, Vincent J. 2003. *Consuming Religion: Christian Faith and Practice in a Consumer Culture*. New York: Continuum.

Mills, Brett. 2009. *The Sitcom*. Edinburgh: Edinburgh University Press.

Min, Pyong Gap. 2003. Immigrants' Religion and Ethnicity: A Comparison of Korean Christian and Indian Hindu Immigrants. In *Revealing the Sacred in Asian and Pacific America*, ed. Jane Naomi Iwamura and Paul Spickard, 125–141. London and New York: Routledge.

Mittell, Jason. 2004. *Genre and Television: From Cop Shows to Cartoons in American Culture*. New York: Routledge.

———. 2010. *Television and American Culture*. New York: Oxford University Press.

Mittell, Jason and Ethan Thompson, eds. 2013. *How to Watch Television*. New York: New York University Press.

Moon, Dawne. 2004. *God, Sex, and Politics: Homosexuality and Everyday Theologies*. Chicago: University of Chicago Press.

Moore, R. Laurence. 1986. *Religious Outsiders and the Making of Americans*. New York: Oxford University Press.

———. 1994. *Selling God: American Religion in the Marketplace of Culture*. New York: Oxford University Press.

Moran, Jeffrey P. 2002. *The Scopes Trial: A Brief History with Documents.* New York: Palgrave.

Morefield, Kenneth R. 2009. "Yes I am Cartman!": Kyle Brovlofski's Cool Judaism. In *The Deep End of South Park,* ed. Leslie Stratyner and James R. Keller, 157–166. Jefferson, NC: McFarland & Company.

Morgan, David. 2007. *The Lure of Images: A History of Religion and Visual Media in America.* London and New York: Routledge.

Morreale, Joanna, ed. 2003. *Critiquing the Sitcom: A Reader.* Syracuse, NY: Syracuse University Press.

Morreall, John. 1983. *Taking Laughter Seriously.* Albany: State University of New York Press.

———, ed. 1987. *The Philosophy of Laughter and Humor.* Albany: State University of New York Press.

———. 1999. *Comedy, Tragedy, and Religion.* Albany: State University of New York Press.

———. 2004. Verbal Humor Without Switching Scripts and Without Non-*bona fide* Communication. *Humor: International Journal of Humor Research* 17 (4): 393–400.

———. 2009. *Comic Relief: A Comprehensive Philosophy of Humor.* Malden, MA: Wiley-Blackwell.

Moslener, Sara. 2011. Don't Act Now! Selling Christian Abstinence in the Religious Marketplace. In *God in the Details,* 2nd edition, ed. Eric Michael Mazur and Kate McCarthy, 197–218. New York: Routledge.

Murphy, Sheila C. 2011. *How Television Invented New Media.* New Brunswick, NJ: Rutgers University Press.

Murtagh, Kevin J. 2007. Blasphemous Humor in *South Park.* In South Park *and Philosophy: You Know, I Learned Something Today,* ed. Robert Arp, 29–39. Malden, MA: Blackwell.

Myles, Robert J. 2015. *The Simpsons* and Biblical Literacy. In *Rethinking Biblical Literacy,* ed. Katie Edwards, 143–162. New York: T&T Clark.

Neal, Lynn S. 2011. 'They're Freaks!': The Cult Stereotype in Fictional Television 1958–2008. *Nova Religio: Journal of Alternative and Emergent Religions* 14 (3): 81–107.

Neusner, Jacob. 1990. Judaism in America: The Social Crisis of Faith. In *Social Foundations of Judaism,* ed. Calvin Goldscheider and Jacob Neusner, 114–133. Englewood Cliffs, NJ: Prentice Hall.

Nielsen Company. 2014a. "Content is King, but Viewing Habits Vary by Demographic." Retrieved from http://www.nielsen.com.

———. 2014b. "Nielsen Estimates 116.3 Million TV Homes in the U.S., Up 4%." Retrieved from http://www.nielsen.com.

Noffke, Jacqueline L. and Susan H. McFadden. 2001. Denominational and Age Comparisons of God Concepts. *Journal for the Scientific Study of Religion* 40 (4): 747–756.

Noll, Mark A. 2001. *American Evangelical Christianity: An Introduction.* Oxford: Blackwell.

Numbers, Ronald L. 2007. Darwinism, Creationism, and "Intelligent Design." In *Scientists Confront Creationism: Intelligent Design and Beyond*, ed. Andrew J. Petto and Laurie R. Godfrey, 31–58. New York: W. W. Norton.

The Numbers: Box Office Data, Movie Stars, Idle Speculation. 2010. "Secret, The—DVD sales." Retrieved from http://www.the-numbers.com.

Ogden, Schubert M. 1976. Sources of Religious Authority in Liberal Protestantism. *Journal of the American Academy of Religion* 44 (3): 403–416.

Olson, Laura R. and Wendy Cadge. 2002. Talking About Homosexuality: The Views of Mainline Protestant Clergy. *Journal for the Scientific Study of Religion* 41 (1): 153–167.

Omi, Michael and Howard Winart. 1986. *Racial Formation in the United States: From the 1960s to the 1980s.* New York: Routledge & Keegan Paul.

O'Neal, Sean. 2014. An Uncensored Version of *South Park*'s Controversial Muhammad Episode Has Surfaced. *The Onion A. V. Club.* Retrieved from http://www.avclub. com.

Oring, Elliott. 2003. *Engaging Humor.* Urbana and Chicago: University of Illinois Press.

Orsi, Robert A. 2005. *Between Heaven and Earth: Religious Worlds People Make and the Scholars Who Study Them.* Princeton and Oxford: Princeton University Press.

Ostling, Richard and Joan K. Ostling. 1999. *Mormon America: The Power and the Promise.* San Francisco: HarperSanFrancisco.

Owen, Suzanne. 2008. *The Appropriation of Native American Spirituality.* London: Continuum.

Pager, Devah. 2007. *Marked: Race, Crime, and Finding Work in an Era of Mass Incarceration.* Chicago: University of Chicago Press.

Palmer, Susan J. 2004. *Aliens Adored: Rael's UFO Religion.* New Brunswick, NJ: Rutgers University Press.

Paolucci, Paul and Margaret Richardson. 2006a. Dramaturgy, Humor and Criticism: How Goffman Reveals *Seinfeld*'s Critique of American Culture. *Humor: International Journal of Humor Research* 19 (1): 27–52.

———. 2006b. Sociology of Humor and a Critical Dramaturgy. *Symbolic Interaction* 29 (3): 331–348.

Parker, Trey, dir. 1999. *South Park: Bigger, Longer, and Uncut.* Written by Trey Parker, Matt Stone, and Pam Brady. Comedy Central Films.

Parker, Trey and Matt Stone, dirs. 1992. *The Spirit of Christmas: Jesus vs. Frosty.* Independently released. Retrieved from http://www.youtube.com.

———, dirs. 1995. *The Spirit of Christmas: Jesus vs. Santa.* Independently released. Retrieved from http://www.youtube.com.

Parkhill, Thomas. 1997. *Weaving Ourselves Into the Land: Charles Godfrey Leland, 'Indians' and the Study of Native American Religions.* Albany: State University of New York Press.

Pennock, Robert T. 1999. *Tower of Babel: The Evidence Against the New Creationism.* Cambridge, MA: MIT Press.

Penton, James. 1997. *Apocalypse Delayed: The Story of the Jehovah's Witnesses.* 2nd ed. Toronto: University of Toronto Press.

Percy, Martyn and Ian Markham, eds. 2006. *Why Liberal Churches Are Growing*. London: T&T Clark.

Petto, Andrew J. and Lurie R. Godfrey, eds. 2007. *Scientists Confront Creationism: Intelligent Design and Beyond*. New York: W. W. Norton.

Pew Forum on Religion & Public Life. 2010. U.S. Religious Knowledge Survey. Retrieved from http://www.pewforum.org.

———. 2013a. Growth of the Nonreligious: Many Say Trend Is Bad for American Society. Retrieved from http://www.pewforum.org.

———. 2013b. A Portrait of Jewish Americans: Findings From a Pew Research Center Survey of U.S. Jews. Retrieved from http://www.pewforum.org.

———. 2015. America's Changing Religious Landscape: Christians Decline Sharply as Share of Population; Unaffiliated and Other Faiths Continue to Grow. May 12. Retrieved from http://www.pewforum.org.

Pike, Sarah M. 2001. *Earthly Bodies, Magical Selves: Contemporary Pagans and the Search for Community*. Berkeley: University of California Press.

Pinsky, Mark I. 2001. *The Gospel According to* The Simpsons: *The Spiritual Life of the World's Most Animated Family*. Foreword by Tony Campolo. Louisville, KY: Westminster John Knox Press.

———. 2007. *The Gospel According to* The Simpsons. Bigger and Possibly Even Better Edition. Louisville, KY: Westminster John Knox Press.

Pinsky, Mark I. and Samuel F. (Skip) Parvin. 2002. *The Gospel According to* The Simpsons: *Leader's Guide for Group Study*. Louisville, KY: Westminster John Knox Press.

Plate, S. Brent. 2006. *Blasphemy: Art that Offends*. London: Black Dog Publishing.

Possamai, Adam. 2003. Alternative Spiritualities and the Cultural Logic of Late Capitalism. *Culture and Religion* 4 (1): 31–45.

Possamai, Adam and Murray Lee. 2004. New Religious Movements and the Fear of Crime. *Journal of Contemporary Religion* 19 (3): 337–352.

Prebish, Charles S. and Martin Baumann, eds. 2002. *Westward Dharma: Buddhism Beyond Asia*. Berkeley: University of California Press.

Prothero, Stephen. 2003. *American Jesus: How the Son of God Became a National Icon*. New York: Farrar, Straus, and Giroux.

———, ed. 2006. *A Nation of Religions: The Politics of Pluralism in Multireligious America*. Chapel Hill: University of North Carolina Press.

———. 2007. *Religious Literacy: What Every American Needs to Know—and Doesn't*. San Francisco: HarperSanFrancisco.

Proudfoot, Wayne. 1985. *Religious Experience*. Berkeley: University of California Press.

Putnam, Robert D. and David E. Campbell. 2010. *American Grace: How Religion Divides and Unites Us*. New York: Simon & Schuster.

Queen, Christopher S., ed. 2000. *Engaged Buddhism in the West*. Boston: Wisdom Publications.

———. 2002. Engaged Buddhism: Agnosticism, Interdependence, Globalization. In *Westward Dharma: Buddhism Beyond Asia*, ed. Charles S. Prebish and Martin Baumann, 324–347. Berkeley: University of California Press.

Raphael, Marc Lee. 2003. *Judaism in America*. New York: Columbia University Press.

Raskin, Victor. 1985. *Semantic Mechanisms of Humor*. Dordrecht: D. Reidel Publishing..

Ratliff, George, dir. 2001. *Hell House*. Cantina Pictures.

Rauschenbusch, Walter. 1967. Christianity and the Social Crisis. In *Theology in America: The Major Protestant Voices From Puritanism to Neo-orthodoxy*, ed. Sydney E. Ahlstrom, 533–579. The American Heritage Series. Indianapolis: Hackett. (Orig. pub. 1907.)

Regnerus, Mark D. 2007. *Forbidden Fruit: Sex & Religion in the Lives of American Teenagers*. New York: Oxford University Press.

Reichenbach, Bruce R. 1988. The Law of Karma and the Principle of Causation. *Philosophy East and West* 38 (4): 39–410.

Reimer, Sam. 2003. *Evangelicals and the Continental Divide: The Conservative Protestant Subculture in Canada and the United States*. Montreal and Kingston: McGill-Queen's University Press.

Richardson, James T. and Barend van Driel. 1997. Journalists' Attitudes Towards New Religious Movements. *Review of Religious Research* 39 (2): 116–136.

Ritterband, Paul. 1995. Modern Times and Jewish Assimilation. In *The Americanization of the Jews*, ed. Robert M. Seltzer and Norman J. Cohen, 377–394. New York: New York University Press.

Robbins, Thomas and Dick Anthony. 1994. 'Cults,' 'Mind Control,' and the State. In *From the Ashes: Making Sense of Waco*, ed. James R. Lewis, 125–135. Lanham, MD: Rowman & Littlefield.

Roof, Wade Clark. 1999. *Spiritual Marketplace: Baby Boomers and the Remaking of American Religion*. Princeton: Princeton University Press.

Roof, Wade Clark and William McKinney. 1987. *American Mainline Religion: Its Changing Shape and Future*. New Brunswick, NJ: Rutgers University Press.

Rose, Stuart. 1998. An Examination of the New Age Movement: Who Is Involved and What Constitutes Its Spirituality. *Journal of Contemporary Religion* 13 (1): 5–22.

———. 2001. Is the Term 'Spirituality' a Word That Everyone Uses, but Nobody Knows What Anyone Means by It? *Journal of Contemporary Religion* 16 (2): 193–207.

Rose, Wendy. 1992. The Great Pretenders: Further Reflections on Whiteshamanism. In *The State of Native America: Genocide, Colonization, and Resistance*, ed. M. Annette Jaimes, 403–421. Boston: South End Press.

Rothstein, Mikael. 2009. "His name was Xenu. He used renegades . . .": Aspects of Scientology's Founding Myth. In *Scientology*, ed. James R. Lewis, 365–387. New York: Oxford University Press.

Rowmanowski, William D. 2005. Evangelicals and Popular Music: The Contemporary Christian Music Industry. In *Religion and Popular Culture in America*, ed. Bruce David Forbes and Jeffrey H. Mahan, 103–122. Berkeley: University of California Press.

———. 2007. *Eyes Wide Open: Looking for God in Popular Culture*. Revised and expanded edition. Grand Rapids, MI: BrazosPress.

Rudin, A. James and Marcia R. Rudin. 1980. *Prison or Paradise? The New Religious Cults*. Philadelphia: Fortress Press.

Rustow, Dankwart A. 1982. *Oil and Turmoil: American Faces OPEC and the Middle East*. New York and London: W. W. Norton.

Said, Edward W. 1979. *Orientalism*. New York: Vintage Books.

———. 1981. *Covering Islam: How the Media and the Experts Determine How We See the Rest of the World*. New York: Pantheon.

Saliba, Therese. 1994. Military Presences and Absences: Arab Women and the Persian Gulf War. In *Seeing Through the Media: The Persian Gulf War*, ed. Susan Jeffords and Lauren Rabinovitz, 263–284. New Brunswick, NJ: Rutgers University Press.

Salomonsen, Jone. 2002. *Enchanted Feminism: The Reclaiming Witches of San Francisco*. New York: Routledge.

Sanford, Stephanie and Donna Eder. 1984. Adolescent Humour During Peer Interaction. *Social Psychology Quarterly* 47 (3): 235–243.

Sanneh, Lamin. 2009. *Translating the Message: The Missionary Impact on Culture*. Revised and expanded edition. Maryknoll, NY: Orbis.

Sarna, Jonathan D. 2004. *American Judaism: A History*. New Haven, CT: Yale University Press.

Schmidt, Lee Eric. 1995. *Consumer Rites: The Buying and Selling of American Holidays*. Princeton: Princeton University Press.

Schudson, Michael. 1989. How Culture Works: Perspectives from Media Studies on the Efficacy of Symbols. *Theory and Society* 18: 153–180.

Scott, David W. 2011. Religiosity in *South Park*: Struggles Over Institutional and Personal Piety Among Residents of a "Redneck Town." *Journal of Media and Religion* 10: 152–163.

Scott, Eugenie C. 2007. Creation Science Lite: "Intelligent Design" as the New Anti-Evolutionism. In *Scientists Confront Creationism: Intelligent Design and Beyond*, ed. Andrew J. Petto and Laurie R. Godfrey, 59–109. New York: W. W. Norton.

Seager, Richard Hughes. 1999. *Buddhism in America*. New York: Columbia University Press.

Semmerling, Tim Jon. 2006. *"Evil" Arabs in American Popular Film: Orientalist Fear*. Austin: University of Texas Press.

Shaheen, Jack. 2003. *Reel Bad Arabs: How Hollywood Vilifies a People*. With a foreword by William Greider. Gloucestershire: Arris Books.

Shanks, Niall and Karl H. Joplin. 1999. Redundant Complexity: A Critical Analysis of Intelligent Design in Biochemistry. *Philosophy of Science* 66 (2): 268–282.

Sharma, Ursula. 1973. Theodicy and the Doctrine of Karma. *Man* 8 (3): 347–364.

Shermer, Michael. 2006. *Why Darwin Matters: The Case Against Intelligent Design*. New York: Times Books.

Shires, Preston. 2007. *Hippies of the Religious Right*. Waco, TX: Baylor University Press.

Shupe, Anson D. and David G. Bromley. 1980. *The New Vigilantes: Deprogrammers, Anti-cultists, and the New Religions*. London: Sage.

———, eds. 1985. *A Documentary History of the Anti-cult Movement*. Arlington: Center for Social Research, University of Texas at Arlington.

Shupe, Anson and Susan E. Darnell. 2006. *Agents of Discord: Deprogramming, Pseudo-science, and the American Anticult Movement*. New Brunswick, NJ: Transaction.

Shupe, Anson and Jeffrey K. Hadden. 1995. Cops, News Copy, and Public Opinion: Legitimacy and the Social Construction of Evil in Waco. In *Armageddon in Waco: Critical Perspectives on the Branch Davidian Conflict*, ed. Stuart A. Wright, 177–202. Chicago: University of Chicago Press.

Silverman, David, dir. 2007. *The Simpsons Movie*. Written by James L. Brooks, Matt Groening, Al Jean, Ian Maxtone-Graham, George Meyer, David Mirkin, Mike Reiss, Mike Scully, Matt Selman, John Swartzwelder, and Jon Vitti. Twentieth Century Fox Film Corporation.

Silver Ring Thing. 2014a. Bare Essentials Abstinence/Purity Series: Session 1—Dealing With Temptation. *Silver Ring Thing*. Video. Retrieved from http://www.silverringthing.com.

———. 2014b. What Is Silver Ring Thing? *Silver Ring Thing*. Retrieved from http://www.silverringthing.com.

Singer, Margaret Thaler with Janja Lalich. 1995. *Cults in Our Midst*. With a foreword by Robert Jay Lifton. San Francisco: Jossey-Bass.

Sklare, Marshall. 1990. Religion and Ethnicity in the American Jewish Community. In *Social Foundations of Judaism*, ed. Calvin Goldscheider and Jacob Neusner, 135–145. Englewood Cliffs, NJ: Prentice Hall.

Skoble, Aeon J. 2001. Lisa and American Anti-intellectualism. In *The Simpsons and Philosophy: The D'oh of Homer*, ed. William Irwin, Mark T. Conard, and Aeon J. Skoble, 25–33. Chicago and La Salle: Open Court.

Slack, Gordy. 2007. *The Battle Over the Meaning of Everything: Evolution, Intelligent Design, and a School Board in Dover, PA*. San Francisco: Jossey-Bass.

Smith, Christian. 2000. *Christian America? What Evangelicals Really Want*. Berkeley: University of California Press.

———. 2003. *Moral, Believing Animals: Human Personhood and Culture*. New York: Oxford University Press.

Smith, Christian with Michael Emerson, Sally Gallagher, Paul Kennedy, and David Sikkink. 1998. *American Evangelicalism: Embattled and Thriving*. Chicago: University of Chicago Press.

Smith, Jane Idleman. 1999. *Islam in America*. New York: Columbia University Press.

Smith, Jessie M. 2011. Becoming an Atheist in America: Constructing Identity and Meaning from the Rejection of Theism. *Sociology of Religion* 72 (2): 215–237.

Smith, Jonathan Z. 1998. Religion, Religions, Religious. In *Critical Terms for Religious Studies*, ed. Mark C. Taylor, 269–284. Chicago: University of Chicago Press.

Smith, Tom W. 1990. Classifying Protestant Denominations. *Review of Religious Research* 31 (3): 225–245.

———. 2012. General Social Survey 2012 Cross-Section and Panel Combined. *The ARDA: Association of Religion Data Archives*. Retrieved from http://www.thearda.com.

Spigel, Lynn and Jan Olsson, eds. 2004. *Television After TV: Essays on a Medium in Transition*. Durham, NC: Duke University Press.

Sri Venkateswara Temple. 1999. Rituals at Sri Venkateswara Temple. In *Asian Religions in America: A Documentary History*, ed. Thomas A. Tweed and Stephen Prothero, 294–298. New York: Oxford University Press.

Starhawk. 1999. *The Spiral Dance: A Rebirth of the Ancient Religion of the Great Goddess*. 20th anniversary edition. San Francisco: HarperSanFrancisco.

Stark, Rodney with Christopher Bader et al. 2008. *What Americans Really Believe: New Findings from the Baylor Surveys of Religion*. Waco, TX: Baylor University Press.

Stark, Rodney and Roger Finke. 2000. *Acts of Faith: Explaining the Human Side of Religion*. Berkeley: University of California Press.

Steffan, Melissa. 2013. Alan Chambers Apologizes to Gay Community, Exodus International to Shut Down. *Christianity Today*. Retrieved from http://www.christianitytoday.com.

Steinberg, Shirley R. and Joe L. Kincheloe, eds. 2009. *Christotainment: Selling Jesus through Popular Culture*. Boulder, CO: Westview Press.

Stone, Jon R. 1997. *On the Boundaries of American Evangelicalism: The Postwar Evangelical Coalition*. New York: St. Martin's Press.

Stout, Harry S. 1991. *The Divine Dramatist: George Whitefield and the Rise of Modern Evangelicalism*. Grand Rapids, MI: W.B. Eerdmans.

Stowe, David W. 2011. *No Sympathy for the Devil: Christian Pop Music and the Transformation of American Evangelicalism*. Chapel Hill: University of North Carolina Press.

Sutcliffe, Steven J. 2003. *Children of the New Age: A History of Spiritual Practices*. London and New York: Routledge.

Swidler, Ann. 1986. Culture in Action: Symbols and Strategies. *American Sociological Review* 51 (2): 273–286.

Swidler, Ann and Jorge Arditi. 1994. The New Sociology of Knowledge. *Annual Review of Sociology* 20: 305–29.

Tanaka, Kenneth. 1998. Epilogue: The Colors and Contours of American Buddhism. In *The Faces of Buddhism in America*, ed. Charles S. Prebish and Kenneth K. Tanaka, 287–298. Berkeley: University of California Press.

Taves, Ann. 2009. *Religious Experience Reconsidered: A Building-Block Approach to the Study of Religion and Other Special Things*. Princeton: Princeton University Press.

Thuesen, Peter J. 2002. The Logic of Mainline Churchliness: Historical Background Since the Reformation. In *The Quiet Hand of God: Faith-based Activism and the Public Role of Mainline Protestantism*, ed. Robert Wuthnow and John H. Evans, 27–53. Princeton: Princeton University Press.

Thumma, Scott. 2006. 'Open and Affirming' of Growth? The Challenge of Liberal Lesbian, Gay and Bisexual-Supportive Congregational Growth. In *Why Liberal Churches Are Growing*, ed. Martyn Percy and Ian Markham, 100–118. London: T&T Clark.

Tumminia, Diana. 2003. When the Archangel Died: From Revelation to Routinisation of Charisma in Unarius. In *UFO Religions*, ed. Christopher Partridge, 62–83. New York: Routledge.

Tumminia, Diana and George R. Kirkpatrick. 1995. Unarius: Emergent Aspects of an American Flying Saucer Group. In *The Gods Have Landed: New Religions From Other Worlds*, ed. James R. Lewis, 85–104. Albany: State University of New York Press.

Turner, Chris. 2004. *Planet Simpson: How a Cartoon Masterpiece Defined a Generation*. With a foreword by Douglas Coupland. Cambridge: Da Capo Press.

Tweed, Thomas A. 2002. Who Is a Buddhist? Night-Stand Buddhists and Other Creatures. In *Westward Dharma: Buddhism Beyond Asia*, ed. Charles S. Prebish and Martin Baumann, 17–33. Berkeley: University of California Press.

———. 2008. Why Are Buddhists so Nice? Media Representations of Buddhism and Islam in the United States Since 1945. *Material Religion* 4: 91–93.

Urban, Hugh B. 2005. Osho, From Sex Guru to Guru of the Rich: The Spiritual Logic of Late Capitalism. In *Gurus in America*, ed. Thomas A. Forsthoefel and Cynthia Ann Humes, 169–192. Albany: State University of New York Press.

———. 2012. *The Church of Scientology: A History of a New Religion*. Princeton: Princeton University Press.

VanArragon, Raymond J. 2007. *Family Guy* and God: Should Believers Take Offense? In Family Guy *and Philosophy: A Cure for the Petarded*, ed. Jeremy Wisnewski, 16–26. Malden, MA: Blackwell.

van Driel, Barend and James T. Richardson. 1988. Categorization of New Religious Movements in American Print Media. *Sociological Analysis* 49 (2): 171–183.

Waghorne, Joane Punzo. 1999. The Hindu Gods in a Split-level World: The Sri Siva-Vishnu Temple in Suburban Washington, D.C. In *Gods of the City*, ed. Robert A. Orsi, 103–130. Bloomington and Indianapolis: Indiana University Press.

Wagner, Rachel. 2012. *Godwired: Religion, Ritual and Virtual Reality*. New York: Routledge.

Wallis, Jim. 2005. *God's Politics: Why the Right Gets It Wrong and the Left Doesn't Get It*. San Francisco: HarperSanFrancisco.

Wallis, Roy. 1977. *The Road to Total Freedom: A Sociological Analysis of Scientology*. New York: Columbia University Press.

Walls, Andrew F. 1996. *The Missionary Movement in Christian History: Studies in the Transmission of Faith*. Maryknoll, NY: Orbis Books.

Waxman, Chaim I. 2005. Patterns of American Jewish Religious Behaviour. In *The Cambridge Companion to American Judaism*, ed. Dana Evan Kaplan, 101–115. Cambridge: Cambridge University Press.

Wellman, James. 2002. Religion without a Net: Strictness in the Religious Practices of West Coast Urban Liberal Christian Congregations. *Review of Religious Research* 44 (2): 184–199.

Wessinger, Catherine. 2000. *How the Millennium Comes Violently: From Jonestown to Heaven's Gate*. With a foreword by Jayne Seminare Docherty. New York: Seven Bridges Press.

White, Martha C. 2012. Lance Armstrong Doping Scandal Hurts Cyclist's Endorsement Career. *NBC News*. Retrieved from http://www.nbcnews.com.

Whitfield, George. 1738. Selected Sermons of George Whitfield: The Eternity of Hell-Torments. *Christian Classics Ethereal Library.* Retrieved from http://www.ccel.org.

Whitmire, Kyle. 2014. Things I Learned During the Alabama Legislature's Ten Commandments Debate Today. *Al.com.* Retrieved from http://blog.al.com.

Wicks, Robert H. 2006. Emotional Response to Collective Action Frames About Islam and Terrorism. *Journal of Media and Religion* 5 (4): 245–263.

Wilder, Courtney and Jeremy Rehwaldt. 2012. What Makes Music Christian? Hipsters, Contemporary Christian Music and Secularization. In *Understanding Religion and Popular Culture,* ed. Terry Ray Clark and Dan W. Clanton, Jr., 157–171. New York: Routledge.

Wilson, Jeff. 2012. *Dixie Dharma: Inside a Buddhist Temple in the South.* Chapel Hill: University of North Carolina Press.

Winter, J. Alan. 1992. The Transformation of Community Integration Among American Jewry: Religion or Ethnoreligion? A National Replication. *Review of Religious Research* 33 (4): 349–363.

———. 1996. Symbolic Ethnicity or Religion Among Jews in the United States: A Test of Gansian Hypothesis. *Review of Religious Research* 37 (3): 233–247.

Wisnewski, Jeremy. 2007. *Family Guy and Philosophy: A Cure for the Petarded.* Malden, MA: Blackwell.

Wojcik, Daniel. 2003. Apocalyptic and Millenarian Aspects of American UFOism. In *UFO Religions,* ed. Christopher Partridge, 274–300. New York: Routledge.

Woocher, Jonathan. 1990. Civil Religion and the Modern Jewish Challenge. In *Social Foundations of Judaism,* ed. Calvin Goldscheider and Jacob Neusner, 146–168. Englewood Cliffs, NJ: Prentice Hall.

Wood, Andrew and Anne Marie Todd. 2005. 'Are We There Yet?': Searching for Springfield and *The Simpsons'* Rhetoric of Omnitopia. *Critical Studies in Media Communication* 22 (3): 207–222.

Woods, Stacey Grenrock. 2009. Hungover with Seth MacFarlane. *Esquire.* Retrieved from http://www.esquire.com.

Wright, Stuart A. 1997. Media Coverage of Unconventional Religion: Any 'Good News' for Minority Faiths? *Review of Religious Research* 39 (2): 101–115.

Wuthnow, Robert. 1988. *The Restructuring of American Religion: Society and Faith Since World War II.* Princeton: Princeton University Press.

———. 1989. *The Struggle for America's Soul: Evangelicals, Liberals, and Secularism.* Grand Rapids, MI: William B. Eerdmans.

———. 1998. *After Heaven: Spirituality in America Since the 1950s.* Berkeley: University of California Press.

———. 2005. *America and the Challenges of Religious Diversity.* Princeton and Oxford: Princeton University Press.

———. 2009. *Boundless Faith: The Global Outreach of American Churches.* Berkeley: University of California Press.

Wuthnow, Robert and John H. Evans, eds. 2002. *The Quiet Hand of God: Faith-based Activism and the Public Role of Mainline Protestantism*. Princeton: Princeton University Press.

Yoffe, Emily. 2007. I've Got *The Secret*: What Happened When I Followed the Best-Selling Book's Advice for Two Months." *Slate.com*. Retrieved from http://www.slate.com.

York, Michael. 2001. New Age Commodification and Appropriation of Spirituality. *Journal of Contemporary Religion* 16 (3): 361–372.

Zaidman, Nurit. 2007. New Age Shop—Church or Marketplace? *Journal of Contemporary Religion* 22 (3): 361–374.

Zeller, Benjamin E. 2014. *Heaven's Gate: America's UFO Religion*. New York: New York University Press.

Zijderveld, Anton C. 1983. Trend Report: The Sociology of Laughter and Humour. *Current Sociology* 31 (3): 1–100.

Zillmann, Dolf. 1983. Disparagement Humor. In *Handbook of Humor Research: Volume I Basic Issues*, ed. Paul E. McGhee and Jeffrey H. Goldstein, 85–107. New York: Springer-Verlag.

Zillmann, Dolf and Joanne R. Cantor. 1996 [1976]. A Disposition Theory of Humour and Mirth. In *Humour and Laughter: Theory, Research, Applications*, ed. Antony J. Chapman and Hugh C. Foot, with a new introduction by Peter Derks, 93–115. New Brunswick, NJ: Transaction.

Zinnbauer, Brian J., Kenneth I. Pargament, Brenda Cole, Mark S. Rye, Eric M. Butter, Timothy G. Belavich, Kathleen M. Hipp, Allie B. Scott, and Jill L. Kadar. 1997. Religion and Spirituality: Unfuzzying the Fuzzy. *Journal for the Scientific Study of Religion* 36 (4): 549–564.

Zuckerman, Phil. 2008. *Society Without God: What the Least Religious Nations Can Tell Us about Contentment*. New York: New York University Press.

INDEX

ABOUT THE AUTHOR

David Feltmate is Associate Professor of Sociology at Auburn University at Montgomery, where he conducts research in the sociology of religion, the sociology of humor, religion and popular culture, religion and mass media, and sociological theory.

Lightning Source UK Ltd.
Milton Keynes UK
UKOW02f1040160317
296761UK00002B/67/P